SECOND EDITION

Mentally Ill in Amityville

⚜

Murder, Mystery, & Mayhem at 112 Ocean Ave.

Will Savive

Del-Grande Publishing Inc.
New Jersey   Hackensack

Mentally Ill in Amityville:
Murder, Mystery, & Mayhem at 112 Ocean Ave.

SECOND EDITION

Copyright © 2012 by Will Savive

All rights reserved. No part of this book may be used or reproduced by any means, graphic, electronic, or mechanical, including photocopying, recording, taping or by any information storage retrieval system without the written permission of the publisher except in the case of brief quotations embodied in critical articles and reviews.

Del-Grande books may be ordered through booksellers or by contacting:

www.delgrandepublishing.webs.com

Because of the dynamic nature of the Internet, any Web address or links contained in this book may have changed since publication and may no longer be valid. The views expressed in this work are solely those of the author and do not necessarily reflect the views of the publisher, and the publisher hereby disclaims any responsibility for them.

ISBN-13: 978-0615639376
ISBN-10: 0615639372
BISAC: True Crime / Murder / General

Printed in the United States of America
Del-Grande date: 7/25/12

*To contact the author, please send correspondence to:
willsavive@live.com.

Contents

Section I Family Portrait

Introduction 1
Life & Death of the DeFeos 4
   "Butch" DeFeo 6
   Dawn DeFeo 9
   Nightmare in Amityville 10
   Investigation 18
   Oral Confession 33
Pretrial 36
The Trial 43
   New Evidence 45
   Going Ballistics 47
   Summary of findings 49
   Autopsy Reports 51
   Insane or Inane? 54
   DeFeo Confesses 55
   Cross Examination 58
   The Prosecutions Witness 60
   Sullivan Tips the Scales 62

Section II The Haunting

The Perfect Psychic Storm 65
   Resident Evil 69
   The Last Night – 28 days later 74
   Should I Stay or Should I Go Now? 76
Media Madness 78
Who Ya Gonna Call? 82
   The Investigation 84
   The Warrens get attacked 91
   Moving Out 92
   More Psychics? 94
The Amityville Horror is born 96
   Amityville Stats - Books & Movies: 98
   Amityville Books 102

Haunting: Fact or Fiction?..103
   Test: 103
Kaplan & Weber 105
Would You Live In This House? 117
   That's Incredible! 119
   Who's House? 124
   List of Owners of 112 Ocean Ave. 127
   The Lutz Children Speak 128
   *Did Duke University Investigate Amityville? 131

Section III A Closer Look

Destined for Amityville 134
   No Trespassing 138
   The "Buddy" System 142
The Needle in the Haystack 146
Interviews with Edward J. Kangesier 153
   Phone Call from Lynn 158
   Ed & the Gang 161
   Amityville Revisited..162
   Gary gets spooked! 164
   Gary and the Horror house 166
   Merv Griffin 169
   Miles Curran 170
   Incest: Motive for Murder 173
Amityville's Hang-Ups with the Curious 177
   The Amityville Horribles 177
   Ed & the Thrill-Seekers 181
   Ed & Mrs. Wilson 182

Section IV Aftermath and Analysis

DeFeo Appeals 186
    Crooked Cops 186
    The Appeal 187
    DNA Testing 191
    After Dawn 194
    Exploring the Possibilities 196
    Kicking up dust 200
    Gates, Osuna, and the FLIP-FLOP 201
    So, what's the real story? 207
    Who let the dogs out? 211
    Mr. Postman 212
    Affidavit Fraud 217
    Domestic Abuse 219
    26 Tales of DeFeo…..222
    Amityville Realtor on New "Horror"…….....................228

    End Notes 234

Preface

    The narrative that follows is a work of fact. Due to the many erroneous accretions that have been written about the DeFeo murders, it seemed to me necessary to dispel many of the myths and misconceptions by documenting this story as a complete reference-guide. My interest in this story stems from the obvious human aspects, as well as my background as an investigative journalist, with a B.S. degree in Criminal Justice with a concentration in Forensic Science.

    My investigation into the events of the Amityville horror house begins with the DeFeo family just before the murders and ends with present-day circumstances. This also includes a detailed section on the Lutz family and their unforgettable story. This book is the chronology of events that was sparked by the heinous murders of six members of the DeFeo family in their quaint suburban home on Long Island.

    I would like to thank Amityville expert, Jason Pyke, for his assistance.

Introduction

Before November 13, 1974, the sleepy seaside village of Amityville, NY—located on Long Island, just an hour outside of Manhattan—was a virtually unknown and uneventful little town. All that changed, however, when police found six members of the DeFeo family dead at their 112 Ocean Avenue home that night. The only surviving member of the family was 23-year-old Ronnie "Butch" DeFeo, Jr. He was later charged and convicted of all six murders and sentenced to six-life terms. Much controversy still exists regarding reports that five of the six family members were found face down in their beds, shot in the back, despite being shot with a high-powered rifle. Many believe that the evidence shows that one person could not have shot all six victims with a high-powered rifle execution style in their beds. Furthermore, it was determined by police reports and examining officials that none of the victims ever got out of bed after the first shots were fired, except for Dawn DeFeo. To add to the mystery, no one ever reported hearing shots fired, yet five-neighbors claim to have heard the DeFeo's dog barking wildly inside of the house at the time of the murders.

Thirty-three-years later many still believe that Ronnie DeFeo could not have executed all six members of his family alone in the time-frame indicated in police documents, and that he must have had at least one other accomplice. Some believe that there is evidence implicating Ronnie's eighteen-year old sister, Dawn DeFeo, as not only the accomplice, but the one who orchestrated the devilish plot, before being murdered herself. However, the fact that Ronnie has told numerous different stories throughout the years has ultimately caused him to lose credibility and damned him to a life behind bars. Why does Ronnie tell such tall tales? Who is he covering for and why? Or is he just a sociopath/psychopath and compulsive liar who gets-off on the attention?

Thirteen months after the murders the home was sold to the Lutz family, who left just 28-days later, literally abandoning the home and all of their possessions. Their claim was that the home was haunted: they say they experienced several nights of intense paranormal activity that led them to evacuate their home, vowing never to return! Their story would ignite a firestorm of controversy and a frenzied American tale of murder, mystery, and mayhem. Their story also made the house at 112 Ocean Avenue in Amityville, NY, the most famous haunted house in the entire world! The Lutzes' experience had a combination of all of the best cases in paranormal history. The story would go on to spawn four movies, five direct-to-video films, numerous books, a T.V. movie, and a CSI-NY Halloween episode, among other things. It also produced a host of critics and non-believers who have been furiously debating the haunting for three decades, leaving the true tragedy of six murdered victims as a briefly mentioned subplot.

The events surrounding the mysterious DeFeo murders—as well as the Lutz family's story—are still much discussed and controversial topics today. Many believe that the house was and will forever be haunted. Others believe the story to be a complete hoax, originated by Ronnie's "false" admissions in court that were further fabricated by the Lutz family, Ronnie's lawyer (William Weber), and Jay Anson, author of *The Amityville Horror*.

The hoax theory was actually originated by admitted Vampirologist, Stephan Kaplan, who was originally scheduled to investigate the house, but was fired by George Lutz before he had the chance. This more than offended Kaplan, and he made a career out of trying to discredit the Lutzes' and proponents of the haunting theory. A closer look at Kaplan and his character, however, reveals a motive for revenge, an obsession with the limelight, and a story of his own that was based on several contradictions and unsupported accusations. William Weber also had an axe to grind with the Lutzes after they turned down his proposal to publish their story in a book he was already working on before he met them. William Weber first claimed that the house was haunted and that he had proof. Later, Weber called dibs on the Lutzes' story, claiming that he and the Lutzes had made-up the haunting story after several bottles of wine. Weber's sorted past and lack of credibility, however, also taint his version of the events.

With all of the hubbub and misinformation surrounding this story it is hard to establish what is fact and what is fiction. Rumors and hearsay have been spinning like a 33-year-old tornado, consuming everything in their path. Everyone has an opinion about Amityville, whether they have any direct relation to it or not. People, who have never stepped into the town of Amityville, let alone the infamous house, can emphatically tell you that the tale is a hoax. Without speaking to any of the Amityville residents or reviewing any of the actual evidence of the case; they claim to have a firm grasp of the facts. Not many hoax-theorists can give you the cold, hard facts. The basis of any of their theories is that Jay Anson's book is a fabrication of the Lutzes' story. This may be true, but it does not dispel the possibility that something supernatural took place there. "Whatever is here [in the house] is able to move around at will," said psychic investigator Lorraine Warren, who was one of the few who entered the house to investigate after the Lutz family fled. "It doesn't have to stay here, but I think it's a resting place."

Consider the following: Did Ronnie DeFeo kill all six of his family members? Was Ronnie afforded a fair trial? Is the Lutzes' story a hoax, or was the hoax theory created by those who stood to gain by affirming the story untrue? Was Jay Anson's book true or a fabrication of the truth? *Most importantly,* what is fact and what is fiction about this story?

SECTION I

FAMILY PORTRAIT

Life & Death of the DeFeos

On paper, the DeFeo family was the living example of the American dream. Ronald Joseph DeFeo, Sr., a.k.a. "Big Ronnie," was born and raised in Brooklyn, New York. After years of hard work and family connections, Mr. DeFeo decided to move his family to Long Island in 1964. After searching the area thoroughly, he chose an exquisite piece of real estate in the quaint village of Amityville, Long Island. Amityville, which means "Friendly Village", was home to about 9,000 residents, and is approximately 35-miles east of New York City. The family moved into 112 Ocean Avenue in Amityville, New York in the summer of 1965. The splendid Dutch Colonial home was built in 1925, and had a lamp post in the front yard with a sign hanging from it that read: "High Hopes;" which the family saw as a mantra for their future.

The roughly 4000 sq. foot home sat on a quarter-acre lot. The village was tastefully affluent, and a certain comfortable serenity seemed to be the pervasive theme. Crime was something that happened "Over there," they would say. Many believed there was no better place to raise a family. The outside of the house had dark shingles with white trim, and it was so long and narrow that it had to be positioned sideways in order to fit onto the property. The front door of the home faced the 237-foot-long driveway that led to the boathouse. The front door also faced the next-door neighbor's side door. The side of the house with the two quarter moon windows—which looked like eyes—faced the street. It was the only house on the block in which the front door did not face the street. The backyard, just outside the patio, was also roomy, and it had a heated in-ground pool.

The inside was just as beautiful as the outside. The two-story home had several rooms, a combination boathouse/garage on the Amityville Creek, and an attic that was so big that it served as a third-floor. There was also a full, livable basement. The living room had an adjoining sun porch; the kitchen had a breakfast nook; there were six bedrooms; a formal dining room with a patio entrance; and the house had two-and-a-half bathrooms. It was every home owners dream!

DeFeo Family:

11/13/1974	Born	AGE
Ronal Joseph DeFeo, Sr.	November 16, 1930	[44]
Louise Marie Brigante-DeFeo	November 03, 1931	[43]
Ronald Joseph DeFeo, Jr.	September 26, 1951	[23]
Dawn Theresa DeFeo	July 29, 1956	[18]
Allison Louise DeFeo	August 16, 1961	[13]
Marc Gregory DeFeo	September 04, 1962	[12]
John Mathew DeFeo	October 24, 1965	[9]

While on vacation in 1970, Mr. DeFeo visited *St. Joseph's Oratory* in Canada. He wasn't very impressed until he returned home and read about the life of Brother Andre—the man who founded the Oratory. Mr. DeFeo was so moved and inspired by Brother Andre's story that he donated money to his foundation. Soon after this he was invited back up to the Oratory as an honored guest. These events led to Mr. DeFeo becoming a very devoted member of St. Joseph's. On the surface the family appeared to have it all; they were a religious family, they had loads of money, and they had access to all of the finer things in life.

Although the family seemed to have it all on the surface, like many other American families, there was a darker side that hid beneath the blissful facade. The DeFeo's were a turbulent family at best. On the exterior they seemed like the perfect Italian-Catholic family, with several religious artifacts in and around their home. Yet, behind the closed doors of the DeFeo home violent behavior seemed to be the norm. As the children grew older the confrontations increased and the physical violence grew more dramatic. Unseen to the average onlooker, the DeFeo family was a time bomb set to explode. It was all orchestrated by the ring leader, Mr. DeFeo, who was known as a violent man that often fell into terrible rages. Fights seemed to break out without provocation, and Ronnie DeFeo, Jr., often took on the brunt of his tirades.

"Butch" DeFeo

Ronald Joseph DeFeo, Jr., a.k.a. "Butch," was the eldest of five children, born on September 26, 1951, in Brooklyn, New York. As an adolescent Ronnie was overweight and was frequently bullied by other kids. Although his father encouraged him to stick up for himself at school, he did not tolerate him sticking up for himself at home. Butch's father was, by many accounts, known as a "Monster." According to Ronnie, his father "used to go around the house beating everyone up." His mother was always yelling and screaming. "It was a crazy house," he asserted. Ronnie tried to run away several times, but they just kept bringing him back. In regard to his turbulent home life he said, "I couldn't take it, I couldn't take it back then, I couldn't take it before this [the murder] happened." Among the many incidents, Ronnie claims that his father beat up his younger brother, Marc, so bad one time that they had to "sew his head up."

The abuse at home began affecting Butch in several different ways. Butch began acting out, much as abused children do. In school Butch became a terror! Butch had a lot of problems with his teachers at Amityville Junior High School. His grades plummeted and he became terribly disruptive in class. Butch began acting out in class: throwing things at his teachers and wrecking their classrooms. Fights with other students seemed to be the norm for him. Soon enough, Butch was thrown out of *Amityville Junior High School* for fighting, bad grades, and a list of other things. One day the Principle of the school drove him home and, from that day forth, he was never allowed back.

The family was concerned about Ronnie and started sending him to see a psychiatrist by the name of Dr. Fried. The sessions helped little; however, Dr. Fried chose clinical methods of therapy, opting not to prescribe him any type of medications. His visits to see Dr. Fried tapered-off by the age of sixteen and his wild ways continued to progress. After Ronnie was kicked out of School, his father became furious. A big fan of tough love, Mr. DeFeo said that he was going to straighten Ronnie out the same way he'd been straightened out when he was Ronnie's age. The result was sending Ronnie to *St. Francis Preparatory School* on Baltic Street in Brooklyn, New York. Ronnie started St. Francis in ninth grade. After wreaking havoc there as well he was sent to *Amityville High School*—still as a ninth grader—the following year.

Ronnie's behavior got so bad and violent outside of the home that most believed him to be incorrigible. However, no matter how much of a bully he appeared outside of the home; in it, his dominance was always eclipsed by his father's. It was in Amityville High School that Butch began taking drugs. He started out with barbiturates and uppers mostly, and then he moved on to heavier drugs, such as LSD and heroine. Heavy drinking also became a regular routine for Ronnie.

The DeFeo's last attempt to turn their son around was a trip to the military. Ronnie passed a military physical and received a letter to report. Days later he was escorted by his father to the Bay Shore Draft Board. From there, Ronnie was taken to Fort Hamilton in Brooklyn, NY. However, just when it looked like he might be accepted and in a good situation, a military psychologist called him in for evaluation and his discharge came soon after that. For reasons unknown, Michael Brigante, Sr., allegedly paid a man $5,000 to keep Ronnie out of the army. After the military, his parents just gave up on him. When all else failed, they just spoiled him rotten, spending piles of money on him. Ronnie always had money!

Ronnie's friends were often afraid to go into the DeFeo home, because they saw Mr. DeFeo as a very intimidating figure. There were even instances when some of Ronnie's friends actually witnessed the 280 pound Mr. DeFeo beating his wife, Louise, in front of them. "He beat her up all the time. All the time; it was nothing new," Ronnie said. "He used to beat everyone in the house up, including myself." Sometimes his father would only hit his mother once, in which case Ronnie claimed he did not have to do anything. Then there were other times when his father seemed to be "going like a maniac" and beating her up badly. In Ronnie's words, "he would have killed her." So he said that he would try to break it up, and his father would then "start beating his brains out." Ronnie never hit his father back; possibly because he was afraid of him, or out of respect. Instead, he would just cover up while his father wailed on him, or he'd simply run away.

By the age of eighteen Butch had been drinking and taking heavy drugs, like LSD, speed, and heroin. Mr. DeFeo gave him a job at the Buick dealership thinking that he might straighten up a bit with more responsibility. However, he slacked off, made his own hours, and still managed to continue to take drugs and get into trouble. Although Butch's hours fluctuated on a weekly basis, Mr. DeFeo still gave him a consistent weekly check. Yet, somehow Ronnie seemed to have much more money than his yearly salary allowed. Regardless, his wild ways and his violent streak grew worse as time went on. One day, Mr. and Mrs. DeFeo were arguing awfully. Ronnie could not stand the screaming, so he ran upstairs and grabbed a 12-gauge shotgun and came back downstairs. "Leave that woman alone," Ronnie said calmly as he pointed the gun at his dad. "I'm going to kill you, you fat fuck! This is it." Ronnie pulled the trigger, but the gun jammed, and no shot was fired. Allegedly unfazed, Ronnie simply lowered the gun and walked back up the stairs—leaving Mr. DeFeo in shock.

Ronnie pissed away money like it was nothing. When he felt that he needed more money he would just ask his parents, steal it from them, gamble, or devise other ways. One day he and a friend allegedly devised a plan to rip off his grandfather's car dealership in Brooklyn. On 1 November 1974, at 2:40 p.m.—just weeks before the murders—Butch and a co-worker from the dealership were ordered to take $1,900 in cash and $20,000 in certified checks over to the bank and deposit them. However, they returned two-hours later and claimed that they had been robbed at gunpoint while in their car waiting at a red light at the intersection of Cortelyou Road and Argyle Street in Brooklyn. Ronald, Sr., was furious and purportedly skeptical of their story. An argument ensued in the parking lot of the dealership between Butch, his father, and the police. Butch screamed and cursed at them when he was asked basic questions about the incident and began banging on the hoods of cars, acting very suspicious.

The police requested Butch's presence at the police station just six days before the murders to view mug shots of criminals that were potentially involved. Butch accepted, but later refused at the last minute.

"You've got the devil on your back," screamed Ronald senior when he heard about Butch's last minute flaking.

"You fat prick, I'll kill you," replied Butch before storming to his car in a rage and speeding off. Twenty-three year old Butch was known around town as real "bad news" by many of the locals. By this time, Ronnie had a sordid history of drinking, drug abuse, and a reputation for violence. He was also known as a gun-buff, collecting many different types of rifles for hunting. Many locals, such as Amityville bar owner, Al Ubert, said that "Alls Ronnie did was drink, gamble and fight." Many, such as next door neighbor, Rufus Ireland, also felt that Ronnie was "not dealing with a full deck." It was also well known to many of the Amityville locals at the time that Ronnie frequently carried around a .38 caliber hand gun.

Dawn DeFeo

Dawn DeFeo had graduated from St. John the Baptist High School earlier in the year and she had been attending secretarial school at the time of the murders. According to Ronnie, Dawn and her father argued all the time and she had begun taking drugs to cope with years of "physical abuse" from their father. Dawn had a boyfriend at the time—William Davidge [17]—who lived in Florida. Davidge later claimed, in a sworn affidavit, that Dawn used mescaline and L.S.D. Dawn had a bad temper that Davidge claimed (in the affidavit) "got out of hand on occasions." Ronnie corroborated these claims by stating that Dawn and Mr. DeFeo did not get along at all. "She was bad," Ronnie said. "She had a bad temper, always fighting."

Only one-week before the murders, Dawn had gotten into a heated argument with her father and mother over moving to Florida to live with Davidge. Dawn was determined to move to Florida "no matter what," according to Davidge in his affidavit. Davidge was friends with Ronnie, as well as the entire DeFeo family, but Mr. and Mrs. DeFeo forbid Dawn from moving to Florida. This caused tremendous hostility between Dawn and her parents. Ronnie would sometimes give Davidge money, such as the time he claimed to have given him money to take Dawn to her senior prom. According to Davidge, "Dawn was only using Ronnie for money."

Nightmare in Amityville

Tuesday, 12 November 1974, started out like any other in the pleasant village of Amityville. Boats lined the canals of the Great South Bay's shoreline, trees lined the streets of Ocean Avenue, and the neighborhood was quiet and tranquil, as usual. The DeFeo's sat down together for dinner that night; later they dressed in their nightclothes and went to bed. For six of the seven family members it would be the last night of their lives. Butch sat in the T.V. room on the second-floor watching the movie *Castle Keep* (an American war film based on a novel by William Eastlake). The violent ending to the movie seemed to further antagonize an already fractured psyche. Moreover, Ronnie had been drinking and shooting heroin that night. Soon after the movie ended Ronnie fell asleep.

He awoke in the morning, and while getting ready for work he noticed that someone was in the bathroom, after hearing the toilet flush. He then saw his brother Marc's wheel chair in front of the bathroom door. Ronald Jr., then left the house and arrived at the Brigante-Karl Buick dealership at 7:00 a.m., that morning. The large car dealership on Coney Island Avenue in Brooklyn was owned by Ronnie Sr.'s father-in-law. Ronnie worked there under his father, who was the Service Manager. Ronald Sr. did not show up for work that day, but this was not very unusual. Mr. DeFeo often went away on business and did not regularly check in with his co-workers. Ronnie, a.k.a., "Butch," called his then girlfriend, Mindy Weiss [19], at 11:00 a.m. The two had known each other for only 6 months, but the relationship had gotten serious quickly. Butch advised her that he was leaving work early that day and wanted to meet up with her. Ronnie did so, leaving work at approximately 12:00 p.m., and headed back to the Amityville area.

Ronnie made his way to Mindy's house—on Harbor Lane East in Massapequa—to spend some time with her. He drove down County Line Road in Amityville to get there and saw his best friend, Robert "Bobby" Kelske, driving in the opposite direction. Kelske was a twenty-five-year old young man whose most recent job was working as a Stone Mason at his father's company. A former Amityville High School football star; Bobby Kelske was between jobs at the time and was frequently seen drinking at the local town bar with Ronnie and a few others.

Both men stopped their cars, turned around, and pulled over to converse. Bobby noticed that Ronnie had his normal work clothes on—a blue shirt and dungarees—and looked like he had just gotten off from work. They had a brief conversation, and then made plans to meet up at their favorite local bar later that night. Ronnie arrived at Mindy's house at 1:00 p.m., and the two went to the *Sunrise Mall* in Massapequa to do some early Christmas shopping. Ronnie seemed to make it a point to inform Mindy that he felt something was odd, because no one at his house was answering the phone. He called his house in front of Mindy, but there was still no answer. It's alleged that Ronnie and Mindy shot heroin together at this time. After spending about two hours with Mindy, Ronnie decided to head over to Bobby's house. He made plans to see Mindy later that night; they planned a date for 7:30 p.m., sharp. Ronnie left Mindy at about 3:00 p.m., and headed directly to Bobby's house. Again, Ronnie made it a point to tell Bobby that he was concerned that no one was answering the phone at his house. Regardless of his trepidation, Ronnie did not go home immediately.

Ronnie's favorite hang out was a local Amityville dive-bar by the name of *Henry's Pub*. The bar, also known as "*The Witches Brew*," was located at 181 Merrick Road. It stood just a quarter-mile from the DeFeo home; at the corner of Ocean Avenue and Merrick Road. On 13 November 1974, the bartender on duty, John Wendal, first saw Ronnie when he [Ronnie] entered the bar at approximately 4:00 p.m. At that time Ronnie sat down for his favorite drink (vodka with 7-up and a lemon peel). Ronnie had a few drinks, but didn't stay very long. Ronnie did return shortly thereafter; but this time, all hell was about to break loose like never before in the sleepy seaside town of Amityville. Ronnie drove back to the bar in his 1970 blue *Buick Electra 225*. Just after 6:00 p.m., Butch dramatically swung open the bar door at Henry's and ran over to his best friend.

"Bobby you got to help me," Ronnie shouted. "I think my mother and father are shot." Ronnie fell to his knees and began crying hysterically. Bobby rushed over to his distraught friend.

"Bobby, you got to help me. Somebody shot my mother and father." Bobby tried to process this shocking revelation.

"Are you sure they're not asleep?" Bobby asked.

"No, I saw them up there," Ronnie replied manically.

"Come on then; let's go," Bobby proclaimed, as he rounded up a few of the other bar faithful and headed over to the house. John Altieri, Joseph Yeswoit, Al Saxton, Bobby, Ronnie, and owner of Henry's Bar, William Scordamaglia, all raced over to the DeFeo home in Ronnie's Buick. The home stood just a few hundred yards from the bar, down Ocean Avenue. When the men pulled up to the home, they heard the DeFeo's sheepdog, Shaggy, barking wildly. The dog was tied up to the kitchen door, on the inside of the house!

"Be careful," someone said just prior to the men entering the home. "Somebody might be in there!"

"I don't care," Bobby yelled, and he opened the unlocked door and proceeded into the house. The rest of the men followed him inside, except for Ronnie. Knowing his way around the house, Bobby ran up the stairs to the master bedroom, which was located on the second floor. Before he could even enter the bedroom he noticed a strange smell. Bobby peered into the dark room, turned on the lights, and saw the bare back of Mr. DeFeo, with a dried up blood trail running down his back and what looked like a bullet hole. Mrs. DeFeo was next to him and had a large orange blanket covering her body. Bobby assumed that she had been shot as well, as he observed no movement.

Bobby got weak, queasy, and felt faint. The other men helped him down the stairs as John Altieri searched the rest of the rooms on the second floor. Altieri entered another room on the second floor and came upon the bodies of Marc and John. Freaked out as well, Altieri rushed downstairs and informed the others of his grisly discovery. Bobby went outside to get some air and to have a word with Ronnie, who was weeping hysterically outside and banging his fist on his car.

"Who do you want me to call from your family," Bobby asked consolingly. Ronnie asked Bobby to contact his grandfather; Michael Brigante Sr. Bobby rushed back into the house to use the phone, but noticed that one of the men had already taken liberties to it. Joe Yeswoit never went upstairs to view the bodies. Instead, he had grabbed hold of the kitchen phone and made a desperate call to police. Yeswoit dialed the newly formed 911 and was transferred to Suffolk County Police Department's emergency dispatch switchboard, which was obviously not used to receiving this type of distress call.

Call to the Suffolk County, NY, emergency dispatch switchboard; 11/13/74 at 6:30pm:

Operator: This is Suffolk County Police. May I help you?"
Man: "We have a shooting here. Uh, DeFeo."
Operator: "Sir, what is your name?"
Man: "Joey Yeswoit."
Operator: "Can you spell that?"
Man: "Yeah. Y-E-S W I T."
Operator: "Y-E-S . . .
Man: "Y-E-S-W-I-T."
Operator: ". . .W-I-T. Your phone number?"
Man: "I don't even know if it's here. There's, uh, I don't have a phone number here."
Operator: "Okay, where you calling from?"

Man: "It's in Amityville. Call up the Amityville Police, and it's right off, uh...Ocean Avenue in Amityville."
Operator: "Austin?"
Man: "Ocean Avenue. What the...?"
Operator: "Ocean ... Avenue? Off a where?"
Man: "It's right off Merrick Road. Ocean Avenue."
Operator: "Merrick Road. What's...what's the problem, Sir?"
Man: "It's a shooting!"
Operator: "There's a shooting. Anybody hurt?"
Man: "Hah?"
Operator: "Anybody hurt?"
Man: "Yeah, it's uh, uh -- everybody's dead."
Operator: "What'ya mean, everybody's dead?"
Man: "I don't know what happened. Kid come running in the bar; he says everybody in the family was killed, and we came down here."
Operator: "Hold on a second, Sir."
(*Police Officer now takes over call*)
Police Officer: "Hello."
Man: "Hello."
Police Officer: "What's your name?"
Man: "My name is Joe Yeswoit."
Police Officer: "George Edwards?"
Man: "Joe Yeswoit."
Police Officer: "How do you spell it?"
Man: "What? I just...How many times do I have to tell you? Y-E-S-W-I-T."
Police Officer: "Where're you at?"
Man: "I'm on Ocean Avenue.
Police Officer: "What number?"
Man: "I don't have a number here. There's no number on the phone.
Police Officer: "What number on the house?"
Man: "I don't even know that."
Police Officer: "Where're you at? Ocean Avenue and what?"
Man: "In Amityville. Call up the Amityville Police and have someone come down here. They know the family."
Police Officer: "Amityville."

Man: "Yeah, Amityville."
Police Officer: "Okay. Now, tell me what's wrong."
Man: "I don't know. Guy come running in the bar. Guy come running in the bar and said there -- his mother and father are shot. We ran down to his house and everybody in the house is shot. I don't know how long, you know. So, uh . . ."
Police Officer: "Uh, what's the add...what's the address of the house?"
Man: "Uh, hold on. Let me go look up the number. All right. Hold on. One-twelve Ocean Avenue, Amityville."
Police Officer: "Is that Amityville or North Amityville?"
Man: "Amityville. Right on ... south of Merrick Road."
Police Officer: "Is it right in the village limits?"
Man: "It's in the village limits, yeah."
Police Officer: "Eh, okay, what's your phone number?"
Man: "I don't even have one. There's no number on the phone."
Police Officer: "All right, where're you calling from? Public phone?"
Man: "No, I'm calling right from the house, because I don't see a number on the phone."
Police Officer: "You're at the house itself?"
Man: "Yeah."
Police Officer: "How *many* bodies are there?"
Man: "I think, uh, I don't know -- uh, I think they said four."
Police Officer: "There's four?"
Man: "Yeah."
Police Officer: "All right, you stay right there at the house, and I'll call the Amityville Village PD, and they'll come down."

Seconds after the call had ended the county dispatcher contacted Sergeant William Smith at the Amityville Police Department and relayed the multiple homicides. Sgt. Smith then radioed Police Officer, Kenneth Greguski, who had just gotten a sandwich from a deli on lower Broadway in Amityville. Greguski sped over to Ocean Avenue and within minutes he had pulled up in front of the house. Butch and all his friends were waiting in the doorway when Greguski arrived. Officer Greguski approached the gentlemen at approximately 6:40 p.m. Butch was crying and animated!

"My mother and father are dead," he screamed as Greguski neared. Greguski, who had been an Amityville police Officer for almost nine-years, wasted no time. He entered the house, bolted up the stairs, and quickly found Mr. & Mrs. DeFeo's bodies in the master bedroom. Greguski was in shock; but the real horror came from what he found next. A father of three children himself, Greguski was horrified to find the two young boys, Marc and John, covered in their own blood. Shocked by what he had just witnessed, he rushed down the stairs and used the kitchen phone to contact village headquarters.

"Sergeant, I have four bodies: a mother and father, and two boys." Butch sat at the kitchen table close by with tears still streaming from his eyes.

"I also have two sisters," Ronnie said while sobbing. Just then, village patrolman, Edwin Tyndall, entered the kitchen. Greguski dropped the phone, and beckoned Tyndall to follow. The two hurried up the stairs to take a further look around. When they returned, they confirmed the worst: Allison and Dawn were also found dead; Allison in her room, and Dawn in the third-floor "guest" bedroom.

"I found two more bodies of young females," Greguski anxiously told headquarters.

"I guess you can say it was the worst call that I ever had," Greguski later recalls, in an interview with the National Geographic Channel. "It was a harrowing site. I wouldn't wish it on anybody, to see a site like I had seen it." Whether they knew it or not at the time, all were witnessing the residential area's worst mass slaying!

DeFeo Crime Scene

Within five minutes Lieutenant Ed Lowe and Amityville's only detective, Pat Cammaroto, arrived on the scene. Amityville's Police Chief, William Kay, was attending a police association meeting that was some 30-miles away when he got the call. Chief Kay rushed back to Amityville to help with the investigation. At

7:20 p.m., Suffolk County Homicide Squad arrived on the scene. Among them were Lieutenant Tom Richmond, Detective Sergeant James Barylski, and Chief Detective George Harrison.

The immediate area in and around the house was soon filled with police. A large perimeter around the house was cordoned off by police to keep back the plethora of curious neighborhood residents that had gathered to get a glimpse of the unthinkable. Suffolk County detective, Gaspar Randazzo, sat with Butch in the kitchen to question the only surviving family member. Randazzo asked Butch who he thinks committed the murders.

"Tony Mazzeo," Butch replied. Mazzeo was a notorious mafia hit-man, who was also a good friend to the DeFeo family at one point. Mazzeo had actually lived with the DeFeo's for a brief time. Butch claimed that he and Mazzeo had gotten into a big argument a few years earlier, and that Mazzeo probably killed his family as a result of that argument.

Mindy was getting anxious, because Ronnie had not shown up or called for their date. Sometime right after 7:30 p.m., Mindy called the DeFeo home to see what was taking so long. To her surprise, Bobby Kelske answered the phone. "There's trouble, big trouble here…" he said. Mindy hung up the phone and rushed over to the house to find out exactly what was going on. Bobby then placed a call to Ronnie's grandfathers, who both rushed over to the house soon after.

Next door neighbor, Rufus Ireland, had an office set up in the front of his house where he was sitting at the time when his friend Al Saxon came rushing into his home and said, "Rufus, I've got something to tell you! You're not gonna believe this! Everybody next door is dead!" Soon after this startling revelation, Detective Harrison approached Mr. Ireland and asked him if he could use his home as a temporary headquarters for police and medics. Mr. Ireland agreed, and the police set up a temporary command post at the Ireland's home for the next few hours.

Fearing that there was still a mad man on the loose, police announced that they needed everyone out of the DeFeo house. Police then escorted everyone to the Ireland home next door, and placed Ronnie into "protective custody." Among the many concerns that the police had, they also did not want the crime scene soiled by the witnesses; they also wanted to keep them around for questioning. At the Ireland home, Suffolk County Detectives, Gerald Gozaloff and Joseph Napolitano, joined in the questioning. Before taking Butch to police headquarters they urged him to give a written statement. In this statement Butch claimed to have been home the previous night until sometime after 4:40 a.m. He also claimed that he saw his Brother Marc's wheelchair in front of the door and heard a toilet flush while walking past the second floor bathroom. After that "he decided to go to work early," he said.

The Investigation

Meanwhile, back at the house Police officers surveyed the crime scene, but they only did a thorough sweep of the rooms that the crimes had allegedly occurred in. Police had an enormous crime scene to investigate and they wasted no time. Officers scurried to and fro, gathering information and possible clues. It was soon clear to anyone involved that this was no dream; it was a real life nightmare.

Police continued to search the premises looking for any obvious answers as to why a whole family had just been butchered. Surveying the area, they noticed that a first floor window of the house was broken. Police did not think it a burglary, because nothing seemed to be missing. Ronnie later claimed that he had broken the window himself after knocking on the door and ringing the doorbell several times, but getting no response. It was then that Ronnie said he discovered the bodies and subsequently rushed to Henry's bar to get help.

Suffolk County Ballistics expert, Detective Alfred DellaPenna, was at his home in Brentwood, NY, when he received a call that there were multiple homicides committed on Ocean Avenue in Amityville. DellaPenna grew up in the Pelican Bay area of the Bronx. He earned a Master of Science degree in police science. DellaPenna headed a crime scene unit that was responsible for 'on the spot' investigations of major crime scenes in the Suffolk County area. DellaPenna had extensive training in firearms and was, by all accounts and degrees, a firearms expert. Yet, nothing could prepare him for what he was about to witness on this night.

DellaPenna was asked to gather up his crime scene unit and head over to the scene. He rushed to Ocean Avenue, not paying much attention to the address. He assumed that he was being sent into the poorer section of Amityville. To his surprise he arrived at one of the most affluent blocks in the area. As he got closer to the home he noticed that there were already a slew of policemen and spectators crowding the area. He made his way to the home on foot and was met first by the Homicide Detective (HD). DellaPenna will never forget what the Detective said to him before he entered. "Hi Al, we've got six big-ones for you this time."

After being briefed by the HD, DellaPenna walked through the crime scene with Deputy Chief Medical Examiner, Dr. Howard C. Adelman. After viewing the bodies DellaPenna went to the kitchen. He was looking for clues to determine if the family had possibly been sedated or poisoned before the shootings. Officers searched diligently for the murder weapon. They searched in and around the house; they searched the Amityville creek behind the house; they searched nearby garbage cans; they even searched the DeFeo's pool; but no murder weapon was recovered. DellaPenna examined the sinks, drains, dishes, silverware, glasses and cups. He even had his unit examine the food scraps in all of the garbages. Ballistics evidence, however, was first priority of DellaPenna and his unit. There were no cartridge casings visible. Normally, ballistics experts must wait for post-mortem inspection—which occurs at a later time—to collect such evidence. But witnessing the size of the wounds of the victims, DellaPenna assumed that the bullets had passed through the bodies. The bodies, however, were not permitted to be turned or shifted, so DellaPenna would have to wait until the bodies were removed to examine the beds.

Police seized a .22-caliber rifle, a shotgun, and a pellet gun, which were all mounted on a wall. Suffolk County Chief Detective's, Patrick Mellon, who was in charge of the investigation, told the press "none of the guns recovered had been used in a long time." Though it was not reported to the press immediately, the police also recovered several weapons in various rooms of the house.

Police Initially Recovered:

- Crossman .38 target Pellgun Revolver [Item #35] from the closet of the master bedroom
- Healthways plainsman pistol [tem #36] in the dresser drawer of the master bedroom
- Marlin .22 caliber rifle [Item #56] Recovered in the 3rd floor Westside bedroom
- Crossman .22 caliber pellet rifle [Item #57] which was mounted on the wall
- Ithaca 12 gauge shotgun [Item #58]
- Starter pistol from the drawer [Item #59]

"It was like an Alfred Hitchcock movie," one investigator told a reporter. "They all lay there peaceful, and on their faces, all in their nightclothes." The scene was so eerie that police whispered when they wanted to say anything; not just because they didn't want to contaminate the crime scene, but also because they were spooked. Although there were several police officers in and around the house, the place remained nearly silent. Police were puzzled by several aspects of the case right from the get-go.

Police were perplexed as to why the DeFeo's dog, Shaggy, hadn't protected the family. Shaggy was a watchdog, according to neighbors, and many were afraid to go into the home with Shaggy running loose; detectives were baffled. Deputy Suffolk County Police Commissioner, Robert C. Rapp, declared: "We have at this time no leads. We've recovered no weapon. We have no suspect."

Police questioned friends and neighbors of the family, trying to get insight on the situation. Reports soon surfaced that Ronnie had bragged to at least one person that his father was "big in the mafia." One neighbor reported that he had an altercation with Ronald DeFeo, Sr., and he too bragged of his organized crime connections. Big

Ronnie threatened the neighbor that he would bring in the mafia to settle the dispute if necessary.

All the family members were found lying facedown—their hands extended above their heads in ritualistic fashion. This bore the ear-markings of a traditional mob killing. So police called in the Suffolk County Organized Crime Control Bureau—led by Chief James Caples—to investigate the possibility of a mob hit. Ronald DeFeo, Sr.'s father, Joseph "Rocco" DeFeo, reportedly had mob ties; but it was Rocco's brother, Peter DeFeo, who was a Mafioso Soldier.

If they didn't know already, the Bureau would soon find out, from their underworld sources, that Peter DeFeo was a captain in the Vito Genovese crime family and one of Genovese's closest associates. Peter's first arrest came back in 1934, when he and others were indicted for the brutal murder of Ferdinand "The Shadow" Broccia. None were ever convicted, however. His second arrest came in 1947, when he was wounded in what police describe as a shootout stemming from a labor dispute. His last charge came in 1968, for attempting to get kickbacks from a Teamster Union pension fund. Although they mulled over the possibility of a 'revenge hit' against Peter, or even Peter as being a suspect in the murders, police eventually exonerated him.

***

When Mindy arrived at about 8:00 p.m., she noticed that the street was blocked off and crowds of people scorned the area. Estimates say that there were upwards of forty neighborhood resident-spectators lining the area, including reporters and camera men. Mindy was frantic and wanted to know what was going on and if Ronnie was ok. She approached a police officer and identified herself. The officer directed her to the Ireland home. Gaining easy access to the Ireland home, she sat and waited to speak with one of the detectives. By this time, Ronnie and his friends had all been escorted to the Ireland home and were being questioned by police. Once in the Ireland home, Mindy took a seat on the couch in the living room and began waiting. Detective Grieco approached Mindy and began questioning her about her involvement with Ronnie and the day's events from her perspective. Mindy introduced herself as

Ronnie's girlfriend and the two began conversing. During the conversation, Mindy was interrupted by a man named Richard Wyssling, who introduced himself as Ronnie's attorney. Wyssling gave Mindy his business card (which was later entered into evidence and labeled *"Exhibit C"*) and asked her to call him if she had any information or any questions about Ronnie.

Along with Ronnie, Bobby Kelske was also facing interrogation in the Ireland home. At first detectives questioned both Ronnie and Bobby together, with a priest present [Reverend James McNamara]. After about ten minutes Bobby was asked to go wait in the other room. Police wanted to isolate Ronnie and Bobby, in an attempt to *divide-and-conquer*. Ronnie's story was falling apart at the seams. Police decided to intensify the questioning and let Ronnie talk his way into more mistakes.

Officer Gozaloff and Sergeant Carmarotto entered the room at some point with a plan to separate the two. Carmarotto escorted Bobby into another room, and Randazzo and Gozaloff turned up the heat. Detective Gozaloff asked Ronnie firmly, "Who killed your family?" However, Ronnie did not answer him. Gozaloff then informed Ronnie that he was going to take him down to the station to continue questioning him, but Ronnie vehemently declined. Ronnie claimed that he did not want to go to the police station, but Gozaloff demanded. They went back and forth for a few minutes, and then Ronnie stood up as if he was going to leave.

According to Ronnie, Detective Gozaloff pushed his face, catching him off guard. Ronnie fell to the ground, but got up quickly. Gozaloff took a step back, slid his coat to the side, and unsnapped the strap on his gun holster. Gozaloff put his hand on his gun and waited for him to make a move, but Ronnie just sat back down. Gozaloff grabbed Ronnie's arm and said adamantly, "Were going to the precinct." Gozaloff then calmed down and began to use his police skills to persuade Ronnie. "It will be better down there," he stated. "All I want you to do is give a statement and then I'll bring you back." Not really having a choice, and feeling confident that they would let him go soon after, Ronnie decided to continue to cooperate with police.

When Bobby exited the room he noticed that Mindy was sitting in another room also being questioned by a detective. Bobby and Mindy were soon escorted out of the Ireland home and asked to wait outside. At approximately 8:00 p.m., they both witnessed Ronnie being escorted out of the Ireland house by several police officers and taken to a police car. Mindy watched in awe as her boyfriend walked past her—just ten-feet away—and looked up at her for an instant, but said nothing. She could see tears in his eyes and she noticed a red mark visible on the left side of his cheek that she later claimed looked like it came from a slap. Ronnie's grandfather, Rocco "Rocky" DeFeo, asked Bobby to go see where they were taking him. Bobby rushed over to the attending officers: "Where are you taking him," he asked. "Get away," one officer said while making a hand gesture to mean the same. "Don't worry about it," the officer continued.

✼✼✼

Mr. Richard Wyssling was an attorney hired *on the fly* by Ronnie's grandfather, Mr. Brigante. Wyssling first arrived at the crime scene at approximately 7:45 p.m. As soon as he arrived at the Ireland house, Mr. Wyssling met with Michael Brigante Sr., Angela Brigante, and their son, Michael Brigante Jr. He then entered the Ireland house and had a conversation with Mindy, Grieco, and Randazzo. Mr. Wyssling spoke to detective Randazzo and informed him that he wanted to speak to Ronnie. Randazzo advised him to wait there for a moment and went off toward the kitchen area and made a phone call. Randazzo left Mr. Wyssling there for about 20 minutes before returning with some bad news. It seems in the midst of Randazzo's timely phone conversation, police had time to slip Ronnie out of the house before Wyssling had a chance to speak to him. "He's at the Amityville jail," Randazzo told Wyssling. Then Randazzo left again, came back and said, "He's at the First Precinct."

After leaving the Ireland house, Ronnie was escorted by Gozaloff to the Amityville Police Station. When they entered, Gozaloff went up to the desk and spoke with the clerk. After a brief discussion, it was determined that they were not allowed to keep him there. This was because it was a felony and was jurisdiction of the

Suffolk County Police Department. Ronnie was then taken to the First Precinct on Rt. 109 in Lindenhurst. Ronnie was immediately taken into the interviewing room, where the questioning continued. Police questioning became increasingly personal and Ronnie felt that the questions had nothing to do with the murders. The line of questioning by police made Ronnie feel very uncomfortable. It was at this time that Ronnie believed that he was now being viewed by police as a suspect.

Fifteen minutes after Ronnie was carted away by police, Bobby was accompanied by Detective Harrison to the First Precinct located at 555 Route 109 in Lindenhurst, Long Island. Police continued questioning Bobby at the precinct, where he remained both a possible material witness and possible suspect in the murders. Bobby was curious to know of Ronnie's whereabouts. Detective Harold Cohen advised him that Ronnie was in the other room in the same building. Bobby remained at the precinct for hours, losing track of time in the process, as there was no clock visible to him. Bobby asked to make a phone call, but he was denied this basic right. He asked to go to the bathroom and again he was denied this basic right. According to Bobby, at no point did officers even offer him any type of food or drink.

After being questioned for about an hour, police informed Ronnie that they were going to perform a "Paraffin Test" on his hands to see if he had fired a weapon. A Paraffin Test was performed on DeFeo at the First Precinct at approximately 9:00 p.m. During the test Ronnie believed that he needed a lawyer present, and he demanded to notify an attorney. Ronnie wanted to call Richard Hartman, an attorney that had previously represented him for a charge that he had against him in Hauppauge. Hartman was also a personal friend of the family for close to six years and had been to more than one DeFeo family function. Detective Gozaloff said to him, "Don't worry; don't worry about it. You'll get an attorney. We'll get you one." Gozaloff kept saying that they'd let him call an attorney, but never did.

At sometime before 11:00 p.m., police performed a paraffin test on Bobby to determine if he had recently fired a gun. Bobby went along with the test as he felt that he had nothing to hide.

Paraffin tests were done on several people that night, including the six-dead-bodies, according to the Assistant District Attorney of Suffolk County, Gerald Sullivan. Somewhere between 11:00 p.m., and 1:00 a.m., Bobby witnessed Ronnie being escorted off the premises. He later learned that Ronnie had been taken to the Forth Precinct located at 345 Old Willets Path in Hauppauge, Long Island. People continued to gather around the crime scene and many of the DeFeo family members—such as Ronnie's aunt, his uncles, and his grandfathers—remained at the scene with no idea where Ronnie had been taken. At approximately 10:30 p.m., police began a conversation with Ronnie's uncle, Vincent Procita, and his grandfather, Michael Brigante Sr. During the conversation Detective Gozaloff boldly asked, "Do you think that Ronnie could have committed the crime?" Procita tells Gozaloff that Ronnie regularly abused drugs. "Who knows what such a person could be capable of," Procita says. Witnessing Procita's outburst, Rocco DeFeo said in a loud voice, "Shut up, this is family!" Suddenly, all cooperation between family members of the victims and police had ceased. Realizing that the family posed a threat to police if they were to get to Ronnie, Gozaloff made a call to Detective Harrison at police headquarters and told him to keep Ronnie away from his family. Gozaloff told Harrison that if the family were to see him at that time, they would cut off the only supply of information available to police.

✶✶✶

At sometime right before 11:00 p.m., Mr. Wyssling arrived at the First Precinct in an attempt to locate his client. There, he spoke to an officer and identified himself as Ronnie DeFeo's attorney. The officer went in the back for about 15-20 minutes. When he returned he advised Wyssling that Ronnie was being held at the Amityville police station located at 21 Greene Avenue in Amityville, NY. Surely the officer was aware that any crime committed in Suffolk County that is considered a felony is immediately the responsibility of the Suffolk County Police Department (SCPD). Amityville police were reduced to traffic duty and keeping spectators back once SCPD came on the scene. Mr. Wyssling left and arrived at the Amityville police station at approximately 11:30 p.m. SCPD had managed to throw Wyssling completely off the trail.

Ronnie spent another couple of hours at the First Precinct before being escorted by Detectives Napolitano and Barrison to the Fourth Precinct. At approximately 11:30 p.m., Gozaloff said that he was going back to the house to investigate further. Ronnie had begun to give a statement at the First Precinct, and continued to add to that same statement at the Fourth Precinct. Ronnie signed an eight-page statement for police there at the Fourth Precinct at sometime after midnight. It was later labeled "*Exhibit 78*." In the statement, Ronnie admitted that his family had mob ties, and that he theorized that the murders were mob related. At that same time, the bodies of his six slain family members were being removed from the house in black plastic bags and transported to the county morgue in Hauppauge.

Mr. Wyssling arrived at the Fourth Precinct at approximately 12:55 a.m., and again, he told the desk officer that he represented Ronald DeFeo. "I understand he's being charged with a number of murders," Wyssling proclaimed. "If you are questioning him I want it stopped and I want to see him now!" The officer made an intercom call to the back area of the police station, which was completely out of site from the main area where Wyssling and the officer were located. The officer eventually left and headed to the back area. The officer returned after about ten-minutes and told Mr. Wyssling that Ronald DeFeo was not there. Mr. Wyssling became very frustrated, angry, and boisterous at this point. "I've been jacked around all night," Wyssling screamed. "This is the third place I've gone to. I demand to see him now!" Sensing that Wyssling was beyond angry, the officer returned to the back area. Minutes later a man came out from the back and identified himself as Lt. David Menzies, the highest ranking police officer in the building at the time.

"Who the hell are you?" Lt. Menzies asked Wyssling.

"I'm Ronald DeFeo's attorney," Wyssling replied. Lt. Menzies continued on his cantankerous, evasive tirade.

"How do I know you're an attorney?" Wyssling was in no mood to take this kind of abuse from a putz with a badge. Wyssling fired back with some sarcasm of his own.

"What do you want me to do, quote the law?" Wyssling then handed him his business card.

"What the hell does this mean?" Menzies rudely asked Wyssling.

The two continued to go back and forth. Menzies wanted to know how Wyssling was going to prove he was an attorney. Finally, Menzies returned to the back area and had Wyssling waiting again. When he returned, Menzies denied Wyssling from seeing his client, which is clearly an unconstitutional act. Meanwhile, worried about her boyfriend's whereabouts, Mindy pulled out Wyssling's business card and decided to give him a call at about 1:30 a.m. On the business card was Wyssling's home phone number. When she called Wyssling's home his wife answered the phone and said that he has not returned yet. Exhausted from the nights events, Mindy decided to get some shut-eye and try Wyssling again later that day. Back at the Fourth Precinct, Wyssling realized that he was not going to get any justice with the police so he left the station at about 1:45 a.m., and returned home.

Bobby was tired as well. He had been at the First Precinct for several hours. At about 3:30 a.m., Bobby gave the police a written statement of his involvement that night, which was an accumulation of what he had already communicated to them. Shortly after providing police with a written statement, Bobby was taken to the Fourth Precinct by two detectives. It was close to 5:00 a.m., when Bobby walked into the doors of the Fourth Precinct. The detectives took Bobby into a room and continued questioning him. They informed him that he would be "leaving soon," because they were satisfied with his statements. Bobby told police that Ronnie owned several guns and was a gun-buff of sorts. Bobby also informed police that Ronnie's father had taken the guns away from him recently, but Ronnie had gotten them back somehow. Bobby also told police that he had a conversation with Ronnie in Ronnie's car a couple of months before about a silencer. Later, in his testimony during the trial, Bobby was never pressed to expound on his conversation with Ronnie about the silencer. This very well may have been because Det. DellaPenna had already determined that there was no silencer used. Bobby was released sometime around 6:00 a.m.

***

Once the bodies were removed from the house, DellaPenna began examining the mattresses. In one of the boy's mattresses he found a shell casing that he believed came from a .35 caliber rifle. Serendipitously, police received a call from Steven Hicks—a good friend of Ronnie's. Steven told police that Ronnie brought a .35 caliber Marlin rifle to his house that he had just purchased. The detail that really caught police's attention, however, was that Steven told them that Ronnie had accidentally fired the weapon in his living room. The bullet went through Steven's living room floor and had never been recovered. DellaPenna was eager to visit Steven's home and see if he could locate the bullet. If so, DellaPenna would then have a chance to run tests to see if the bullet was an exact match with the bullets used in the murders. This test would also help DellaPenna determine whether or not the gun used in the murders was the same gun sold to Ronnie by Chuck Tewksbury (the .35 caliber Marlin rifle in question).

Five different neighbors reported being awakened by the DeFeo's dog at around 2:30 a.m., from the loud barking. Each neighbor also reported going right back to bed after, as this was a frequent occurrence. Although the dog's barking could be heard, none of the neighbors reported hearing any shots fired. Police were puzzled as to how this could be. Police began to seriously consider the possibility that the family may have been drugged. Dr. Adelman offered a statement to the press, and seemed as puzzled as the rest of the investigators. "I cannot offer any explanation as to why all the victims were lying face down. But it appeared to me that they were all asleep when they were killed," Adelman said. "It is bizarre that they were all in the exact same position," he added. The pervasive theme was that the victims were drugged, but police wouldn't confirm anything until they ran further tests. Adelman told reporters that it could take up to a week to find out the results. Reporters pressed Adelman for his response to the family being drugged. Adelman said, "I don't know how else they could keep quiet at the time of the shootings." Adelman did explain that there were no needle marks found on any of the victims, and police were looking into the possibility that the family's last meal was drugged. Other questions began forming from this, such as where was Ronnie during the murders, and how did he escape the drugging and subsequent slaughter? Detectives were interrogating Ronnie to find out just that.

During the early morning hours of 14 November 1974, DellaPenna and the Homicide Detective headed over to Steven's home to try and recover the bullet. The bullet hole was located in the living room floor of the house. Police pulled back the rug to expose the hard wood floor where the bullet had pierced. Steven told police that there was a small crawl space below the house where the bullet was probably resting. DellaPenna crawled beneath the house into the dark and damp crawl space in search of the bullet. He was armed with only a flashlight as he sifted through the sand and debris looking for the bullet. DellaPenna positioned himself directly under the small circle of light coming from the bullet hole in the floor above.

Although DellaPenna searched diligently for the bullet, he was no match for the lack of light and proper tools, not to mention the cold. DellaPenna called off his search and decided to call in a recovery team. The following day an *Emergency Service Group* recovered the bullet and delivered it to DellaPenna in the lab. After tests were conducted, DellaPenna found that the bullet recovered from Steven's home was an exact match with the bullets that had been used to kill the DeFeo family.

Reports began to mount heavily against Ronnie. Many felt that Ronnie was bad news, and several people reported stories that corroborated this. Newspapers contacted a local Long Island bar owner who told them that Ronnie had threatened him after he had fired a barmaid whom Ronnie had been dating. The owner told reporters that Ronnie stood outside the bar and was firing a pistol in an attempt to intimidate the bar owner into hiring the girl back.

"Nothing indicated that he could have resorted to violence of this kind," said William Benjamin, principle officer of Suffolk County's Babylon Probation Office. Ronnie was convicted of grand larceny, for the theft of an outboard motor, in September of 1973.

On 14 December 1973, Ronnie was sentenced to one-year of probation. In April of 1974, Ronnie's then girlfriend had contacted police and told them that Ronnie was still using drugs. Upon inspection, probation officers noticed fresh needle marks in DeFeo's arms. On 29 May 1974, Judge Harry E. Seidell granted probation officers the right to randomly search Ronnie at their own discretion. Ronnie's probation officer told police that Ronnie had been given fifteen urine tests between June and October, and two of them showed traces of quinine—which is frequently used to dilute heroin. The five-foot-seven, 155-pound DeFeo was also a major suspect in a more recent robbery case at his grandfather's Buick car dealership in Brooklyn.

At 8:45 a.m., Detective George Harrison entered the filing room and observed Butch sleeping peacefully on a cot. Harrison began shaking Butch until he awoke. Butch looked at Harrison all crusty eyed and said, "Did you find Mazzeo?" Harrison did not respond. The look on Harrison's face was stone cold.

"You have the right to remain silent," Harrison said in a professional tone. "Anything you say can and will be used against you in the court of law. You have the right to an attorney. If you cannot afford one..." Butch sat up quickly on the cot and protested his innocence.

"I didn't kill anyone! I told you who the killer was!" The evidence had already begun mounting against the bearded twenty-three-year-old.

Things were only going to get worse for Butch, starting out with Gozaloff and Napolitano's immediate departure. The two detectives were relieved by two of the fiercest officers on the Suffolk County Police force, Detective Dennis Rafferty and Lt. Robert Dunn, who were determined to get a confession by any-means-necessary. These two gentlemen had built up quite a reputation for getting oral and written confessions over the years—some legal and some illegal, allegedly. Coincidentally, *Newsday* had just printed an article on Tuesday, 5 November 1974, about police brutality in Suffolk County. In the article they cited that, over a 30-month period, there were *93 brutality complaints* filed against Suffolk

County Officers. Rafferty and Dunn were among the one's complaints were filed against.

At 6:45 p.m., on 14 November 1974, Suffolk County Deputy Commissioner, Robert C. Rapp, sitting along side Chief Mellon, announced the arrest of Ronald DeFeo, Jr., in a press conference. Police told the press that DeFeo showed little sign of remorse and did not act like someone whose entire family had been murdered. The bodies had been taken to the county morgue, where it was determined that the family had been dead since, at latest, 7:00 a.m., on the morning of November 13th.

Detective Harrison signed the complaint against Ronnie. Harrison said during Ronnie's confession, Ronnie said, "I took the rifle and ammunition from my room, and then I shot my brother Marc like this." Harrison said that Ronnie then stood up and acted out the killing. During his confession Ronnie also said that after he shot his brother Marc, he watched the boy's body twitch and convulse. No motive was offered for the crime, as Rapp refused to discuss the evidence in the case. Although, newspapers were reporting that the motive for the murder was money and that Ronnie was the beneficiary of a $200,000 life insurance policy. Police reported that the murder weapon had not yet been recovered, but they were expecting to find it soon.

Christopher Berry-Dee, a British criminologist, author, and Director of *The Criminology Research Institute*, had a chance to interview Ronnie in 1994 at the Green Haven Correctional Facility for a TV documentary series called, "The Serial Killers". He also used the interview for a chapter in his book titled, *Talking with Serial Killers*. Berry-Dee interviewed just about every other major player in the Amityville story as well. Berry-Dee stated that Ronnie had repeatedly demanded his lawyer, but was denied. Berry-Dee stated that "the officers continued interrogating him for more than 21 hours without the presence of a lawyer. During this entire time DeFeo was illegally denied the services of an attorney, he was even denied the use of a toilet and was deprived of food and water."

Later at his preliminary hearing, Ronnie described what was done to him. He claimed that he was knocked to the ground and kicked repeatedly. Ronnie claimed that, later while seated in a chair, officers put a phone book on his head then took a blackjack and kept beating on the top of the phone book with it. This lasted for a good ten-minutes, according to DeFeo. "By this time I was crying," Ronnie continued. "I was sick and I was hurt pretty bad. I couldn't take anymore. But I wasn't going to sign a statement saying I did it."

✽✽✽

Police would continue their sweep of the house, collecting evidence for several days following the murders. In the early morning hours of November 15th, Detective John Shirvell was doing a routine investigation of the crime scene. The bedrooms where the murders had taken place had been inspected thoroughly. Butch's room, however, was only briefly examined, because allegedly none of the murders were committed there; although that was not actually a legitimate excuse for not checking it for evidence. At the time police were not aware exactly what weapon was used to commit the murders. Shirvell decided to take a quick look around Ronnie's room at about 2:30 a.m. Upon doing so, Shirvell found a pair of long rectangular cardboard boxes labeled *Marlin rifles, .22, and .35.* Shirvell returned to the station and tagged the boxes as evidence. Shirvell did not know at that time that the .35 caliber Marlin was the murder weapon. It was only later, when forensic examiners revealed that a .35-caliber Marlin rifle was used in all of the killings, that Det. Shirvell realized the magnitude of his findings.

Another piece of evidence soon surfaced that also helped to incriminate Ronnie further. Next door neighbor, Mrs. Nemeth, recalled her son telling her that he had heard the DeFeo's dog howling wildly at about 3:20 a.m., on 13 November 1974. Mrs. Nemeth was not a big fan of Ronnie either. She told police that Ronnie had once threatened to punch her in the face, because he accused her daughter of throwing rocks at the statue on the DeFeo's lawn. Since other neighbors had reported hearing the dog bark at 2:30 a.m., police were able to narrow down the time of the murders even further.

This first admission by Mrs. Nemeth helped police begin to build a case against Ronnie. Since all of the victims were found in their nightclothes and found dead in their beds, police were left thinking that the murders occurred sometime during the late night of November 12th, or the early morning hours of November 13th. Through witness reports and other evidence, police were able to determine the time of the murders as occurring at approximately 3:00 a.m. Ronnie claimed that he left the house that morning at around 4:40 a.m., and that he didn't notice anything unusual before he left. This helped police put Ronnie at the scene of the crime at the time the murders took place.

Oral Confession

Other evidence was also beginning to be confirmed by police, and they also started to notice serious inconsistencies in Ronnie's version of the events. After being questioned for several hours during the day of 14 November 1974, Ronnie finally broke down and confessed to the murders.

"It all started so fast. Once I started, I just couldn't stop. It went so fast…"

Ronnie told police the gut-wrenching details. The interrogation went on for several hours and Ronnie was forced to reiterate the murders numerous times. Just as he does now, Ronnie would recant certain statements, adding new details with each new version he uttered. Nearly every statement he made contradicted the previous one. Police said that at one point Ronnie said that he killed Dawn "because she took too much time hogging up the bathroom," and that he killed Allison because "she annoyed him." His whole family he called, "fat fucks and fucking pigs," and he said that his mother's cooking, "tastes like shit!" Police were looking for statements from Ronnie that they could be sure only the killer would know. Ronnie's testimony remained consistently vague; however, there were a number of times that Ronnie told police very graphic details of the killings. When asked to reconstruct the murder of his youngest brother, police claim that Ronnie shrugged his shoulders and said, "I remember that after I shot him, I stood there and watched his feet twitching." Detective Dunn said that "if ever Ronnie was truthful, he was truthful on that occasion."

Ronnie told police that after the murders he calmly cleaned up, showered, trimmed his beard, and then collected all of the shell-casings and the bloodied clothes. After wrapping them up in a pillow case, Ronnie went outside and tossed the rifle into the river near his home then drove to Brooklyn, New York to go to work. Ronnie drove on the Belt Parkway to get to work, and always got off at the same exit. This time, however, Ronnie exited the parkway before the actual stop and was searching for a garbage-can to dispose-of the evidence. Abandoning that idea, Ronnie stopped at a red light, exited the vehicle, and emptied the pillow case and its contents into a storm drain/sewer across from the Shell Gas Station at the intersection of Seaview Avenue and 96th Street before going to work. At around 6a.m., Ronnie arrived at work. He revealed to police the precise location of the sewer in Brooklyn where he dumped the evidence; he even drew them a map.

Under Ronnie's direction, police were able to recover:

- A rifle carrying case (in excellent condition)
- A pillow case (containing various items of blood stained clothing)
- A few boxes of live ammunition
- All eight spent shell casings from the scene of the murders

Ronnie admitted to police that he threw the gun into the canal behind his house. It wasn't directly behind his house, so he again drew police a map where to find it. On 15 November 1974 (Friday morning), Chief Mellon assigned marine scuba divers to search the murky Amityville Creek behind the DeFeo home for the murder weapon. Police recovered the weapon from the water at the end of the *Richmond Avenue Dock*. After it was recovered by the divers, it was immediately given to DellaPenna for inspection. The first thing DellaPenna checked was the end of the barrel. He found no "outside threads," which indicated to him that there had been *no silencer* used. Police considered the possibility that Ronnie may have intended to kill himself, because the rifle was cocked when they found it.

DellaPenna cleaned the gun using regular water to remove as much of the salt as possible. He also submerged the rifle in kerosene to stop any further oxidation, which stopped rust from forming. Back at the lab, DellaPenna disassembled the rifle piece by piece. He continued to run tests on the rifle for several hours. Once tests were done and the weapon had dried, DellaPenna gave all parts a thin coat of oil and reassembled the weapon. Once put back together, DellaPenna began test-firing the weapon to try and duplicate the exact markings found on the murder bullets. Striation marks (or microscopic scratches) inside of the barrel of the gun transfer onto the bullets when they are fired. These marks are unique to each barrel, which allows forensic investigators to identify a weapon from the bullets fired from it. After several tests, DellaPenna concluded that the gun found in the canal had "without question fired all eight bullets used in the murders."

At sometime during the morning hours of November 15th, Chief Mellon told reporters that police had recovered a *.35 caliber Marlin Lever Action rifle (Model number 336C)* out of the river right behind the DeFeo home. Although there were several suspects considered by police, as the investigation went on they were starting to believe that Ronnie was the sole killer in these murders. In several of Ronnie's stories he admitted to being the lone-gunman; however, in others stories he claimed to have unnamed accomplices. Police continued to listen to his various versions, using each to piece together the crimes. Police then concentrated on the physical evidence, which all further implicated Ronnie and Ronnie alone. Police searched the house for footprints and impressions. They also swept the scene for serological evidence on cigarettes, glasses, and receptacles. From these tests police were able to determine that there was no evidence of any outsider's presence during the night of the murders. Also, Police were never able to find a single piece of credible evidence that put anyone else in the house during the time of the murders.

Pretrial

DeFeo's lawyer, Leonard Symons, represented him at his bail hearing just two days after the murders. Symons also represented Ronnie back in September of 1973, when he was put on probation for theft of an outboard motor. Symons requested that a psychiatric examination be given to his client, but Judge Donald Auperin turned down defense council's request. Symons said that he would make a second request—this time in writing—for the examination adding, "I have doubts about the defendant's ability to help his own defense." Symons also stated that DeFeo had "new bruises" that he had received during questioning.

Detective Harrison added the dramatics when he explained how DeFeo described the shooting of his brother, Marc. From Harrison's testimony, Ronnie was arraigned on one-count of second-degree murder. Suffolk County District Attorney, Henry Wenzel, reported that evidence in all six murders would be presented to the Grand Jury. Ronnie was sent to the county jail in Riverhead at 3:00 p.m., where he would await indictment. The bodies of the deceased DeFeo's were later brought to Guidetti Funeral Home at 33 Spring Street in Manhattan for the wake.

On Monday, 18 November 1974, DeFeo was brought in front of District Judge Ernest L. Signorelli for arraignment. Signorelli noticed that Butch looked pretty beat up. In fact, Signorelli felt so strongly about Butch's appearance that he ordered an immediate Medical Examination. The examination was conducted later that day in the Suffolk County jail by a jail physician. The results were later marked as "Exhibit B."

The resulting document stated that "a subsiding bruise on the abdomen, a subsiding bruise on the left leg, and healing abrasions of the spinal area." Although the jail physician claimed in the report that the bruises were between "four to seven days old"—apparently to protect the Suffolk County Police Officer's responsible (one can deduce, as he was the "jail physician")—several witnesses testified that those bruises were not there previous to Butch being taken away by police. The police and the D.A. had claimed that Butch received the injuries during the alleged fist fight between him and his father just two days before the murders. Patrolman Kenneth Greguski, who later became Amityville's police chief, allegedly told Christopher Berry-Dee that when he first arrived on the scene and witnessed Ronnie, "He [Ronnie] was pretty upset and had been crying...but there were no injuries to his face at all."

The prosecution was headed by Assistant District Attorney of Suffolk County, Gerald Sullivan, who seemed hell-bent right from the get-go to see that Ronnie Joseph DeFeo, Jr., get the maximum penalty for all six murders, and he would do everything in his power to accomplish just that. Shortly after the arraignment it was decided that instead of having a preliminary hearing—to decide whether there was enough evidence to force the defendant to stand trial—the case would be taken directly to the Grand Jury (GJ). The GJ is made up of twenty-three random citizens that must hear evidence of the crime and vote to issue an indictment against the defendant. Sullivan presented the evidence and the GJ wasted no time in returning with an indictment. It was easy based on the fact that Sullivan claimed that Ronnie confessed his guilt to the interrogating officers. Given the drastic nature of the crimes, it's easy to understand how this case was immediately sent to the grand jury. With allegations of an oral confession, including Ronnie leading police to the murder weapon (as well as other evidence) the prosecution had all they needed to proceed directly to the grand jury for an indictment. The proceedings lasted only a half-hour.

On that same day, the DeFeo funeral mass was held inside of *St. Martin of Tours Church,* at 35 Union Avenue in Amityville. The service was scheduled to be private, but the response from sympathizers was overwhelming. Eleven priests were on hand for "The Mass of the Resurrection," where nearly 1000 mourners and curious-onlookers were in attendance. More than 300 people were turned away at the door. Heavy police detail chaperoned scores of onlookers during the ninety-minute funeral service. The sermon was given by Reverend James McNamara (The same clergyman who witnessed part of Ronnie and Bobby's interrogation). The Reverend spoke optimistically about the departed DeFeo's. An example of this is when he said, *"Through death, they have been given new life and become more like Jesus, because they have seen him. We must not confuse our sorrow with their joy."*

Just two hours after the six coffins were lowered into the ground at St. Charles Cemetery in Pinelawn, a Suffolk County Grand Jury indicted DeFeo on six-counts of second-degree murder. A spokesman for the county jail in Riverhead said that Ronnie made no request to attend his family's funeral. As 300 mourners—each with a red carnation in hand—watched the bodies of the deceased being lowered into the ground, Father McNamara again read from the scriptures. It was at this point that Mr. and Mrs. Brigante were seen breaking down for the first time. Long after the bodies were lowered into the ground, Joseph "Rocco" DeFeo held rosary-beads and starred at the graves.

On Tuesday, November 19th, Ronnie was brought to the chapel of the Suffolk County jail, instead of the Suffolk County Courthouse, for his arraignment. Chief of the District Attorney's Trial Bureau, John L. Buonora, said, "We have reason to fear for his [Ronnie's] safety and decided a maximum security facility was far better than an open courtroom." Police feared that a young mob-thug might try and 'make a name for himself' by doing away with Ronnie to avenge the killings.

Ronnie's Grandfather, Michael Brigante, Sr., hired Jacob Siegfried for a substantial amount of money to represent his grandson Ronnie in court. Soon after his hiring, Jacob Siegfried took a statement from a man by the name of Augustine F. DeGennaro (a.k.a. Augusto DeGennaro), who told him that Dawn had tried to get him to kill her father for a share of money she claimed was stashed in the house. He also said "she had asked him to get hold of an unmarked gun and flavorless sleeping tablets. She said her brother was in on the plan, as he wanted to get away from the family too. Coincidentally, police recovered a small metal box from the DeFeo house. The box was found just past the master bedroom entrance, in a small hole in the ground under the rug. The box was empty when found by police. They questioned Ronnie as to what was in the box, but he never told them.

On 15 January 1975, Siegfried filled a motion with the Suffolk County Superior Court asking that the indictment be dismissed, because it was based on "insufficient evidence." In the motion, Siegfried requested that the D.A. make available any copies, records, memoranda, or summaries of the confessions or admissions being offered at the trial, immediately. Siegfried went on record, stating that the defendant [Butch] was "deprived of his rights under the Fifth and Sixth Amendments of the Constitution of the United States, primarily his right to council." Siegfried also claimed that the only possible evidence that connects Ronnie to the murders is the unlawfully obtained confession, obtained by unlawful methods and means. Siegfried requested that the court have a hearing on the admissibility of the confession. Siegfried had to know that the court would deny a request of this nature. He knew this, but I believe he made it a point to go on the record with his gripes for the sake of a future appeal. In legal terms this is known as *"Fruit of the poisonous tree."* It is a legal metaphor in the United States used to describe evidence that is obtained illegally; whereby stating that if the source of the evidence (the tree) is tainted, then anything gained from it (the fruit) is tainted as well and therefore should be inadmissible against the defendant. So, if the confession led to the finding of the murder weapon and other evidence, then it should all be excluded.

Regardless of the reasoning nature of the aforementioned document submitted by Siegfried, the presiding judge, John Jones, denied all requests on 11 March 1975. This ruling by Jones left Siegfried with no choice but to go the route of an insanity plea for his client. There was only one problem; this was completely against his client's wishes. Ronnie was so angry with Siegfried's attempted persuasion for him to plead insanity that he threatened to strangle his own lawyer, not really helping his credibility out at all. Although Siegfried was paid more than $40,000 up to that point by Mr. Brigante Sr. to represent his grandson, he would withdraw from the case because future money was not provided and for other reasons.

On 7 July 1975, the Suffolk County clerk appointed William Weber, from the firm of *Mars and Burton* in Patchogue, New York, to represent Ronald DeFeo, Jr. Just prior to his appointment, Weber had been acting as Judge Signorelli's campaign manager in his bid for election to Surrogate Court. In a private conference with Weber and Signorelli, Prosecutor Sullivan claimed that he had no objections with the association. However, later in his book, *High Hopes*, he wrote: "I had not finished maneuvering. I was about to engage in a time-honored strategy that defense lawyers and prosecutors have honed into an art form. Some call it—judge shopping."

Weber went right to work, filing a supplemental omnibus motion on 22 July 1975, to obtain evidence, as well as a host of other requests. One of the requests from Weber was to have the county pay for a polygraph test for the defendant regarding his police brutality claims. On 1 August 1975, Judge Signorelli ruled in favor of Weber's omnibus motion, granting him access to copies of the reports and photographs in the prosecution's possession. However, Judge Signorelli made a shocking announcement in a hearing on 15 September 1975, which all but annihilated the defense's chances of a fair trial. "I deem it advisable to disqualify myself from the case, and I am going to ask the administrative judge to reassign the case." Signorelli had withdrawn himself from the trial, with the help of Sullivan—who had apparently applied some type of pressure on him. One week later Sullivan's "judge shopping" was complete, and Justice Thomas Stark was chosen to preside over the DeFeo trial. Criminologist, Christopher Berry-Dee, claimed that "Judge Stark & Sullivan in turn, engineered the removal of Signorelli from the case and elected for Thomas M. Stark, who could be guaranteed to bat for his side." According to Berry-Dee, Stark also told him, in reference to the judge shopping, "In hindsight this was quite wrong, but things were different back then."

Preliminary hearings were held on September 22, 23, 24, 25, 26, and 29 in Riverhead, NY to determine the admissibility of four pieces of evidence:

- The oral confession
- The .35 caliber Marlin
- The clothes obtained from Ronnie's person on November 14, 1975
- The evidence recovered from the "Storm Drain" in Brooklyn, NY

Unfortunately for Butch, during these hearings, it was his word versus the word of Suffolk County Detectives—Rafferty and Dunn. Since Rafferty and Dunn never recorded the confession, as well as the fact that Ronnie refused to sign a written confession of this nature, it was up to Stark to determine who was more credible. Ronnie had claimed that the blood found on his clothes was his own, from beatings handed down by Dunn and Rafferty during interrogation. Rafferty, however, claimed that the blood on Ronnie's pants was his sister's. Rafferty posed the theory that the blood on Ronnie's pants came from a blood-covered cartridge-case that Ronnie had picked up and wiped on his shirt and jeans when he went around cleaning up after the murders. Another thing that was frustrating for Butch was that fact that there was no such thing as DNA testing at the time. Since it was claimed to be his sister's blood, and there was no DNA testing at the time, their blood-types would have been identical and therefore indistinguishable.

Although Detective Rafferty testified that he witnessed Butch confess orally to the crime, Lt. Robert Dunn testified to something entirely different. When asked by William Weber while on the stand, "Did you hear Ronald DeFeo state during the interview that he committed the crime?" Lt. Robert Dunn answered, "No, I did not." On Wednesday, 1 October 1975, after six days of preliminary hearings, Judge Stark made his choice, denying all four requests of the Defense. During the judgment, Stark stated that Rafferty's and Dunn's testimonies were "basically accurate and credible." He further stated, "No police officer used or threatened the use of physical force upon the defendant. The oral incriminatory admissions and statements obtained from the defendant...were not involuntary."

With Stark's judgment, Weber knew that the trial would be commencing immediately, and Weber was not prepared to do so at that point. Weber needed more time to build his defense. He did not receive the granted paperwork from the district attorney's office until August 27, and he didn't have enough time to prepare for trial. Weber had also begun working with a private investigator by the name of Herman Race, who was hired by Mr. Brigante Sr., on 22

September 1975. Race, a former New York City supervising police detective, did not have much time to investigate the case.

Weber made a request to Justice Stark for a 60-day adjournment, claiming that he needed more time to prepare his defense. One of these reasons he claimed, was because Race had proof that there were multiple killers and accomplices involved and multiple weapons used in the murders. Although Race had only been on the case for about a week, Justice Stark refused Weber's requests and began jury selection on Monday, 6 October 1975. Weber was left with no other alternative but to persuade his client to plead insanity or face the maximum penalties that could be handed down by law.

As criminologist Christopher Berry-Dee explains, "Of course, it goes without saying that as soon as DeFeo was taken into police custody he was denied his lawful civil rights. He was threatened, beaten, and denied the services of an attorney to a degree common to Third World nations, and this is a shocking indictment against those who are sworn in to protect and uphold the Law." It was known that Judge Signorelli was an impartial judge and was aware of the mistreatment of the defendant. Since he and Weber were good friends, Sullivan and others feared that Signorelli would hand down a verdict of 'Not Guilty by Reason of Insanity,' which is why Sullivan's good friend, Judge Thomas Stark, was brought in to side with the prosecution. As Berry-Dee further theorizes, "With police, judicial, and political corruption rampant throughout Suffolk County, the last thing the police and prosecution needed was an unbiased judge."

The Trial

Butch was brought to trial on 14 October 1975, almost one-year after the murders. Prosecutor and Assistant District Attorney for Suffolk County, Gerald Sullivan, gave an impressive and revealing opening statement.

> *"Ladies and gentleman of the jury, each of you will be changed to some degree by this case. You will leave this courtroom after rendering a verdict, perhaps a month from now, carrying with you an abiding memory of the horror that occurred in that house 112 Ocean Avenue in the dead of night eleven months ago...I'm confident that at the end of the case you will come back into this courtroom and find Ronald DeFeo, Jr., guilty of six counts of murder in the second degree."*

In his opening speech, Sullivan reveals that Ronald Sr. may have been standing when he was hit with the first shot, claiming that "the trajectories of each bullet which entered his back were different," according to the Deputy Chief Medical Examiner, Dr. Howard C. Adelman, who examined the body at the murder scene and at the Suffolk County Medical Examiner's office in Hauppauge, where he later conducted the autopsy. Mrs. DeFeo was also found with two shots in her back, lying next to Mr. DeFeo. Although they walked the crime scene and investigated it together, DellaPenna and Adelman have two different views of what took place. DellaPenna testified that the .35 caliber Marlin rifle, to the exclusion of all other weapons, had without a doubt been employed in the killing of the DeFeo family. Dr. Adelman testified that he told Chief Mellon, Lt. Richmond of the Suffolk County PD, and the Daily News—while in his office on 14 November 1975—that he was "Mystified as to how all six DeFeos could have been killed by a single gunman."

One year after the trial had commenced, Adelman stated that his opinion has not changed since then. Although Sullivan used some of Dr. Adelman's theories, he clearly did not co-sign on his above statement. Sullivan also offered evidence indicating that Allison DeFeo might have been awake at the time she was shot. According to Sullivan, Allison awakened when her killer entered the doorway. Allison raised her sleepy head and was fired upon. The bullet went through one ear and exited out the other, killing her instantly. After ejecting an empty cartridge onto the floor, into a pool of Allison's blood, the killer then moved to Marc and John's room. The two boys lay parallel to each other. Marc had been suffering from a football injury and needed a wheel chair to get around. That wheel chair was found at the foot of his bed later by police. The semantics used by Sullivan were revealing as well. Sullivan was elucidating that he believed Ronnie to be the lone-gunman, painting a dark picture of a single person moving from room to room, referring to him as "The Killer."

Sullivan and others suggested that Marc was ordered by his doctor to sleep on his back, and that he needed help to turn over. However, Marc as well was found by police lying on his stomach. Both boys were shot once in the back. The shooter stood somewhat to the rear and alongside the children when the two shots were fired. Both bullets went through their bodies and became lodged in their beds. Sullivan claimed that there was no definitive evidence to indicate whether either of the children had awoken prior to the shots being fired. Sullivan then claimed that he would offer proof, however, that Dawn DeFeo very well may have been awake when the killer approached her on the third floor.

Right from the onset of the trial, several key pieces of testimonial-evidence seemed to be ignored or overlooked. Looking back, many have pointed out the dubious trend forming by the amalgamation of Stark & Sullivan. During the trial, Herman Race—private investigator for the defense—stated under oath:

> *"Your Honor, I can say with almost a reasonable certainty there is more than one person involved in this. There was more than one gun used, and I would say with very reasonable certainty there is another*

party involved in this. When I say another party, I mean more than one, your Honor."

Race claimed that at least one, maybe two, of the victims were shot in other rooms and dragged back to their bedrooms. Race claimed that he witnessed trails of blood stains on the carpet. Regardless, his testimony was never really taken into consideration. Moreover, although police believed that the victims were drugged—and despite police reporting initially that Ronnie confessed to drugging the family's food on the night of November 12th—all test results came back negative for drugs in the systems of all of the victims.

New Evidence

Journalist, Rick Moran, claimed that he had a chance to speak to some of the officers involved in the original investigation sometime after the murders. One of them, Suffolk County Police officer, Michael Shaner, told Moran "prior to the murders, a car was constantly in the area, within view of the house. It displayed 'US Department of Health (USDH)' parking permit" and was always occupied. Another source, NYC Drug Taskforce Agent, Jim Sutton, told Moran that the Department of Justice Drug Enforcement Administration (DEA) often used the USDH label during their surveillance operations.

Moran claims that he has several friends who are DEA officers in Manhattan on West 57th Street. One of them, he claimed, promised to get back to him and confirm whether there was an agent stationed in front of the DeFeo home during the time of the murders. A week later Moran received a call from a DEA operative who claimed that he had the DeFeo home under surveillance at the time of the murders. The agent claimed that Mr. DeFeo Sr. was in fact "suspected of involvement in an elaborate scheme to bring wholesale drugs into the US from ships traveling into the NYC region, on a route just south of Long Island." The agent claimed that Mr. DeFeo Sr. would, reportedly, take his boat from his boathouse and meet up with an ocean-going ship in the Great South Bay canal. After transferring the drugs to DeFeo's boat he would return home, package the drugs in the boathouse, and transport them out of Amityville via car or truck. Allegedly, the order came to watch the house after one of the DeFeo children was heard bragging about this process. Word reached all the way back to the DEA's office, and the order was given to investigate. No incidents of the "alleged tracking" were ever witnessed.

However, the most shocking claims from the agent had nothing to do with his drug trafficking investigation. The agent allegedly told Moran that he happened to be parked on the street-side of the house in view of the front door during the time of the murders. The agent claims that he "heard the muffled roars and saw the muzzle flashes from the murder weapon as the killer walked from room to room on the second floor of the house." The agent also added that soon after, he witnessed "Dawn DeFeo leave the house in a long nightgown and winter snorkel jacket with what looked like a rifle in hand." He then says that "she drove out of the driveway in the direction of a finger of land occupied by the homes." He then witnessed Dawn return a few minutes later without the rifle in hand. This same agent then said that he "saw Butch leave the house the next morning. Twenty-four hours later, another man came to the house and within minutes, the area was swarming with police." This story leaves much to be desired in the way of accuracy, but it is worth discussing. The fact that this agent never contacted the police, even as an anonymous source, to report what he had seen is quite distressing, in and of itself.

Although this is pretty interesting information, and should certainly be considered, it is third party hear-say. Moreover, Moran states, "Everyone in the house, except for Dawn DeFeo, was shot with a rifle. Dawn by contrast was the only one who had gunpowder residue on the shoulder of her nightgown. That, forensic experts will tell you, would suggest she fired the rifle." Though this sounds like a very plausible concept to the layperson, Detective DellaPenna's scientific explanation of the evidence strongly-contradicts Moran's assertions. However, DellaPenna's explanation is absolutely correct, from a scientific perspective.

Going Ballistics

Suffolk County Ballistics expert, Detective Alfred DellaPenna, testified that there was a powdery residue found on Dawn's nightgown. According to the DellaPenna Ballistics Report, Item #16 - partially-burnt particles of Nitrocellulose gunpowder were found on the left shoulder of Dawn's dress. Ronnie and others contest that the "partially-burnt" Nitrocellulose gunpowder that was found on Dawn's dress could only be caused by her firing the gun and could not have been caused by any type of struggle that she had with her killer.

In Dawn's autopsy report, it states, *"No powder marks or fine speckled indentations are noted surrounding the entrance wound."* This entrance wound was near the left ear. Detective Alfred DellaPenna explained that the reason why Dawn had this gunpowder residue on her is because she was so close to the muzzle of the gun when it was fired, and that there is no connection whatsoever between Dawn firing a weapon and the particles found on her dress.

DellaPenna said, "There are two areas of discharge residue: one is what comes out of the muzzle of the weapon and deposits itself on a wound or clothing area; the other are gasses or particle matter that come out of the weapon when a shot is fired, and this comes out in a gaseous manner and deposit themselves on the hands of the shooter. So there are two different areas firearm-discharge resolution you're looking for: one is you're trying to say this person has fired a weapon; and the other you're saying that that person was close enough to the muzzle of the gun when the discharge occurred and they received some of those particles of powder on their wound or on their clothing."

After reviewing Dawn's autopsy report, Detective DellaPenna's explanation, and those who assert that this information points to Dawn firing the weapon, I decided to contact a forensic colleague of mine, Mr. John Nixon, to help clear up some of the misconceptions in this area. Mr. Nixon is a firearms & ballistics expert witness, and engineering expert witness, whose primary area of expertise is in firearms & ballistics. His specialty experience is with firearms, guns, ammunition, ballistics, trajectory, accident, reconstruction, wounds, safety, trigger, design and failure. He also has been in practice for over 19-years and has deposed/testified in 28-cases in the last 4-years. After supplying Mr. Nixon with DellaPenna's video analogy of the particles on Dawn's nightdress and some other evidence, he provided a detailed explanation of the possibilities.

> **Mr. Nixon:** Alfred DellaPenna is correct in his comments. Propellant particles exit the muzzle; the vaporous deposits are what they are looking for on the hands (GSR or PGSR to be specific) PGSr = primer gunshot residue and is comprised of 3 main elements - lead, barium, and antimony. The propellant residue from the muzzle (unburned propellant particles) is just nitrocellulose graduals. The PGSR particles are spherical and about 5 microns in size – about the size of a virus. You can see the propellant residue with the naked eye."

I asked John to simplify this explanation in his own words for the reader. I also asked him a bunch of other questions and sent him more case evidence. His responses clear-up any misconceptions about Dawn firing a weapon.

> **Mr. Nixon:** When you fire a gun the bullet goes away from you (except for suicide of course) and any unburned propellant particles go away from you too. This was a Marlin rifle, so the muzzle of the gun (when shouldered) would be a significant distance from the shooter's body (3.5 to 4 feet - I can provide an accurate measurement if you wish). If there were unburned propellant particles on the dress, and not around the wound, that would be odd. Is it possible that the propellant particles were from another shot that missed? I've not seen all the details on this crime, so I can't theorize too much.

Later in our discussion I did advise him that the official reports state that there was only one shot fired in the room that Dawn had been found dead in and presumed killed in as well.

Mr. Nixon: Propellant particles are a sign that a gun was fired in your direction, not away from you. PGSR is a sign that either a gun was fired in your direction or, if on the hands, that you *may* have fired a gun. PGSR has been dropped by many labs because of the ease with which transfer and cross contamination occur. The particles on the hands are so small that they are invisible to naked eye. They show up under the electron microscope. There may have been some unburned particles in the hair that were not recorded. This assumed that the wound was closest to the muzzle - hence if you have propellant particles on the dress, you would expect them on the wound. If the head were turned correctly the dress may have been closer to the muzzle than the wound, so that may explain it. *You would not find any particles on her if she was shooting the gun.* The absence of stippling around the wound would indicate a muzzle-to-wound distance of at least 2 feet, and possibly as far as 3 feet.

Summary of findings

These particles were found on Dawn's left shoulder, which are consistent with the bullet entry, located just under the left ear. There could be many reasons why there was residue on Dawn's left shoulder and not directly around the wound. One reason could be that after Ronnie successfully wrestled the gun away from her, she could have put her shoulder up in a defensive posture as an instinctive reaction, bracing herself for the shot. This would have left little room between the entrance wound and the top of her shoulder. Larry Ragle, retired Director of Forensic Sciences in Orange County, California, describes this process in his book entitled *Crime Scene*. "During discharge, the flash, hot gases, and waste products (muzzle debris) will leave distinct distance-related information if held in close proximity to the target, from full contact up to thirty-six inches and more...this term or composite patterns are called 'powder burns' by some authorities. The soot—partially burned and unburned gunpowder—will leave a different yet reproducible pattern at each distance fired, which can be compared to the questioned pattern to establish distance" (pg. 195).

In response to Mr. Nixon's question regarding the possibility of particles found in Dawn's hair, Ragle explains a possible answer when referring to a similar case. "There was too much blood matted in the victim's hair for any powder burns or residue to be recognized...there was no evidence of tattooing to indicate the proximity because the hair and blood masked the evidence" (Pgs. 141-142). Unfortunately, the absence of close-up photos of Dawn DeFeo's wounds leaves much to the imagination. Regarding police procedure in such a case, Ragle explains, "Clothing on the body that retains visible evidence of firearm debris must be removed and collected at the crime scene before the body is moved or placed in a body bag for transportation" (pg. 196). This is to avoid smudging, smearing or cross contamination of the evidence. Indications in police reports, from what I have seen, do not indicate whether Dawn's clothes were removed before or after transport.

(So, to summarize this section...) As Detective DellaPenna explained there are two ways that a weapon discharges residue: the first is from backfire which appears on the hands of the shooter, and the second is from gunpowder particles that exit the barrel of the weapon and lodge themselves onto the victim. Both are commonly referred to as "Gunshot Residue" (GSR). Firearms create a large amount of pressure when fired, causing gases to leak back onto the hands of the shooter through small openings on the sides of the weapon. This is due to the enormous back pressure created when the weapon is fired. When the primer at the back of the bullet is struck by the firing pin, the primer blast blows particles from the primer explosive back onto the hand(s) of the person holding the weapon, in vaporous form.

These primer particles contain lead, barium, and antimony. These particles can be positively identified up to 48-hours of the person firing the weapon. (The only exceptions are .22 caliber weapons, because the rim fire cartridges have the primer mixture sealed inside the casing). These particles should not be confused with the particles found on Dawn's nightdress, as they differ dramatically! The Gunpowder residue exiting the barrel contains unburned gunpowder particles, partially burned gunpowder particles and or even carbonaceous soot from completely burned gunpowder. Being a high velocity rifle [.35 caliber Marlin] this type of GSR is expelled further than with a handgun, for instance. The range varies from 3 to 5 feet, sometimes even a bit further. This means that the shooter of the rifle could be standing a considerable distance (muzzle-to-garment distance) from the victim and residue from the barrel could still be found on the victim. At shorter distances would obviously create a greater concentration of residue on the victim.

Paraffin tests have been deemed by the forensic community as unscientific for many reasons. One reason, as indicated by Mr. Nixon, is a strong chance of cross-contamination. Another reason is that the mere handling of a weapon may leave nitrates on the skin, even without firing the weapon. So, although it is not an exact science and shouldn't be treated as such, if on the hands it can still determine, to a high degree, whether a person fired a weapon or not. That being said, controversy still lies in the Paraffin test results that Deputy Medical Examiner for Suffolk County, Dr. Howard C. Adelman, claims were done on Dawn's hands and came back negative. Ronnie's current wife, Tracey Lynn DeFeo, filed an application with the SCPD requesting public access records for the tests done on Dawn DeFeo's hands. The results that she received from the SCPD were: "After a diligent search, the record cannot be found."

Autopsy Reports

The Toxicology Report was conducted on 15 November 1974. Surprisingly, no blood or urine was tested. The only urine tests done were performed on 27 November 1975, and they were only performed on Ronald Sr., and Louise. Oddly enough, Dr. Adelman conducted autopsies on only 5 of the six DeFeo victims. Dawn

DeFeo was assigned to Dr. Irving Rappaport at the Suffolk County Medical Examiner's office. It was alluded to by Gerald Sullivan during the trial that "Paraffin tests" were conducted on all of the victims. Dr. Adelman claimed in a video interview that there was an examination done on Dawn's hands. That examination consisted of "finger-nail scrapings" and "other" tests on the hands to see if there were any hairs or fibers from her aggressor, indicating a struggle.

Dr. Adelman claimed that all of these tests came up negative. Dr. Adelman also states, "We did extensive toxicology, not only on the blood and urine, but on all of the organs that we removed. And it turned up zero. There wasn't anything in their bodies. So, they were cold sober at the time they were murdered." However, a closer look at the toxicology reports on all of the victims shows that there were no blood or urine tests performed on either Allison or on Dawn. The only blood and urine tests that were done were performed on Mr. & Mrs. DeFeo. Furthermore, the autopsy reports indicate that rigor mortis was "complete" in each victim, with the exception of Dawn. Steven Morris, Editor of *The New Criminologist* website, explains:

> "The autopsy indicates that in each victim, with the exception of Dawn, rigor mortis was complete. Dawn suffered only partial rigor. Livor mortis was anterior. All other victims were anterior, confluent, violaceous and fixed."

This appears to indicate that Dawn was killed sometime after the rest of the family. This key-issue was not considered during the trial, even though there appears to be sufficient evidence to refute a simultaneous murder. Morris continues his bewilderment with the autopsy results:

> "Adelman also claimed that urine and blood tests were performed on the victims (there was some suggestion that the parents may have ingested LSD) and found them to have been sober at the time they were shot dead. This testing was said to have occurred on November 27, 1974, two weeks *after* the

murders...There is no direct evidence that blood from any of the victims was ever actually tested. Samples of blood, liver, kidney, brain tissue, bile and gastric fluid had been submitted, but no positive results of such tests upon them are in existence, with the exception of urine results for Ronald DeFeo Sr., and his wife, Louise."

In Prosecutor Sullivan's book, *High Hopes*, he states that Dawn DeFeo had been menstruating at the time of her death. Sullivan explains that this is the reason for the sheeting beneath her blanket being sodden with blood. Morris sharply points out that "The official autopsy performed upon Dawn DeFeo reveals the absence of any menstrual blood on the sanitary napkin she had in place at the time of her death. The fact that she was using one would indicate that she anticipated her menstrual cycle, yet reveals an inconsistency with that posited by Gerard Sullivan, in that the blood on her sheet was not of menstrual origin."

Livor mortis (postmortem lividity) is the settling of blood, by gravity, in the vessels of the dependent areas of the body. Livor mortis starts 20 minutes to 3 hours after death and is congealed in the capillaries in 4-5 hours. Maximum lividity occurs within 6-12 hours. The blood becomes "fixed" (i.e. changing the position of the body will not cause livor to shift) in dependent areas in approximately 8 to 10 hours.

Rigor mortis—the stiffening of the muscles after death—usually appears 2 to 4 hours after death and is fully developed in 6 to 12 hours. The muscles begin to become noticeably and increasingly rigid and the joints stiffen. This is all assuming that all six victims had "normal" temperature at the time of their deaths, as well as the assumption that their bodies cooled at a uniformed rate. It is safe to say that decomposition would have occurred at a rather steady rate for all, even considering the fact that Dawn was the only one found on the third floor. This would not account for such a variation in decomposition.

Since the toxicology reports indicate that Dawn was only in *partial rigor,* and in the rest of the victims *rigor was complete* and livor was *fixed*; this would indicate that Dawn was killed a significant time after the rest of the family. A rough estimate can determine that Dawn was killed some 3-5 hours after the last family member was shot (this is a rough estimation based on the facts provided). Again, this was never mentioned at the 1975 trial. Quite the contrary, all explanations of the crime given at the trial—whether by police, the medical examiner, the prosecutor [Gerald Sullivan] or Ronald DeFeo himself—acknowledged that all six murders were committed within about a fifteen-minute window; although this physical evidence seems to indicate otherwise.

Insane or Inane?

Throughout Ronnie's testimony, Weber would hand him the crime scene photos of his family members. Ronnie would look at the picture and say, "I've never seen these people before in my life." Many say that this seemed odd and did not go along with the rest of his demeanor. Ronnie seemed coherent and clear in his answers other than these brief moments of what seemed like contrived answers. Ronnie spoke of memories of his family vividly and in great detail. However, when he was suddenly handed a photo of the crime scene, he claimed that he didn't know them. It seemed very strange, contrived even. On the other hand, when shown pictures of his house or his families' belongings, Butch goes into great detail explaining them clearly and coherently. The only time that his testimony becomes inconsistent with the rest of his demeanor, is when he looks at the crime scene photos of his family members.

Again, this seemed to be inconsistent or incongruent with his character at the time. Moreover, Butch shows no remorse throughout the trial. When it comes time to look at the pictures, it just reads like bad acting. Years later, Ronnie would say that William Weber told him to say that he killed the whole family. He said that Weber told him that he would get off on an insanity plea and be out to collect his money for the impending book that Weber was working on in a few years. Aside from the immoral intent and irresponsibility by the two, it was a very silly strategy that backfired on both men. It was karma rearing its destructive head at two men who thought that they could outsmart the system without using any smarts. Furthermore, an innocent person doesn't admit to killing six family members under any circumstances.

DeFeo Confesses

Ronnie has told several different stories throughout the years and has been his own worst enemy. Following the advice of William Weber, in regards to the insanity plea, and making up stories has not served him well. However, several of Ronnie's stories have put the gun in his sister Dawn's hands. Perhaps the most striking testimony of the trial is the one he gave that supports the theory of a demon in the house. Though he attempted to retract these statements some years later and debunk the ghost theory; his 1975 testimony is indeed terrifying, and paints a picture of a demonic presence that led him around the house, reinforcing the Amityville legend. One thing is certain, it's the most detailed account that he has given publicly.

Ronnie testified that on the weekend before the murders, there were several arguments between Dawn and his parents. While he was on the second floor, Ronnie claimed that a big fight had broken out on the first floor and he heard the commotion. This fight was more severe and not the normal household bickering. Although Ronnie never alludes to the nature of the argument on this occasion, others postulate that the fight was indeed over Dawn wanting to go to Florida to see her then boyfriend, William Davidge.

Ronnie was upstairs on the second floor watching T.V. when he heard the quarreling. The fighting was intense, and Ronnie couldn't take it anymore; so he went down to break up the fight. When Ronnie arrived on the first floor his father had his hands around Dawn's throat, violently choking her. Somehow Dawn broke free of the hold and ran into the kitchen and grabbed a butcher knife.

"She was trying to kill my father," Ronnie stated. Ronnie then got in the middle of them and tried to break it up. Someone hit him in the process, but he wasn't sure who. Ronnie told Dawn, "You'd better get out of the house; you'd better get out of here! He's going to kill you!" Ronnie told Dawn to leave and come back after their father had cooled off, and she did.

"I should have let them kill themselves," Ronnie said about the incident. The fighting between Dawn and their parents continued. Ronnie claimed that they were fighting everyday.

"Everyday Dawn was constantly fighting with my father. I mean, it was just day after day. They never took a break." Just a couple of days before the murders, Ronnie claimed that another fight broke out between Dawn and their father that was similar to the one described above. Dawn again ran and got a knife; Ronnie broke up the fight and held his father back while shouting for Dawn to leave the house. When she returned, Dawn approached him and said that she was going to kill everyone in the house. Ronnie said that he told Dawn, "Listen, if you're going to kill everyone in the house, you let me know, I'm getting out of here first." Ronnie said, "It didn't make no difference to me who she killed." After this, Ronnie went back up to the second floor to watch T.V.

Later that night, at about 11p.m., a war-movie by the name of *Castle Keep* was showing on T.V. Ronnie remembers watching the whole movie; he even explained the ending clearly. After the movie, Ronnie recalls another program coming on. He couldn't remember what program it was, because he fell asleep soon after it had started. When he awoke, he felt someone kicking him. *DeFeo Testimony*:

> "Somebody came down there and started kicking me. When I got up the T.V. was off; the lamp was off; the room was pretty dark. All I know is somebody was standing there with a rifle in their hands and the hands that the person had were black. I thought it was my sister Dawn, to be quite honest about it. I remember taking the rifle away from her…she seemed to disappear. I remember taking the rifle from there and going into my mother and father's room with it. I walked in the door; I didn't go that far in the door, a few feet, maybe. And I just started to shoot. I don't know if it was three or four times, but I started to shoot the gun, fire the gun. The gun did not make any

noise; there was no noise in the house. There were no lights on at that time, as far as I remember. The only light that was on was the bathroom next to Allison's room. They left that light on in that bathroom. That was the only light I can remember being on that floor. And after I shot my mother and father I put the gun down on the floor. I went back in the sitting room and sat down in the chair."

"The next thing I heard, it didn't sound like it was close; it sounded like it was real, real far away. I heard shots going on, gun shots. And when I did get up to look, I could have sworn it was my sister that came out of that room and ran up the stairs with a rifle in her hand. This whole time I was very, very calm. I wasn't mad; I was completely calm. I walked up the stairs and I remember seeing Dawn loading the rifle. And I remember fighting with her. I know I wanted to throw her out the window of her bedroom. That was on the third floor; it was pretty high. I was going to throw her out the window, but I didn't throw her out the window. I remember pushing her into her bed, and somehow, I don't remember what point of time I got the gun, but I remember pushing her down. And I shot her. Well, after that I heard footsteps. When I came out of the room, I could have sworn I saw somebody else running down the stairs. So I ran down the stairs. When I got down to the first floor, the front door was open. And I went out the front door. I might have been on the stoop and went as far as the driveway in the front of my house. I saw somebody or *something* running across the Ireland's front lawn. That's what I believe did happen in that house. Whether it's my imagination or my mind playing tricks on me, I don't know."

While in jail during the trial, Ronnie had made a list of the top-ten people that he wanted to kill once he was found not guilty by reason of insanity. A court officer testified as to the existence of this list. It was Weber's aim to prove that Ronnie made the list "in jest" for the court officer in the jail. Judge Stark was number three on the list, Sullivan number two, and a juror even made the cut. As Weber was discussing the list, Ronnie said to him, "Hey stupid, you're number one on the list."

Cross Examination

Ronnie continued to spill the beans to Sullivan. Ronnie claimed that after the murders, he went to work. While at work, Ronnie claims that he didn't know that he had killed anyone, but he said that he "thought he did something." Sullivan followed up by asking Ronnie, "You thought you had killed three people, isn't that true?" Sullivan was alluding to Ronnie's earlier testimony, when he admitted to killing his parents and Dawn. Sullivan was just not buying Ronnie's story. He believed that Ronnie was of sound mind when he committed the murders, and he was determined to get him on all six counts; but he wanted to at least affirm that he killed three before moving on.

Buick dealership employee, Lucy Burkin, testified that on Tuesday afternoon—the day before the murders—Ronnie Sr., left work at 2:00 p.m., to go home and have a confrontation with Butch about the dealership robbery, of which Ronnie was the prime suspect. Ronnie claimed that there was no confrontation. In fact, Ronnie claimed that Arthur Bellin and two others robbed the Buick dealership in Brooklyn. He said that he didn't know who the other two were, but a man by the name of Frank Boyd may have also been involved. Ronnie claimed that he knew that for sure and so did his father. Ronnie was not sure who the two other people were who aided Bellin. Sullivan accused Ronnie of being the one who set up the robbery. Sullivan also asserted that Ronnie gave Frank Boyd ten-percent of the proceeds from the robbery. Ronnie denied any involvement.

Ronnie's side of the story was that Arthur Bellin was driving and someone with a gun jumped in the back seat of the car, put a gun to his head, and demanded the money. Ronnie claimed that he could not identify the person in the back seat, but said he thought that it might have been Frank Boyd. Contrarily, Ronnie told police that he could not identify any of the assailants. When the police asked Ronnie to look at mug shots of possible assailants, Ronnie refused. This led police to believe that Ronnie was involved in the crime. Police then notified Ronald Sr., and advised him that his son was now the prime suspect.

Ronnie said several times under oath that he was not sure if the person who handed him the rifle in the basement or the person who walked out of Marc and John's room with the rifle was his sister or not. Again he answered with, "My mind was playing tricks on me." Sullivan didn't believe a word of Ronnie's testimony. Sullivan was determined to prove that Ronnie was of sound mind when he killed his family, and that he is a cold-blooded killer. Sullivan did his homework and dug deep to find corroborating witnesses. John Kramer was a fellow inmate of Ronnie's in Sick Bay. Kramer testified that Ronnie told him in jail that he had stolen jewelry and money the night before the murders. Ronnie testified that there was no jewelry in the house, that it had been put in a safety deposit box. It was later confirmed that Ronnie was telling the truth about the safety deposit box.

"I wouldn't kill anybody for money," Ronnie said. "If I wanted money, I'd rob a bank." Ronnie testified that he had heard about John Kramer from other inmates.

"Kramer was a guy who was known to testify against people to save his own skin," Ronnie said.

Another inmate, James Devito, testified that Ronnie was boasting that he would not be in jail long, because he was using the insanity defense. Several times Butch seemed to contradict himself during his testimony. At times he would sound sympathetic: like the moment when he said that he loved his family and that he was very proud of his brother Marc. Then there were other times when Ronnie seemed completely insensitive: like when he claimed that he didn't care who was killed in the house. He also flip-flopped back and forth about not really being sure what was happening to being fully aware and in control of the situation. At one point, DeFeo said during his testimony, "As far as I'm concerned, if I didn't kill my family they were going to kill me. And as far as I'm concerned, what I did was self-defense and there was nothing wrong with it. When I got a gun in my hand there's no doubt in my mind who I am. I am God."

Sullivan tried to prove to the jury that Ronnie was nothing but a cold blooded killer. Sullivan did this in many ways. One way was by provoking Ronnie and insulting his intelligence. Another was by provoking Ronnie into downplaying the murders, even having Ronnie explain how good it felt to kill his family.

"You felt good at the time?" Sullivan asked.

"Yes sir, I believe it felt very good," Butch responded.

"Is that because you knew they were dead, because you had given them each two shots?"

"I don't know why. I can't answer that honestly."

"Do you remember being glad?"

"I don't remember being glad. I remember feeling very good. Good."

At one point Ronnie completely lost his cool and threatened Sullivan's life. While on the witness stand, DeFeo shouted, "You think I'm playing? If I had any sense, which I don't, I'd come down there and kill you now."

The Prosecutions Witness

Perhaps the best example of the dynamic of the trial is the testimony of Ronnie's aunt, Phyllis Procita. Phyllis was the grieving sister of Ronald DeFeo, Sr. Phyllis was called as a witness for the prosecution, pertaining to her conversations with Ronnie about the murders while he was awaiting trial. Ronnie had managed to tell Phyllis several different stories of what occurred on the night of the murders. In turn, Weber tried to use Mrs. Procita's testimony to prove to the jury that Ronnie was insane. The first occasion that Phyllis had to visit Ronnie in jail was on 18 December 1974. She brought a friend of hers on that particular visit who happened to be a nun. The second time she visited Ronnie was on January 6th. Neither time did they discuss the events of the murders. However, on January 30th, Phyllis decided to ask Ronnie what had happened. Ronnie said that he was asleep in his bedroom when he was awakened by gunshots. Ronnie then said he hid in a crawl space in his room, and he stayed in there for a long time—until he was sure that 'they' were gone. Phyllis asked him why he didn't telephone for help, and Ronnie said that the phones were dead.

"Why didn't you call the police?" Phyllis asked.

"They would have never believed me."

"You should have called grandpa."

"I didn't want grandpa to see the mess, it would have killed him," Ronnie asserted.

On 24 February 1975, Phyllis and Ronnie discussed the murders for a second time. This time, Ronnie's story changed dramatically from the first one. Ronnie said that his friend came over late on the night of November 12th. His friend either came to buy drugs, or just get high with him, Phyllis said. The friend then fell asleep in the T.V. room and Ronnie could not wake him up. Ronnie then said that he had to go out, so he told Dawn to try and wake his friend up, and he [Ronnie] left. When he came home he found his family murdered. When Phyllis told Ronnie that his story didn't make sense, Ronnie ignored her and didn't answer.

In a future visit, Ronnie told Phyllis that Bobby Kelske killed the family and that she shouldn't trust him. Another time, Ronnie blamed Augusto DeGennaro (the man who Ronnie's former lawyer, Jacob Siegfried, claimed was approached by Dawn to commit the murders) for the murders. Most of Ronnie's stories were outlandish; however, Ronnie seemed to throw-in a possible clue here and there. One time, Ronnie told Phyllis that "his father was shot in the hall, and he [Ronnie] carried him to the bed." This may not have been too far from the truth, because there was some evidence that indicates that when Mr. DeFeo was shot the first time, he was standing. Another time, Phyllis asked Ronnie, "Would you ever cover-up for somebody and take the rap?"

Why not?" Ronnie said. "What makes you think I'm not covering for my sister, Dawn?" Phyllis found it ridiculous, and blew-off this story from Ronnie more than any other.

Weber tried desperately to use the testimony to prove Ronnie insane. Weber questioned Mrs. Procita as if she were a trained psychologist, asking her if she thought that Ronnie's words were "rational or irrational" during her many visits. Sullivan showed his superiority, blocking Weber's line of questioning with timely objections. Weber's attempts ultimately failed, and Ronnie came out of it looking more like a pathological liar and sociopath, rather than clinically insane.

Sullivan Tips the Scales

Sullivan's strategy was to use several witnesses to paint a portrait of Ronnie, showing that he was sane and capable of committing these murders. What Sullivan did not count on was the fact that Ronnie DeFeo Jr., himself, would take the stand and basically do Sullivan's job for him. On the stand, Ronnie went into his act of insanity at the covert request of Weber. Weber showed Ronnie a picture of the victims. Ronnie's response was, "I never saw this person before in my life. I don't know this person." Later he told Weber from the stand, "Did I kill them? I killed them all. Yes, sir. I killed them all in self-defense." Some members of the jury reacted in disgust, but Sullivan didn't flinch. He knew what Weber was trying to do. However, the plan completely backfired on Weber and DeFeo, and the only thing that Ronnie's poor acting job was about to earn him was a one way ticket to the big-house.

Sullivan attacked Ronnie during his cross examination. He spoke of inconsistencies in Ronnie's testimony and what he told police. Sullivan still had a loose end, though: he needed to find and prove Ronnie's motive for committing the murders. Even with his outlandish statements on the stand; without a motive, Ronnie may well have gotten away with the insanity defense. Sullivan was desperate to dig up a motive. Sullivan's first attempt to prove motive was a jewelry stash that the DeFeo's kept in the house. Sullivan explained that Ronnie had stolen the jewelry, and when his father found out Ronnie killed them all. Later in the trial it was found out that the jewelry was placed in a safety deposit box at the European Savings Bank in Amityville. Now even more desperate than before,

Sullivan sent Detective Rafferty around to friends of Ronnie to coerce them to say that there was jewelry in the house and that Ronnie had stolen it. That plan backfired when the witnesses denied and actually exposed the attempt, by signing sworn affidavits explaining the attempt by Rafferty. In regards to this, Christopher Berry-Dee (criminologist) says, "Judge Stark dealt with this serious issue with his usual air of casual indifference and that was the end of it."

During Sullivan's search for a motive he also had to fight off attempts by Weber to prove his client insane. Weber used well-known psychiatrist, Dr. Daniel Schwartz, who had become popular as the psychiatrist who found David Berkowitz [The Son of Sam] criminally insane. Coincidentally, Berkowitz was another Long Island killer who claimed a type of possession. Sullivan believed that the whole trial pretty much came down to Schwartzes' testimony, and he knew that Schwartz had previously ruled that Ronnie was criminally insane. Instead of directly questioning his witness, Weber let Schwartz give the jury a mini-lecture on psychosis, disassociation, and the criminally insane. It turned out to be a mistake on Weber's part, and allowed Sullivan to capitalize and challenge several things stated by the doctor during his lecture.

Sullivan focused on something that Schwartz had pointed out about Ronnie's "clean-up" after the murders, which Schwartz claimed to have used a figurative admission of insanity. Sullivan seemed to fluster Schwartz early on in his cross-examination. Sullivan claimed that Ronnie's clean-up was "indicative of a person who had gone to very careful lengths to remove evidence of the crime," therefore proving his sanity. Schwartz argued that, "it's evidence of someone who is trying to remove evidence from himself." Schwartz actually quoted Shakespeare's, *Macbeth*, when Lady Mac Beth said, "What, will these hands ne'er be clean?" Schwartz pointed out that Lady Mac Beth was not hiding the murder from anyone, but that she couldn't live with the blood on her hands.

Sullivan ridiculed Schwartz on his analogy, asking him sarcastically if he was basing his psychiatric opinion on a work of fiction. Sullivan argued that Ronnie had taken everything out of the house that would have connected him to the crime. Schwartz grew visibly angry and said, "What you are talking about is trivial compared to six bodies." Schwartz had testified that it was of neurotic nature that Ronnie had thrown all of the evidence in one sewer-drain location. Schwartz claimed that the police were no friends of Ronnie, and that he removed the evidence not to conceal the crimes, but so that he didn't leave clues for the police. With this line of questioning, Sullivan basically proved that Ronnie was acting with clear purpose when he removed the evidence from the scene.

In New York State, 1st degree murder can only be charged if the victim is a Police Officer or the killer is already serving a *Life* sentence. On Wednesday, 19 November 1975, a year and five days after the murders, the jury began their deliberations. The first vote came back 10-2, with two jurors still unsure of Ronnie's mental state at the time of the murders. On Friday morning, the jury asked for a reading of Detective Rafferty's testimony. After further review of Ronnie's testimony, on Friday, 21 November 1975, a unanimous jury of six-males and six-females delivered a guilty verdict, convicting twenty-four-year-old Ronald Joseph 'Butch' DeFeo, Jr., of six counts of murder in the 2nd degree. Two weeks later (On 4 December 1975), he was sentenced to six-consecutive 25-to-life sentences. It was the longest trial in Suffolk County history to that point.

Section II
The Haunting

The Perfect Psychic Storm

"If we hadn't had the house blessed, I don't know how things would have turned out - or what may have happened. Until there was a threat like that of some kind perceived by whatever was there... the events in the house were all very subtle."
—George Lutz

George Lee Lutz was a twenty-eight-year-old, ex-Marine, who owned a land surveying business that was passed down to him by his family. Kathleen Connors was a twenty-eight-year-old full-time waitress. The two were married in July of 1975. Kathy lived with her three children: Danny [9], Chris [7], and Missy [5]. George lived alone with his hyper dog, Harry, which was a cute mix between Malamute and Labrador retriever. The kids loved George and Harry, and accepted George as any child would a father; although George was not, biologically. Harry quickly became just another member of the family. George was a non-practicing Methodist and Kathy was a divorced Catholic, and neither had daily thoughts of religion on the brain. Oddly enough, the couple got married in a Presbyterian Church. Soon after marriage, the family began searching for a home; and like the DeFeo's, they decided that Long Island's South Shore would be the best place to live out their dreams. The homes in the area were pricey, possibly too pricey for the family, but they were fixated on buying a home in that area.

They soon contacted realtor, Edith W. Evans, who was working for Conklin Realty in Massapequa Park, Long Island at the time. Evans had been an Amityville resident since 1965, herself, and she knew the beauty of the area. After finding out the Lutzes' tight budget for house-shopping, Edith didn't have many options. She decided to show them the former DeFeo house at the asking price of $90,000. The price was more than George wanted to spend (some speculate it was more than he could afford). The Lutzes immediately fell in love with the house. George was determined to follow through with the sale after seeing how much his wife really wanted the house. The family had looked at some 50 houses before they were taken to 112 Ocean Ave. It was love at first site. "All the things that we had talked about were found in one place," Kathy said. "Charming" was the word that first came to mind when she first saw the beautiful house. "Do you believe this?" George asked Kathy in awe. "No, I don't believe this," he replied. The two shared a laugh as they both basked in wonderment.

Once the tour of the home was nearly completed, Edith took the couple back to show them the boathouse. Edith saw that George and Kathy were just ecstatic about the home. It was then that she decided to reveal to them the reason why the price of the home was such a bargain. "I don't know if we should have told you before you saw the house, or if now's the appropriate time," Edith said. The couple looked at her, puzzled. "This is the DeFeo house, and I don't know if it'll change your views" she said. George and Kathy were aware of the DeFeo murders, but they did not realize—until that moment—that they were at the infamous residence.

Ronnie's trial had not yet completed at that time. Edith had been reluctant to tell the Lutzes about the tragic events that took place at the home just 11-months earlier. Even she was surprised when the Lutzes had no problem with her admissions of what had occurred in the home. The couple was sold on the house, but felt it imperative to discuss the details with the children first. George and Kathy's main concern was that the kids might hear rumors when they went to school, but the children claimed that they loved the house and that it wouldn't bother them either. The couple made a few more visits to the house and then decided that, with the sale of their other two homes; they would have plenty for the down payment. Moreover, since the house had been on the market for close to a year, George wisely offered Edith $80,000 for the sale of the home. Edith graciously accepted.

The entire Lutz family moved all their belongings into the house on Thursday, 18 December 1975, just two weeks after DeFeo's sentencing. Earlier in the week, one of George's friends—

who was a practicing Catholic—insisted that they have a priest bless the home, because of the recent brutal murders that had taken place there. George thought it a good idea, and made arrangements to have Father Ralph Pecoraro—from the Diocese of Rockville Centre—come and bless the house on move-in day. Reportedly, George had met the priest while getting an annulment for his first marriage. George was previously married to a Catholic woman, and as part of the annulment proceedings he had to go down to the diocese office to do an interview. The interviewee was Father Pecoraro. It was the only priest that George knew to call at the time. "Father Ray," as they called him, arrived as scheduled, and even he was impressed by the immensity of the home.

Father Ray started on the first floor, going room to room, performing a routine blessing ritual. However, when Father Ray went upstairs and began blessing Marc and John DeFeo's former bed room—which the Lutzes later called the sewing room—it set off a chain of events that still leave many speechless and spellbound to this very day. Father Ray had a bible in his right hand and a salt-shaker-type object filled with holy water in his left hand. As he did in all the other rooms, he began by walking around the room reading a certain verse from the bible while sprinkling holy water throughout the room. Years later, Father Ray agreed to do an exclusive interview with TV series *In Search Of,* hosted by Leonard Nimoy, where he said:

> "I was blessing the sewing room. (Pause) It was cold! It was really cold in there! And I thought, 'Gee, this is peculiar,' because it was a lovely day out. It was winter, yes, but it didn't account for that type of cold. I walked around the room sprinkling holy water and I heard a rather deep voice behind me say, 'GET OUT!' It seemed so directed towards me that I was really quite startled. Then, I felt a slap on the face. I felt somebody slap me, and there was nobody there!"

Perhaps the most intriguing thing about the interview is that Father Ray agreed to talk with *In Search Of* only if he could remain anonymous. During the program he remained in a dark silhouette. He also received heavy criticism and flak from his own and other church parishes. Anonymity was imperative to Father Ray, and he soon disappeared from public view altogether. He was transferred to another diocese, but remained a priest. He has not earned a cent for his story, and is currently deceased.

After Father Ray felt a hard slap on the face, he quickly turned around and noticed that he was the only one in the room. Terror stricken, he immediately fled and returned to the first floor, where George and Kathy were still busy unpacking. In haste, Father Ray claimed that he had a prior engagement to attend and had to get going. George and Kathy noticed that he looked quite disheveled. Being a bit naive, George went to give Father some money for his time. "No, you don't charge for this, and you don't charge friends for this," he said. Father Ray told them nothing of the incident, but left them with a warning: "You know; I felt something really strange in that one upstairs bedroom. Don't spend too much time in that room and don't use it as a bedroom." George and Kathy did not really think to ask why, since they had no knowledge of the prior event and because they did not believe in the occult; their un-superstitious minds did not process the desperation in his voice. George and Kathy both had already decided to use it as a sewing room, so they were not very concerned. "That's good," Father Ray replied. "As long as no one sleeps in there; that's fine." With that, Father Ray quickly left the scene.

Harry was a year-and-a-half old at the time and was "fearless" before moving into the house, according to George. While the Lutzes were moving their stuff to and fro, they chained Harry to the dog run so they could move their stuff and not worry about him running away. But Harry was acting very strange that day. In what seemed like a fit, "Harry climbed over the fence, but the chain was too short for him to get all the way over," and Harry hung choking to death on his own noose-like leash. George and the family rushed over and lifted him back into the pen, saving the dog's life. The incident was a scary one that shook-up the family.

Resident Evil

Although latent to the family at first, they were soon besieged by an unknown entity. Whether the actions of the priest angered the entity or sparked the events to come; it would soon become all too evident to the Lutz family that there was an evil presence occupying their property. Right from the beginning the temperature in the house was eerily bizarre. The house would go from warm to cold instantly, fluctuating some 40 to 50 degrees one way or the other. In the dead of winter George was frequently seen by neighbors chopping wood for their fireplace. They believed that it was a problem with the heating system, so they contacted local heating specialists to come to the house. After three visits from the inspectors, they were never able to determine the cause of the problem. During one specialist visit, Kathy explained that "the repair man witnessed the furnace functioning, yet there was no heat. The temperature of the house was 40 degrees, but the thermostat read 80."

According to the Lutzes (on the Merv Griffin Show, 1979), the first incident that occurred that made the Lutzes question the possibility of an unknown presence was when they were meditating one day in the house. The Lutzes frequently practiced *Transcendental Meditation*—a technique which claimed to produced a state of "restful alertness." The process became popular after the first of many studies was published in the early 1970's in *Science, American Journal of Physiology* and *Scientific American*. One day the Lutzes were meditating in their living room and Kathy's hand was touched, and it wasn't George. Kathy told George about it, describing the touch as a "comforting feeling." It didn't happen for several days after; but the next time that it happened it was not so comforting.

Strange odors began to emanate in the house and the family could not figure out where they were coming from. At first they blamed the kids, thinking that they may have spilled perfume or something else; however, the mysterious odors would travel from room to room, sometimes when the kids were not even home. Flies began appearing in the dead of winter, mainly in the sewing room on the second-floor, but also in Dawn's old room on the third-floor. At first, just a few appeared. However, as time went on, the number of flies increased, until there were hundreds. George and Kathy would kill all the flies only to return and see the flies had grown in numbers.

George and Kathy began noticing drops of green gelatinous slime scattered about the house. Again they blamed the kids, thinking that they might have mixed up a slimy concoction and made a mess; but the next time it happened the kids were at school. "It was like drops of gelatin on the carpet, going from room to room" George explained. He would often wake up in the morning and see this strange phenomenon. George began waking up between 3:00 a.m. and 3:30 a.m., feeling restless, uneasy, and often hearing strange noises in the house. He would regularly get out of bed at this time and walk around cautiously to discover what was causing the noises. Oddly enough, as he perused around the house the noises would suddenly cease. George did not know at that time that this was the estimated time of the DeFeo murders.

The bathrooms also began to show the effects. The toilet bowls began to turn black from a burnt-type substance. Many think that it was the water itself that was black or blood-like (because this is what was shown in the movie); however, it was the actual China on the bowl that turned black, not the water. It started in one bathroom, and then quickly spread to all the others. The bowls were still black when investigators later arrived. The family also began seeing a substance, similar to what was on the bowls, oozing from the keyholes of the doors.

As the weeks went on, the evil resident grew more insolent and its acts more audacious. No one escaped the affects of the horror house, even the children. Danny, Christopher, and Missy were model children before moving into the house, as George and Kathy described on the TV show *In Search Of*. However, as the weeks went on, the children became unruly and their parents were forced to punish them regularly. They noticed a dramatic change in them. Missy began telling her parents about a friend that visited her in the house by the name of Jodie. She claimed that Jodie could take any form; from the smallest animal or doll, to an enormous size.

Missy claimed that Jodie gave her a choice of the form it would take; either a little boy, or a pig. Being a five-year-old girl, Missy chose the pig. At first, George and Kathy did not take their young girl's stories very seriously, writing it off as the imagination of a child. However, as the weeks went on and the strange events continued, the couple began to wonder. One day Missy told her parents that Jodie told her that she [Missy] will live in the house forever. This concerned the couple, who were having enough problems trying to keep their own sanity.

George began undergoing personality changes, snapping at the family and fighting regularly with Kathy. The feeling of confusion and misplaced anger were the prevalent themes in the mind of George Lutz. For no reason, George would lash out at Kathy and the kids. George's only concern was to keep warm by keeping the fire going. He was continuously seen chopping wood outside the home. George began having strange "thoughts," he clarified, not "feelings." These thoughts, he believed, were "not of his nature;" they were coming from some other entity. He knew the thoughts were not his own.

It was then that George began to wonder just what went on before they moved into the home. George began wondering if this entity had influenced Ronnie DeFeo's actions. George also noticed that he, himself, looked strikingly similar to Ronnie DeFeo Jr. George visited *The Witches' Brew* a couple of times and had a few drinks. He attempted to get some information about Ronnie and what really happened at the house. In an interview with Bill Jensen in 1999, Officer Pat Cammaroto recalls being in the Amityville police station the day that George Lutz came in and gave them a gun. "He brought in the gun and said he was afraid of having the gun "cause the house was haunted," says Cammaroto. George claimed that he was scared what he might do to his wife and kids if he kept the gun in the house. In Kaplan's *Amityville Conspiracy* book (page 35), Kaplan claims that an unnamed officer told him "he [George] had an impulse to shoot his wife and kids." Amityville enthusiast, Jason Pyke, informed me that "George said the reason for handing in his handgun was because he was going into Manhattan on business and you were not legally allowed to take firearms with you; so he left it there overnight and simply collected it the next day." In Mr. Pyke's opinion, either Kaplan made it up or the police were making George out to be a madman, because they were fed up with being called out to the house for false alarms.

Kathy continued to feel the embrace of an invisible force, even smelling a woman's perfume at certain times. At first it was comforting, but as time went on the touches became more menacing. It got so bad that there were instances when Kathy actually passed out from fear during these encounters. George and Kathy began waking up at 3:15 a.m., to horrifying screams of anguish. George would jump out of bed and inspect the house, only to realize that it wasn't anyone in their family, and, upon further inspection, he found no other person(s) in the house.

George and Kathy were becoming increasingly worried about their daughter Missy. She began acting stranger and stranger. Missy continued telling more and more stories about this imaginary friend. Missy claimed that Jodie could only be seen by those that it chose. Missy even drew a picture, of what appeared to be a pig or a cat (in crayons), that she claimed was Jodie. While George and Kathy tried to explain to her one night that Jodie did not exist, Missy pointed to the window and said, "Jodie is outside and wants to come in." George and Kathy looked towards the window and saw two bright red menacing eyes peering through the window from the outside. In shock and fear, Kathy stood up and hurled a chair at the window. As the chair hit the wall they heard a squeal and they saw the eyes quickly vanish. Kathy picked up Missy and raced into the other room; while George raced over to the window. George looked around in a panic, but there was nothing in site.

During George's episodes of waking up at 3:15 a.m., he had overwhelming urges to go out and check the boathouse, for some unknown reason. Sometimes he would go out two-three times a night to check out the boathouse. One night, coming back from the boathouse, George looked up into Missy's room and saw the shape of a figure, but could not make it out. The figure was ominous and bizarre enough that it frightened him. He quickly rushed up to Missy's room, but found nothing there.

George and Kathy believed that the situation was now becoming critical. Another incident, of witnessing a rocking chair in motion as if some unseen force was clearly maneuvering it, prompted the family to place a call to Father Ray for help. The phone would ring, Father Ray would answer, but noise interference prevented any type of communication with him. Similar instances occurred when they tried to contact Father Ray again in the future. Father Ray found blisters festering on his hands and decided to call the Lutz family to warn them that something odd was occurring. Similarly to the Lutzes' phone calls to him, the call again was blocked by static interference. The static only occurred when calling Father Ray and vise versa. Telephone repair men came to the house three times to check the phone lines, but found no static and no interference when testing the lines. Father Ray did not believe that the marks on his hands were a result of a psychosomatic response, but that it was something to do with his blessing of the house.

Intense cold began to seriously affect George—to the point that he neglected his work and hygiene and constantly chopped wood and sat in front of the lit fireplace that never actually warmed him. One day sitting in front of the fire, George noticed a demonic face etched into the brick of the fireplace. Desperate for action, George and Kathy decided to take matters into their own hands and bless the house themselves. On 8 January 1976, they grabbed a silver crucifix in an attempt to cleanse the evil from the home. George held it with both hands, Kathy grasped onto George's arm, and they began walking around the house trying to rid it of the evil resident. "That's when things really got bad," recalled George. "We tried to kick out what was there, and it didn't want to go." They continued blessing each room, saying the Lords prayer, and commanding the entity to leave in the name of God. "We heard a chorus of voices scream out, 'will you please stop!'" George explains. They quickly realized that not only did their mock ceremony not work, but it seemed to have actually angered the spirits even more.

That night they went to bed and fell into a deep sleep. Kathy was awoken by George at 3:15 a.m. George looked at Kathy and was horrified. Kathy reached out to him, but George slithered away from her furiously. Kathy didn't know why George was so frightened. She looked up and caught her reflection in the mirror and was terror stricken by what she saw. Her hair had turned grayish-white, her face was severely wrinkled, deep impressions covered her face and forehead, and drool dribbled down her tight mouth: Kathy had aged 40-years, into an old hag! By morning, she looked back to her old self, but the effects of the aging process had taken a toll on her. Kathy's mother visited the next morning and bore witness to the gruesome after affects of Kathy's aging process.

Missy seemed to be the most affected of the children. Kathy recalls that Missy would sing constantly in one bedroom in the house. "Silent night, holy night, all…" (Missy leaves the room; she stops singing abruptly once she crosses the threshold of the doorway) However, upon returning to the room, she would pick up the lyrics of the song from the exact word she had stopped from previously: (Missy returns to the room, crossing back over threshold) "…is calm, all is bright."

The Last Night – 28 days later

"The last night in the house, we knew that there was a terrible, terrific storm going on outside. Later, people checked the reports for the area, and say that there was no such storm. I don't really care what the weatherman said. For us… there was a storm raging that night." --George Lutz

According to the Lutz family, every night of their 28-day torment something un-godlike occurred, but the last night in the house was the worst by far. In twenty-eight days, George had lost approximately twenty-eight pounds—managing to lose roughly a pound a day. As George recalled on the *Merv Griffin Show* (1979), "The last night, the noises downstairs on the first floor were just incredible; it sounded like fifty…a hundred people tuning up instruments and slamming doors. The front door would slam; Harry our dog would get up, get sick, and then lie back down again for no reason. Doors upstairs, across from our bed, would open and close. The boy's beds, over our bedroom, were being dragged across the floor; and we could hear them, but we couldn't get up out of bed and do anything about them. Ya just couldn't move; there was just no way you could get up to move."

George later claimed in an interview with TV show *Primetime Live* that he was laying in bed, there was no pressure on him, yet he was unable to move. The children's beds were slamming violently up and down on the floor, just over head, and he could not get up to help them. At that moment in the interview, his jaw began visibly shaking and he put his head down to gather himself. "How long did that last," he was asked. Without hesitation, and in a stern voice, George replied, "All night!"

At 3:15 a.m., that very night, Kathy's body levitated several feet off of the bed. George lain in shock as he watched his wife float into the air, helplessly. "That's the hardest thing for people to accept," he stated on *Primetime Live*. Doors opened and closed and multiple horrifying screams echoed throughout the house in stereo. I will never be able to set aside what had gone on that night [The last night]," George said. "All night," George continued. "And the boys, the way they looked and what they said when they came down that morning."

The family had finally had enough! Contrary to the fictional version, the next morning, 14 January 1976, the Lutzes did not flee the house immediately. Instead they sent their kids to school. The couple was finally able to contact Father Ray, who advised them to go and stay at Kathy's mother's house for a while to clear their heads. When the children returned from school, the family decided to leave. As they were attempting to flee the home, however, bizarre things again began occurring. The temperature began fluctuating rapidly, the walls started making a creaking sound (like on a ship) and George claimed to have seen a hooded demon pointing at him from the stairs.

Finally they all piled into the van, but it wouldn't start! George explained this, however, as a common problem that he fixed easily. But they were not out of harm's way just yet. While driving away they heard pounding on the outside of the van. The sounds lasted for several miles on their way to Kathy's mother's house. Pictures of the house months after show closets still full, the refrigerator heavily stocked, and the children's toys left behind. Pictures also reveal that the beds were made, which indicates that they did not immediately rush out of the home in the morning. Also, the family left the house with two days worth of clothing each, which is a bit trivial and can easily be translated into *'Leaving with the clothes on their backs;'* relative to what they left behind.

George and Kathy fled the house at 112 Ocean Avenue and sped towards Kathy's mother's (Joan Connors) home in Babylon, NY. Naturally, the family was utterly traumatized. Still, they were resolute on getting some help, ridding the home of whatever it was that was plaguing it, and moving back in. "When we left," George explains, "we didn't know we weren't coming back. We didn't know that what we were leaving behind we would never see again." It was indeed Father Ray who talked the couple into going to Kathy's mother's house for a night to get some sleep.

"Why don't you just go there, get some sleep, and we'll talk some more," Father Ray told them. Father Ray seemed to have sensed the severity of the situation more than the Lutz family did at the time. They were caught up in it; this was their dream home. They really weren't sure what was happening to them. It was only after spending a few nights away from the home that they began to realize what was going on. It was like a demon-detox.

Should I stay or should I go now?

It was never George and Kathy's intention to give up the house. They believed that if they got help from knowledgeable sources, these sources could rid the home of the evil and they would be able to move back in. Once at Kathy's mother's house, George believes that the force followed them. Kathy again levitated and they still felt an evil presence, but they believed that being out of the house cleared their thoughts, and the force was just not as strong outside of the house. Strange things also continued to happen to father Ray, and some of these incidents were witnessed by his superiors at the diocese, although they would never admit it publicly. Instead, they referred George and Kathy to the *Psychical Research Foundation* (PRF) located on the campus of Duke University in

Durham, North Carolina. On 24 January 1976, the PRF sent a field investigator, by the name of George Kekoris, to conduct an interview with the couple. After hearing the shocking events, Kekoris and the PRF decided to make the case their top priority, and they planned to run a complete scientific investigation of the house.

In hindsight, as the family's lives began to stabilize, they started to realize that they had been through something quite extraordinary. Still was the matter of what to do with the house. They became obsessed with the happenstances of their 28-day stay, and sought to find out more information about the house and its history. The couple again began asking around about the previous owners and the circumstances of their deaths. They were shocked to learn that Ronald DeFeo, Jr., had recently claimed in court that he heard voices in the house. A chill rode up the spines of George and Kathy Lutz! Was there some type of connection between what had happened to them and the murders of the previous owners? Was Ronnie possibly provoked or possessed by the evil resident to kill his family?

These questions made George and Kathy actively seek out Ronnie's lawyer, William Weber. The Lutzes contend that their initial involvement with Weber was to find out all the information they could about the DeFeo's and if DeFeo experienced any similar phenomenon as they had while in the home. They met Weber at Kathy's mother's house in late January of 1976, and the Lutzes briefly described their story to Weber. The next time the couple met Weber he arrived with Paul Hoffman (who introduced himself as a criminologist working on the DeFeo case) and Bernard Burton (a law partner of Weber's). The Lutzes recorded the meeting and recounted their experiences to the group. The forty-five minute tape recording was the first on record that the Lutzes would give. "It was at that time that we [George & Kathy] learned the extent of each other's individual experiences," explained George in regards to hearing the tape afterwards. Up to that point, they had not even known the magnitude of each family member's own terrifying ordeals. Based on the Lutzes' version of their story, Weber was attempting to get Ronnie DeFeo, Jr., a new trial by claiming "Possession."

Media Madness

The house at 112 Ocean Avenue in Amityville, NY, was already news before the Lutz family even stepped foot in the house. According to several Amityville locals that I have spoken to, the name "horror house" was already given to the much maligned property locally, which was known for its legendary occult history. Many believe that Ronnie DeFeo did not cause the phenomena, but was affected by an already present demonic force on the property. Research proves that the *Shinnecock Indians* resided in the area for some time. The home at 112 Ocean Avenue used to house Indians that were deemed insane, evil, or possessed, according to many sources. It has been said that these Indians were imprisoned there by other tribal members. However, this rumor [of insane or possessed Indians being imprisoned at that exact location] has yet to be proven as fact.

With Ronnie DeFeo's trial still 'hot' in the news, it only took one more straw to break this camel's back. When the Lutzes returned from George's grandfather's funeral in early February, they were informed by a reporter that their story was becoming a much sought after scoop. They immediately thought that Weber was behind the leak to the media. On Saturday, 14 February 1976, George Lutz picked up Long Island's, *Newsday*, and saw an article about his family's recent ordeal. "*DeFeo Home Abandoned; Buyer Calls It Haunted.*" The family was stunned to see that not only had their story been leaked to the press, but that the contents of the article were filled with lies and misinformation. The article caught on, spawning shrouds of people to flock to the house to get a curious peak. The following Monday another article was printed in the same paper, claiming that the first article attracted so many locals that it kept the police busy most of the night. This started a vicious cycle of events. One article would spawn curiosity seekers, which in turn caused more articles, and so on and so forth. The national media slowly began to report the story, such as *Channel 5 News* in New York, which reported from outside of the home. But again, there were several inconsistencies and a lot of misinformation in their report.

The second article that had been printed by *Newsday* on Monday, 16 February 1976, contained a quote from a man by the name of Dr. Stephan Kaplan, who was the self-proclaimed head of the *Parapsychology Institute of America* and *Vampirologist*. In the article Kaplan claimed that he intended to do an investigation of the house and warned that no amateur "should mix into these things, because they do not know how to handle a hostile spirit." George was desperate at that point and knew very little, if nothing, about the paranormal. Without actually investigating Kaplan's background, George figured that he'd contact Kaplan and give him a try. During their first phone call, George gave Kaplan only one requirement: that he not speak a word to the media. Kaplan accepted and began preparing his investigative team, which allegedly included several witches.

Earlier that very day, Kathy was contacted by William Weber, who requested that she and George be present at a press conference being held at his office in Patchogue, New York. Weber made his intentions known, claiming that the Lutzes' story abets his clients' [Ronnie DeFeo, Jr.] appeal. The couple did not really want to attend, but Weber warned that *Newsday* demanded they attend, and threatened they'd show up at their children's school if they bailed. At the conference, the Lutzes were very reluctant to give any details of what had occurred. "Let me put it this way," George said. "We moved out of the house mainly because of the concern for our own personal safety. We felt threatened." They also alluded to Kaplan, stating that the "proper people and organizations" were conducting an investigation, but never actually mentioned any names.

On Thursday, 19 February 1976, an angry George Lutz contacted Kaplan. Lutz had seen an article earlier that day that was printed in the Long Island Press, *'Ghost Hunt: Expert to probe forces in DeFeo house.'* George was livid. He must have had a healthy skepticism about Kaplan to begin with to terminate his involvement in the investigation so quickly. Though George had stated that he didn't want media involvement in the story and he had just done a press conference; his logic is plausible considering the circumstances. First, George was adamant about one thing: Kaplan not going to the press. Kaplan broke confidence in the one area that George had asked him not to. Second, George never gave up any details of the story at the press conference. When George was pressed by the reporter and asked "what happened," George said, "Probably the easiest thing to do is to tell you what didn't happen." George skated eloquently around the questions. He didn't even mention who was investigating, but did mention that the "proper people and organizations" were looking into it.

What also made George skeptical of Kaplan during that phone call was Kaplan's motive for leading the investigation. "Kaplan told me that *Channel 7* was going to make him a star if he let them film his investigation," George said. Prior to this conversation with Lutz, Kaplan was allegedly planning on showing up to exorcise the house with six witches and a *Channel 7* News team. Kaplan must have been crushed, because the next day the *Long Island Press* published a story entitled; *"Ghost Hunter Smells A Hoax."* Kaplan was hell bent on getting famous from this story one way or the other. If he couldn't be the famous investigator who exposed the story, he would become the infamous investigator who would expose a hoax. It was the very first allegations of a hoax, but certainly not the last. Kaplan was quoted in the article saying that "If he [George Lutz] does not invite me in the house, then I would have to believe the possibility that a hoax was being presented." Kaplan also contradicted himself by saying, "I am bowing out because I don't like the set-up."

First he claimed 'hoax' if he was not let in the house then he claimed that he was bowing out on his own accord. Kaplan continued such contradictions and odd behavior for the next twenty-years, until his death in 1995. Without anything to back him up, Kaplan capriciously suggested in the same article that the Lutzes personally knew Ronnie DeFeo, Jr., and that their story was a set up and an attempt to assist with Ronnie's appeal. They later learned that Kaplan had no prior experience in parapsychology, but referred to himself as a professional Vampirologist.

In reality, the Lutzes did not have to do anything from this point on. Their story was quickly spreading and taking on a life of its own. What they were concerned about was that their story was being erroneously misrepresented by those who had no knowledge of the events. Behind the scenes was the scheming William Weber, who unbeknownst to the Lutzes had already signed a contract, dated 14 February 1976, with his law partners, Fredrick Mars and Bernard Burton; he also included Paul Hoffman, who was scheduled to write the book. "Hoffman was introduced to us as a criminologist working on the DeFeo case," claimed George. "It wasn't until later that we learned that Hoffman was actually a journalist." To their surprise, Hoffman had been hired by Weber to write a book about the DeFeo case, and later they would ask the Lutzes to have their story included in an epilogue.

The plan had been set in motion by William Weber before the Lutzes even knew about it. The original book that the men were going to write was the story of the DeFeo murders. But because the Lutzes' story was growing more popular by the minute; they wanted to include the Lutzes' story in their book as an epilogue to corroborate their *possession* defense. The Lutzes received a fresh contract in the mail from Weber days later, offering them a percentage of the book deal. The Lutzes were aghast over the contract when they looked it over and found that Ronnie DeFeo, Jr., was going to get five-percent of the proceeds.

The Lutzes were appalled that they might have to give a percentage of the proceeds to a person who was convicted of murdering his family. George looked at it as though "Weber was paying DeFeo for the murders," which may have been inadvertently so. However, it was William Weber who was trying to cash in on the tragedy. The Lutzes were also upset that Weber had lied to them, claiming that Paul Hoffman was a criminologist, when he was actually hired by Weber as the proposed writer of the book. At that point, the Lutzes broke all contact with William Weber and as Weber described in *The Real Amityville Horror* documentary, "...they disappeared off of the face of Long Island."

Who Ya Gonna Call?

The Warrens believe that the DeFeo's were in a state of "phantomania" at the time of the murders, which in effect paralyzed them, making them unable to cry out for help.

Interest in the Lutzes' story grew and continued to garner national attention. *Channel 5 News* was determined to get the rights to the story, and they assigned their news assistant, Laura DiDio to cover it. DiDio and the Lutzes hit it off immediately and she gained the Lutzes confidence right from the start. The Lutz family now needed someone whom they could put their faith and trust into. They were even getting more desperate as time went on. With the betrayal of Kaplan and Weber behind them, the Lutzes found a friend in DiDio. "I got in touch with George Lutz and said, 'Your family needs help,' because they were clearly terrified," recalled DiDio. "Look," DiDio told George. "You need to be put in touch with some credible people who can help you if this really happened as you say it did." The Lutzes respected the fact that DiDio was a straight shooter. Laura contacted a well known pair of psychic investigators by the name of Ed & Lorraine Warren.

The Warrens were a devout Roman Catholic married couple. They were also well-known demonologists and paranormal specialists based in Connecticut. The Warrens were the world's foremost team of psychic investigators, who had investigated a plethora of cases involving psychic phenomena. The scope of the Warren's investigations consisted of the paranormal, the supernatural, and the preternatural; they were the real life Ghost Busters. The Warrens were experienced in phenomenon caused by human spirits, poltergeist activity, and demonic or inhuman hauntings. Though Roman Catholic in denomination, they've worked with people from just about every religion. Ed was a blue-color paranormal investigator and many of their cases relied on Lorraine's proclaimed clairvoyant and trance-medium abilities. They had worked on a myriad of possession and exorcism cases up to that point.

On 6 March 1976, the Warrens set out to investigate the house at 112 Ocean Avenue in Amityville, NY.

Accompanying them were:

- **Steve** - Camera Man - *Channel 5 News*

- **Marvin Scott** - Anchorman - *Channel 5 New*

- **Laura DiDio** - News Assistant - *Channel 5 News*

- **Mary Pascarella-Downey** – Psychic & Director of a prominent psychic research group in New Haven.

- **Dr. Brian Riley**, British Parapsychologist, and his wife, **Alberta Riley**, a deep transmedium-psychic.

- The Warren's personal **Photographer**

- **Dr. Alex Tanous** and **Dr. Karlis Osis** from *The American Society for Psychical Research* in Manhattan.

- **Jerry Solfvin**, a senior research associate from the *Psychical Research Foundation* in Durham, North Carolina.

- **George Kekoris**, field investigator from the *Psychical Research Foundation* in Durham, North Carolina.

- **Keith Harary**, from the *Psychical Research Foundation* in Durham, North Carolina.

One of the various rumors floating around about Amityville is that Tanous and Osis were field investigators from Duke University; who were associated with the Parapsychology Laboratory of Duke University—headed by Dr. Joseph Banks Rhine. This was actually not the case.

- *See the end of the chapter for clarification on Tanous and Osis affiliations.*

Being an experienced paranormal investigator did not help Lorraine's nerves in this case; she was terrified before even entering the house. In an interview with Paulington in 2005, Lorraine described her feelings when she received the call from Laura DiDio about the Amityville horror case: "I just had an odd feeling. I wasn't comfortable. Why I wasn't comfortable, I don't have an answer for that. Why would the case be any different than any other case?" she asked herself. "I just felt personally threatened." In fact, Lorraine felt so threatened that she called up a clergyman she knew and asked him to go into the house with her in spirit.

The Investigation

With the team of psychics and reporters assembled, they met at the house on 6 March 1976, just before nightfall, and set up for what would become known as the most famous investigation into the psychic realm of our time. Ed and Lorraine Warren met George and Kathleen Lutz at a pizza parlor near the house earlier to discuss the details of the investigation. Lorraine and her husband had met the Lutzes one time prior to this: at Kathy's mother's house on St. Joseph's day, 19 March 1976 (Father Ray was also in attendance). At the pizza place, George told the Warrens that Father Ray had warned them not to go back to the house, because it "would give the spirits recognition and bring them right back." Lorraine agreed with Father Ray's assessment. The Lutzes later traveled to the house with the others, but would not step foot on the property.

Bizarre things started occurring almost immediately after the group entered the house at 112 Ocean Avenue. An overwhelming impression of sadness was the general consensus of the group throughout their research of the house. According to Laura DiDio, the first strange thing that happened was that the *Channel 5* cameraman, Steve, bent over clutching his chest once he reached the second floor landing and began complaining of stabbing chest pains.

Psychic, Mary Downey, was not familiar with the DeFeo case up to that point, but claimed that she had the overall impression of a male teenager in the house that had done something horrendous. The psychics felt even greater bad vibes from the house as they entered the second floor. The metaphoric-scent of a brutal crime having occurred there was strong and fresh. Suddenly Downey looked up at the window above and saw the face of a young girl looking in at her. "Then I heard crying, weeping," Downey recalls. She kept her cool and used her knowledge and training to summon the girl towards the white light.

Lorraine was adamant that the spirits in the home were not just those of the murdered DeFeo family, but that of evil spirits from the bowls of hell:

> *"You're not dealing with a haunting that's come about as the result of a tragedy of murder [the DeFeo family murders]; you're dealing with something that has the wisdom and cunning of the ages. You're looking at what caused this. When a person is open and vulnerable to his own psychoses [and could accept that he] could kill every member of his family, nobody is going to put up a fight. Nobody is going to try to suppress themselves. It's a mystery, it's a puzzle. But that's how cunning the Devil can actually be — he'll outwit you... It was the same thing that had affected [DeFeo] and brought about that tragedy. It was evil."* --Lorraine Warren

Lorraine began seeing visions of several bodies lined up, all wearing white sheets. Mary Downey also began seeing something similar; claiming that she saw hooded figures that looked like monks. Downey became extremely frightened when she saw the monks close the door behind them and began gawking at her.

Lorraine received nonstop clairvisual and clairaudial messages and all had menacing, extant demons. Walking up the stairs, Lorraine described a powerful force, like a rush of water bouncing off her chest, holding her back.

Lorraine continued up the stairs to the 2nd floor and entered into the sewing room. Accompanying her was anchorman, Marvin Scott. Suddenly, Lorraine stopped in her tracks, turned and looked at Marvin.

"What's wrong," Marvin asked.

"I hope this is as close to hell as I'll ever get," Lorraine stated in dramatic fashion.

Lorraine then entered Missy's room. She knew it was Missy's room by psychic interpretation. She also clairvoyantly made the assumption that Missy's room had the DeFeo's furniture in it. In other words, the furniture in that room—bed included—belonged to the DeFeo's. The only thing that was changed on the beds were the mattresses; Lorraine claimed that all beds in the house had the same frame and box spring that the DeFeo's had been slaughtered on.

Ed Warren had a strange feeling as well. He had usually relied on the clairvoyancey of Lorraine for indication, but something was drawing him into the basement. Ed separated from the group and traveled alone into the cellar. Once in the basement, Ed saw thousands of pinpoints of light that momentarily blinded him. When his eyesight slightly recovered, he saw shadows through the lights. Suddenly an unseen force lifted him off of his feet and sent him crashing to the ground. Ed's only recourse was to use religious resistance to fight off the disturbing presence. He quickly began chanting bible verses, commanding the demons to release their evil grip. It was over as quickly as it began, and it was at that moment that Ed realized there was an evil present in the house. Terrified, because he had never experienced such an encounter; he rushed back upstairs and rejoined the others.

Meanwhile, downstairs Downey continued getting strong sensations, and she went into several deep trances. At one point she opened up a bottle of holy water that she had packed and began sprinkling it around while chanting; "Get thee behind me Satan," several times. As Downey began dowsing the floor with holy water she describes, "And you could hear, like, water on a hot stove."

Lorraine describes that on the third floor, she clairvoyantly encountered Ronald DeFeo Sr., or an evil spirit that resembled him. "This encounter was so awful, and he was so sinister, that she felt there was absolutely nothing she could do to help—or eject—his spirit from the house." Lorraine explained that their mission was to do research, not really to rid the house of spirits. These spirits were certainly resistant to any type of religious intervention, by all accounts.

Later, the group all gathered on the first floor. At sometime after midnight, they decided to have a séance in order to summon the spirits and ask them what they wanted. Five members sat at the table for the ceremony, all holding hands. Field investigator, George Kekoris, was one of the five at the table. George was skeptical of the group that had been assembled.

"It was like a side show," Kekoris said, "with self-styled psychics seeing spirits here and there." As Lorraine began to speak, Kekoris was not impressed. "It was like the Twilight Zone," he said. Suddenly, Kekoris felt his hands getting cold, "sort of numb-like," he explained. Then, he felt his hands sliding from the table, his teeth began chattering, and his heart started racing uncontrollably. Kekoris broke from the séance abruptly, and was unaware what had just happened to him. "My common sense told me to attribute it to nothing but the power of suggestion," he later said.

During this ghoulish ceremony, it was reported that one of the investigators actually passed out cold from fear. According to Lorraine, "Two of the investigators began complaining of severe heart palpitations, and Alberta Riley had become visibly upset during the séance. With her hands covering her face, she almost broke out into tears. "Whatever is here, it's something that comes at you and makes your heart speed up," she said in a teary sounding voice, as she rocked back and forth with her left hand on her head. Downey actually became so ill that she had to be taken outside and never entered the house again." By the end of the investigation, Lorraine Warren was convinced that whatever it was that was in the house never walked the face of the earth in human form. Jerry

Solfvin claimed that he felt nothing in the house, but he admits that his participation was informal, and "not for investigative purposes."

Alberta Riley was a distinguished and attractive English woman who had practically spent her whole life as a psychic up to that point. Alberta had seen it all, but she was not ready for what she would experience in the spooked Long Island home. Alberta was deeply shaken by the experience in the Amityville house that night! "I saw things I never knew existed, things I never thought could exist in this universe," she told Gerald Brittle, author of best-selling book, *The Demonologist*. In an exclusive interview with Brittle, Alberta said that she was so shaken by what she had seen in the horror house, that she quit the psychic profession right-then-and there. "I don't want to know any more," she said adamantly. "This has been enough. My attention now goes to God."

Though nothing happened for the T.V. cameras, two particular unexplainable instances—that have yet to be explained—materialize sometime after the first investigation of the house. Lorraine had brought a relic of the late Padre Pio Da Pietrelcina with her for protection. The relic of Padre had been sent to Lorraine weeks earlier by a complete stranger. Padre Pio was a famous Italian priest who is best known for baring all five stigmata-like wounds of Jesus Christ for 50-years. Padre Pio died in 1968. She claimed that no one knew about the relic except for her and her husband Ed. When Lorraine saw Father Ray after the investigation he said, "Who do you think brought you out of the house?" Feeling like she was back in Catholic school, Lorraine said, "God, I guess, father."

"Padre Pio," Father Ray said, to Lorraine's amazement.

"How do you know that?" Lorraine asked inquisitively.

"Padre Pio told me so," Father Ray miraculously answered.

Lorraine was in awe and amazement. For one thing, Padre Pio passed away back in 1968. Another thing was that only Ed knew about the Padre Pio relict Lorraine had carried into the house and he told no one. Approximately one week after the Warrens first visit to the horror house, they were contacted by the photographer that accompanied them into the house. "I'd like to show you something that's in one of these pictures, because I don't understand it," the photographer said. Lorraine and Ed met up with the photographer and looked closely at the tiny proof sheet pictures that they used back then. "You're going to have to blow these up, I can't tell by that," Lorraine pronounced. After they blew the picture up, they received one of the most shocking visuals they had ever seen. In the picture, an image of Padre Pio's face had materialized on a moose head that was hanging on the wall of the house. No one in the group, including Lorraine, knew Padre Pio or what he looked like. Lorraine began praying to Padre Pio. "If it's really you in the picture, I need to know who you are," Lorraine said in her prayers to Padre Pio. "And I need you to help me to better understand why you appeared to me." Lorraine continued praying to Padre Pio over and over. Continuing on their speaking engagement-tour, the Warrens went out to the University of La Hoya in California. That Sunday they attended the mass of the Good Sheppard, accompanied by two men from ABC TV. Lorraine was adamant that no one there knew anything about Padre Pio's recent appearance to her. After the mass, a stranger approached Lorraine outside the church and said; out of know where, "Did you know Padre Pio?"

"I knew of him," Lorraine said. "Why?"

"You're going to be in La Hoya tonight?" the stranger asked.

"Yes, Ed and I are going to be at La Hoya tonight."

"There's a Solician school for boys, and there's a priest that served with Padre Pio, and he's a visiting priest," the man said. Though Padre Pio was a very popular figure at the time, this was certainly an odd coincidence.

"Really," Lorraine said with excitement. "What's his name?"

"Father Ralph Negrai," the stranger replied.

Ed and Lorraine were stunned and taken aback by the sudden promulgations of the stranger. Ed encouraged Lorraine to contact the priest and set up a get together, which Lorraine willingly obliged. Lorraine wasted no time calling Father Negrai, expressing to him her excitement to meet a priest who worked with Padre Pio. Father Negrai graciously agreed. Ed and Lorraine went to meet Father Negrai, who spoke broken English and was a lovely man, according to Lorraine. Father Negrai knew Padre Pio quite well, serving with him back in Italy. Ed was anxious to show Father Negrai the photo that they had taken at the horror house that vividly resembled Padre

Pio. Without advanced notice of what he was going to show, Ed set up his projector and showed Father Negrai the picture-slide on the wall. Suddenly, Father Negrai fell to his knees, made the sign of the cross and said, "Padre Pio!"

"Father," Lorraine called. "Why would he appear to me?" Father Negrai looked up at Lorraine and profoundly stated, "You must have asked him to." Padre Pio Da Pietrelcina later became a saint of the Catholic Church on 16 June 2002, in Rome.

The second bizarre incident caught on film occurred when the group had set up a tri-pod-camera on the second floor facing Missy's bedroom during the session. The camera fired off picture after picture; a flash photograph was taken every few moments. Several rolls of film were used over the course of the investigation of the house that night. George had the photographs catalogued by his secretary years later in California, who happened to be pregnant at the time. "Every time she picked up this one particular picture the baby inside her jumped," recalled George.

"Low and behold, in the doorway on the second floor, in one room," DiDio recollected, "there is the distinct image figure of a little boy peering out from the doorway."

"There were no children in the house that night," DiDio explains. Some say the blonde-haired-boy in the photo—with a classic 70's shirt on—was one of the murdered DeFeo boys. Perhaps the scariest thing about the photo is the boy's glowing eyes, which Brittle suggests is a common characteristic of a demon. The boy was peeking out of the room and clearly did not want to be seen by the camera.

"When I called Missy and asked her, 'who was this,' she said, 'oh that's the boy I used to play with there,'" said George with an I-told-ya-so-type grin on his face. George claims that was the first he and Kathy had heard of that from Missy. Even to this very day, the pictures validity has yet to be disproven or theoretically challenged. Marvin Scott claimed that he felt nothing during the 6 March 1975, investigation, and that the two hours that he spent watching the movie with a rowdy bunch of pot-smoking moviegoers was scarier than the six-hours that he spent in the house.

The Warrens get attacked

Even though the Warrens had been involved in cases such as levitation, blood coming from someone's eyes and all sorts of bad things, they left the house that night more terrified than ever for their own safety. Lorraine sensed the danger first hand from the thing that she claimed personally threatened her. During the car ride home, they felt that an evil entity was following them. When they finally got home, Ed took his briefcase and went to the basement, which was where his office was located; Lorraine went upstairs to the bedroom. Lorraine had picked up a brown manila folder from the post office earlier and opened it up. In the envelope was a book on Padre Pio.

While reading the first paragraph of the book, Lorraine noticed that her two dogs—a Belgian sheep dog and a Border collie—were acting strange, "as if they were drugged." Lorraine continued to try and get through the first paragraph, but felt a strong sense of confusion. She looked at the dogs and noticed that the hair on their backs was standing up. She sensed that a force trying to reach out to her, something she described as "diabolical confusion." Suddenly, she was rendered motionless and could not move. There was a security button close by, and she wanted to press it to notify her husband, but she was paralyzed.

Then, a blistering, devilish sound, which could only be descrbied as someone shaking "big sheets of metal," reverberated through the house. Suddenly, a cyclone of wind swept a huge energy of darkness up from the lowest level of the house. The black energy swept through the dinning room, the living room, and eventually to her bedroom. She looked up and saw a massive black figure in the doorway. Fear shot through her body as she made a sign of the cross and said, "In the name of Jesus Christ, I demand you to leave and go back where you came from." Seconds later, Ed came running into the room, got into bed and under the covers next to Lorraine, and put his hands on hers'. "Honey, do you have any idea what just happened?" he asked. Ed had also witnessed the black shadowy abomination.

Ed was in the basement pondering what he had seen and felt in Amityville, when a door slammed. Ed sat up in attention and heard footsteps. Suddenly, a dense, dark mass entered the room, and the temperature immediately dropped to icy cold. Then Ed heard a sound of wind, which he described as a "wind cone." Ed knew that he was witnessing a diabolical infestation. "It was so dark and evil," Ed recalls, "that I knew it was a devil, not just a demon." The force came within two feet of him; Ed was terrified. He grabbed a wooden cross that he had handy. Ed also happened to have Holy Water on his desk that he used for the investigation. He threw the holy water at the figure, made the sign of the cross, and commanded it to leave in the name of Jesus Christ. All of a sudden, it was gone!

"What was in that house can never be explained," Lorraine Warren told Brittle. "What we encountered was a true spirit of perdition. It knew all our vulnerabilities and it went after them. It tried, and it tried very hard, to ruin our lives. It even tried to physically kill us. So when I think of Amityville, I don't just think of what happened to George and Kathy Lutz. I also think of what happened afterwards. Because once it was done with the Lutzes this thing came after us. We became the new threat. We became the new threat because we were working with the church. Our work in Amityville was not to satisfy the media's curiosity; our work was to justify the need for an exorcism. That's why we were attacked: to prevent us from succeeding in our work. So when someone says, 'The Amityville case isn't real', I feel insulted. *I know it's real. I lived it.* And I still live with it today."

Moving Out

With the preliminary investigation completed, it was determined that the spirits haunting the grounds at 112 Ocean Avenue were not going anywhere anytime soon. It was advised by many that the Lutz family give up their dream home for good. Not only did the Lutzes refuse to go back into the house, but—at the request of Father Ray—they also decided to abandon all of their possessions. Father Ray believed that their possessions might by then have been infested with the negative energies inhabiting the house.

George contacted Doug Capra and Benjamin Mattana Jr., (who owned Nassau County Harley Davidson)—two of his friends—to go into the house and prepare their belongings. Capra had already been at the house when Benny arrived at about noon on Easter Sunday, 1976. Benny had brought his girlfriend, Frances Victoria Ardito, along with him, but she refused to step foot onto the property. After some time of moving clothes and furniture, the two men went into the boathouse to look at George's speedboat. Curious and probably bored, Benny's girlfriend walked down to the boathouse and met up with the guys. However, she complained that she was feeling uneasy and returned to the car shortly after. Oddly enough, Frances Victoria was arrested a week later and charged with Benny's murder. Frances Victoria Ardito had been found incompetent to stand trial and was institutionalized. She died while incarcerated. Even more bizarre; according to George Lutz in a 2005 radio interview with *Magick Mind Radio*, Benny had eaten some of the food in the fridge, although he was specifically told not to. Coincidentally, Frances Victoria had a son by the name of Gerald Ardito, who was arrested in 1993 for strangling to death his ex-fiancé, Marie Daniele, with pantyhose in Room 3431, on the top floor of the luxury hotel near Grand Central Terminal. He was convicted of manslaughter in 1994.

Later (April or May), there was an auction of their belongings, but the Lutzes did not attend. Looking back on it, George believes they netted around $1,600 (the low amount was mainly due to repairs that had to be made to their boat, the fact that they still owed over $10,000 on it and that the auctioneer had a 10% take on the auction). The leftover food was donated to the Salvation Army. They gave one of their last office cars to a person at the JFK ticket counter. They got rid of the van due to mechanical problems. They left another car at Father Ray's rectory and were able to salvage one of their motorcycles.

The Lutz family decided that they would move as far away as they could from the home without leaving the states. George, Kathy, and her kids left Kathy's mother's house and headed for the airport.

When they arrived, they handed the curbside porter their keys and the title of their vehicle, and headed for a fresh start in sunny San Diego, California. The family arrived in California on Mother's Day, 1976, and attempted to put the pieces of their broken lives back together. Although they had abandoned the house in February, they continued to make payments on it through July or August, according to George Lutz in his 2005 interview with *Magick Mind Radio*. After that, George claims that they gave the house back to the bank, because they didn't want the responsibility of selling it to someone else.

More Psychics?

Psychics and paranormal specialists from all over the world were itching to investigate the horror house and see for themselves what was going on. This case was a psychic's dream. Parapsychologist, Peter Jordan, who also had a chance to investigate the house in 1977, said "Amityville was on the tips of everyone's tongue" back in those days. Jordan states that the Amityville story is "a compendium of all of the most horrific things that have ever happened in the paranormal, all in one case." Every one of these "so called" professionals had a theory, and everyone of them could tell you, point blank, what was happening, whether they had visited the house or not.

Among the many to come out of the woodwork was Dr. Hans Holzer, a Parapsychologist known at the time as America's most famous ghost hunter. Holzer contacted William Weber and was hired by Weber to investigate the infamous home in Amityville. On 13 January 1977, Hans Holzer went to the horror house with William Weber, Laura DiDio, and world-renowned deep transmedium, Ethel Johnson Meyers. Hans believes that a transmedium is required when entering grounds that are haunted. A tranmedium's job is to go into a semi-trance state and connect with the spirit through a channeling session—using a trained ear to hear the spirit, and vocal cords to speak to it.

DiDio described the physical transformation that Myers had undergone during the session as "eerie" and "shocking." Not knowing anything about the houses history, Meyers stepped out of the car and said, "There's an Indian around here." DiDio claims that once in the house, Myers "developed an Adams apple;" and as Weber described, "After a while, this lady began talking in a strange gibberish language." Once the séance got under way, Meyers began to communicate with the spirit that lingered on the grounds of the house. "Her voice dropped several octaves," DiDio explains; and she began speaking with who she claimed was an Indian chief, whose tomb nearby the house had been disturbed. During the séance, Hans asked Ethel questions and Meyers was to interpret the Indian Chief's answers and relay them to the group.

> **Hans**: Why are they angry?
> **Meyers**: Because this has been a sacred place and...this is over the very, very special Chief's school...I can't move my face.
> **Hans**: And what does he make them do? [Presumably asking, what does he make the people in the house do?]
> **Meyers**: Violence of... deaths... I don't know, my skulls cracked and my necks stretched.
> **Hans**: What will the male do under those circumstances?
> **Meyers**: Anything the Indian desires him to do...

After the séance, Hans came out with the theory that the house was only occupied by one Indian Chief, and not a demon or one of the DeFeo victims. Hans believed that the Chief just wanted people to get off his land. Another one of Holzer's theories was that during the DeFeo murders, no one awoke or heard the blasts from the rifle, because the *sound barrier was blocked* by the *paranormal forces* in the house.

The Amityville Horror is born

In just a few short months of leaving the Amityville horror house, the Lutzes' lives were turned upside down. Their world had spun into a media storm of controversy, and the town of Amityville was turned into a tourist attraction from hell. However, the thrill seeking intrusions had not reached their peek just yet. At the Univ-Con Convention at Penn State University in 2005, George Lutz was interviewed by radio personality Lou Gentile. Lutz recounted the story of how he was put in contact with Jay Anson.

"A friend of mine who sold textbooks to colleges looked at this (Weber contract) and said, 'I know someone who you should talk to before you ever consider such a thing.' I said, 'Well we're not even considering this – this is just an absurd idea,' but he introduced us then to Tam Mossman who was an editor at Prentice-Hall Books – Prentice Hall Trade Division. Tam Mossman was Jane Roberts – who did the *Seth Speaks* books – her editor. And I went and looked those up, and bought them and read them, and learned about – even thought there was some really strange stuff in those books, that this was a guy who knew what he was talking about – what he was doing – who understood the paranormal at least one particular perspective, and I was now dealing with a credible company. He made a recommendation of someone he knew – Jay Anson – and asked that we meet with Jay."

With all of the misinformation and fabrications circulating about their story, the Lutzes decided to set the record straight and give their account in the form of a non-fiction novel. Tam Mossman, who specialized in publishing books on the occult, met with the Lutzes in March of 1976 to discuss the events of their nightmarish stay in Amityville. The Lutzes handed Mossman audio tapes that they had recorded which chronicled their stay in the house. Mossman later commissioned his friend and writer, Jay Anson, who was working in Manhattan at the time for a company called *Professional Films*. Anson had previous experience with the occult while doing a documentary on the making of the 1973 blockbuster movie, *The Exorcist*.

Anson listened to the Lutzes' tapes and took it upon himself to interview others involved as well, including Father Ray. In fact, it was Father's testimony that convinced Anson that he had a possible *hit* on his hands. Anson got to work on writing the story immediately, sometime in April of 1976. Anson had never even met the Lutzes prior to writing the book. The Lutzes moved far from Long Island, settling in San Diego, California for a time. Despite the common misconceptions that the Lutz family was well-off after the book deal, George was forced to sell his family business that was worth $250,000 for only $30,000 up front and $20,000 over the next three-years. The family also had to live on food stamps and they briefly delivered Reader's Digest magazines door to door and sold Amway products to make a living.

Meanwhile, Anson continued penning his masterpiece but, once involved, even he was affected by the aftershock of the events. Anson did an interview in March of 1979 with Writer's Digest. In the article, Anson claims that he gave the first few chapters of the book to a friend to review. That night, the female friend and her two children died in a house fire. Everything in the house was destroyed beyond recognition, except for the manuscript! Not long after that, Jay Anson suffered a heart attack during the writing process. Although he was bed ridden, Anson managed to complete two chapters a week, ultimately finishing the book.

In September of 1977, "The Amityville Horror" hit bookstores and immediately became a runaway bestseller. Estimates of the sales of the book are around ten million copies sold in the U.S. to date from its numerous editions.

The Amityville Horror, the movie, was released on 27 July 1979, and was based on the 1977 bestselling novel: *The Amityville Horror - A True Story*, by Jay Anson. The film was directed by Stuart Rosenberg, whose first movie was *Cool Hand Luke* in 1967. *The Amityville Horror* starred: James Brolin, Margot Kidder, Rod Steiger, Don Stroud and Murray Hamilton.

Amityville Stats - Books & Movies:

- Jay Anson wrote *The Amityville Horror: A True Story*, before he ever met George or Kathy Lutz. Anson used audio taped interviews of the couple explaining their experience's to write the book.

- The producers of the movie rejected Jay Anson's screenplay that was based upon his bestselling novel, and instead chose Canada native, *Sandor Stern's* version. Needless to say, the movie caught on like wild-fire and was a massive box office success. The film made more than $86 million in the United States alone; and an American icon was born.

- *The Amityville Horror* movie was filmed at a Dutch Colonial style home in Toms River, New Jersey (Outside scenes). The owners of 112 Ocean Avenue at the time [The Cromarty's] and the town of Amityville would not let them film there.

- The owners were given $15,000 to allow the house to be used and it was quickly remodeled to look like the infamous house of 112 Ocean Avenue. [72]

- The Toms River, New Jersey Volunteer Fire Company was used to provide *the rain* during one of the outdoor scenes.

- It is estimated that the production pumped some $250,000 into the local Toms River economy. [72]

- James Brolin appeared on Good Morning America beside George & Kathy Lutz. On the program, Brolin said, "Do I believe them [the Lutzes], yes I do. Looking over the story, I can't say that I believe the book totally, but sitting with these people, it's hard to deny a lot of the facts." [36]

- James Brolin said that he was originally sent the script first, while he was working on another movie. He thought it would make a "terrific movie." The agency then suggested that he pick up a copy of Anson's book. Brolin was shocked that there was a book, and the next day, to his amazement, he found out it was a "true story." Brolin smiled and said, "I didn't know what I was getting into." After the movies release, several newspapers began reporting strange happenstances with anyone involved with the house. They called it *The Amityville Curse*. [36]

- James Brolin said, on the first day of filming the *Amityville Horror*, he stepped into the elevator of his third floor apartment and pressed the button for the lobby. Before he reached the lobby, the floors shuddered, and the car grinded to a halt! The lights of the elevator flickered violently, before plunging him into complete darkness. He screamed for help, but no one heard his cries. He remained in the elevator for nearly 30-minutes. (House of Evil) [68]

- A friend of Jay Anson's was driving home after receiving a copy of the final draft of the book, which he put in his car's trunk. Driving down the road, he saw what he believed to be a large puddle ahead. It turned out to be a sinkhole. The car went into it. Of course, the front end goes down into the hole, raising the trunk above water, thus saving the book. [68]

- A truck was delivering large pieces of lumber to the house in Tom's River, New Jersey, where the first movie was being filmed. On its way to the house, the truck lost its load, killing the people in the car behind it. [68]

- A photographer went to take pictures of Anson immediately after photographing the Amityville house. While he was in the author's home his car caught fire and billowed orange smoke. [68]

- Anson's editor picked up a complete manuscript of the book at his office. His car caught fire, and he discovered that all the bolts on his engine had been loosened. [68]

- Anson said he loaned a woman friend of his some early chapters of the book. She and two of her children suffocated in a fire that night. The only item in the apartment not damaged by fire was the manuscript. [68]

- Toms River police and ambulance workers were used as extras.

- If the Lutz family was just out to make money, they sure did a very poor job! The Lutzes' total earnings for revealing their story was reportedly less than $300,000. While Jay Anson's book earned him several million dollars, and the Total Domestic Gross of *The Amityville Horror* movie was $86,432,000. The movie made $7,843,467 in its opening weekend. Not bad for (1979) numbers. It opened in 748 theaters around the United States during its first week. [70]

- The original film's theatrical success was followed by two sequels; *Amityville II: The Possession* (1982), and *Amityville 3-D* (1983)

- These films were followed by five direct-to-video sequels released from (1989) to (1996), which include: *The Amityville Curse* (1990); *Amityville 1992: It's About Time* (1992); *Amityville A New Generation (1993); and Amityville Dollhouse (1996).*

- The film was also remade in April (2005), and was parodied in *Bloodbath at the House of Death* (1984) and Scary Movie 2 (2001). In (1989), a TV-movie was released entitled *Amityville: The Evil Escapes.* There was also a *CSI-NY (2007) Halloween episode,* which played-off the Amityville Horror House.

- Ryan Reynolds played George Lutz in *"The Amityville Horror (2005)."* George Lutz was not happy with the way he was depicted by Reynolds. [34]

- In *"The Amityville Horror (2005),"* George Lutz filed a lawsuit against the film for defamation, libel, and breach of contract. In the film, Lutz is shown killing the family dog with an ax, and building coffins for his own family. [34]

- The (2005) remake of the film *The Amityville Horror* was shot on location at a private residence on Silver Lake Road in Wisconsin. At this location stood a 100-year-old house, which had reportedly been unoccupied for 40-years. [71]

- A scary character in the film was Jodie DeFeo. She was a fictional character and not one of the murdered DeFeos. She is the last character seen in the (2005) remake.

- Ryan Reynolds admitted that the movie was not based on reality: *"I don't know if my opinion is neither here nor there. I just wanted to tell the story as best I could, according to the script. It's not a biography of George Lutz so I never met George. I never got into what he's like as a man and a person. I know that something awful happened in that house. We know that six murders happened in that house. We know a family moved in there a year later and lasted twenty-eight days; we know that. My job was just to bring that character to life in the script."* [69]

- Final casting for the (2005) movie wrapped on August 2, 2004. Kathy Lutz died of respiratory disease on August 17, 2004; days before the start of the new film's production.

- Amityville II: The Possession and Amityville 3-D, were also filmed in Toms River. [72]

Amityville Books

After the original novel, twelve other books were written:

Murder in Amityville – by: Hans Holzer
The Amityville Horror II – by: John G. Jones
The Amityville Curse – by: Hans Holzer
The Secret of Amityville – by: Hans Holzer
Ghosts in Amityville – by: Jack DeMolay
Amityville: The Final Chapter – by: John G. Jones
Amityville: The Evil Escapes – by: John G. Jones
Amityville: The Horror Returns – by: John G. Jones
Amityville: The Nightmare Continues – by: Robin Karl
The Amityville Horror Conspiracy – by: Stephen Kaplan
The Night the DeFeos Died – by: Ric Osuna
Mentally Ill in Amityville: Murder, Mystery, & Mayhem at 112 Ocean Ave. – by: Will Savive

Haunting: Fact or Fiction?

On 19 June 1979, four weeks before the Lutzes appeared on Good Morning America, they took a polygraph test conducted by Professional Security Consultants, Polygraph and Security Specialists, Chris Gugas & Michael Rice, in California. The test consisted of a series of questions pertaining to the Lutzes' 28-day stay in Amityville. Both examiners had reviewed a copy of Anson's book beforehand, which represented the Lutzes' experiences. Gugas and Rice conducted an extensive pre-test interview with George and Kathy to ensure that both had an understanding of the evaluation that was about to take place. Following the pre-test interview, stimulation tests were conducted to determine whether the two would be "suitable subjects" for a polygraph examination. Satisfied with the results, Gugas and Rice began the examination. Both George and Kathy were interviewed separately for further accuracy.

Test:

Chris Gugas asked George Lutz the following questions while George was attached to the lie detector machine:

1. Are the details you gave me on your frightening experiences at the Amityville house true?
2. When you fled your Amityville house, were you in fear of your life and the well being of your family?
3. After leaving Amityville did you and Kathy both levitate at your mother-in-law's house?
4. During your 28 days in Amityville, did you experience unexplained flies and disturbing odors on several occasions?
5. At the Amityville house, did you hear what sounded like a marching band tuning up in the middle of the night?

George Lutz answered "YES" to all of the five questions.

Michael Rice asked Kathy Lutz the following questions while Kathy was attached to the lie detector machine:

1. To the best of your ability did the events of that Amityville house as recorded on your tapes actually happen?
2. Are all the events discussed in your interview today true and correct?
3. While in the Amityville house did you actually see yourself as an old woman?
4. While in the Amityville house were you embraced by an invisible being?
5. While in your Amityville bed did you actually feel the presence of an invisible being over you?

Kathy Lutz answered "YES" to all of the five questions.

During the examination, instruments were used on each subject to test blood pressure, heart rate, respiration, and electrodermal resistance. Irrelevant and controlled questions were also mixed in to both examinations, which is standard procedure for these types of tests. They both passed with "flying colors," Kathy later boasted on Good Morning America, and she was absolutely correct. Mr. Gugas determined that "George Lee Lutz answered truthfully to all his critical questions asked in the examination," and Mr. Rice determined that Mrs. Lutz "answered truthfully to all critical questions listed above and that no deception was indicated to any of those questions."

For those who question the validity of the tester's, Chris Gugas is one of the most prominent polygraph testers to have ever lived. Gugas founded the *National Board of Polygraph Examiners*, and the *California Academy of Polygraph Sciences*. At one time, Gugas was also the President and executive Director of the *American Polygraph Association*. Gugas has also been called as a polygraph expert before civil, criminal, as well as federal courts. In 2002, a USA article (entitled *Telling the truth about lie detectors, by* Dan Vergano) reported that a 1997 survey of 421 psychologists estimated the accuracy of a polygraph to be at approximately 61 percent, which is slightly better than chance. Still, this evidence holds a lot of weight when it comes to the Lutzes' credibility.

Kaplan & Weber

Despite the Lutzes' lie detector test results produced by Gugas and Rice, the critics were still not satisfied. One of the most vocal critics, of course, was again Stephen Kaplan, who claimed the test "a sham," and Gugas a "ringer." Though Kaplan continued his outlandish accusations, he still never provided any type of proof to back them up. Aside from his attacks on George and Kathy Lutz, Kaplan was also a vocal critic of the Warrens after their investigation results were made public. Kaplan and the Warrens became regular sparring partners on several radio programs throughout the years. Despite the fact that Kaplan claimed that he had proof that the Lutzes' story was a lie, and that the story was an overall hoax, he never offered proof. In fact, Ed Warren offered Kaplan $5,000 to make public his Amityville-hoax proof, but Kaplan declined. The Warrens later offered a $3,000 reward to anyone who can prove that there was a conspiracy to create the Amityville story. Though Kaplan called the Warrens "frauds" and "charlatans" on many occasions, he did offer an apology in 1982 on the *Joel Martin Radio Show* on WBAB in NY. With Joel Martin playing peace maker, Kaplan backed down to his rivals.

Joel Martin: How do we want to clear this up?

Ed Warren: If Dr. Kaplan would simply write their newspaper a letter that the Warrens are not charlatans. We do not go out to hoodwink the public. This would satisfy us.

Joel Martin: Is this agreeable to you Dr. Kaplan?

Stephen Kaplan: Sure.

Ed Warren: We have never talked about Dr. Kaplan on any programs unless we have been directly attacked.

Joel Martin: Okay what about this business of alleged threats made by each other?

Stephen Kaplan: I think it was a misunderstanding. I think we are both nervous of each other because we are in strange fields. I get a feeling people think I cohort with vampires. Maybe the Warren's cohort with fighting against demons and bringing with them. I think there was a lot of nervousness involved.

Joel Martin: Okay have we performed an exorcism tonight? Are all the bad spirits and bad feelings gone?

Ed Warren: Well, I want to thank you very much Joel for bringing us together...

Joel Martin: I don't want thanks...

Lorraine Warren: Well you deserve thanks for clearing the air.

Stephen Kaplan: I am here because I think you folks were wrongly criticized very wrongly and I think it ought to been corrected.

Joel Martin: Alright I hope for the future you work together or don't work together as the case may be, but with no impugning or derogatory remarks about reputations.

Stephen Kaplan: The forces of Evil are stronger in terms because they are more united than we are. It would not shock me that in the future somewhere that Ed and Lorraine Warren and I get together on certain cases if need be against forces which have hurt the public and the people.

Joel Martin: Is the animosity over?

Stephen Kaplan: I have no animosity to the Warrens.

Joel Martin: Is the misrepresentations over?

Stephen Kaplan: I feel happy that it is over; that the frustration is over; that my obsession with the truth because sometimes that truth is not truth is over.

However sincere Kaplan may have seemed at the time, he still continued his claims; and in 1995 he released his book, "*The Amityville Horror Conspiracy*, which claimed that there were several people involved in the hoax, including the Warrens. Kaplan died, though, before the book was released. It's the opinion of many that Kaplan's book has more inconsistencies in it than Anson's book. In Kaplan's book, he claimed that Marvin Scott's T.V. coverage of the Warren's investigation took place on 24 February 1976, when in reality, it took place on 6 March 1976. This is just one of the many misnomers set forth in Kaplan's book.

***

Aside from Amityville, Kaplan had made several outlandish statements that, unlike the Lutzes' statements, have never been challenged or discussed. Many acknowledge that he was a vampire hunter, but for some reason that has not really sunk into the heads of the people that use his logic to discredit Amityville. Kaplan made a career out of attempting to make something of fiction into "historical fact" by claiming that vampires live among us. Moreover, according to the Los Angeles Almanac, Kaplan was quoted in 1995 as saying, "Los Angeles was home to 36 vampires; the *highest* concentration of vampires in the world." He claimed that vampires thrived there, because of L.A.'s "acceptance of the unusual." Speaking of unusual, Kaplan also stated, "Vampires are not to be feared. They are pleasant people who require only a very small amount of blood." Kaplan also wrote a book entitled, *Vampires Are* (ETC Publications, 1984), where he tries to convince people that vampires are in fact real.

According to Stephen's wife, Roxanne, S. Kaplan graduated from a city college in New York with a Bachelor's degree in sociology and later earned a Master's degree in communication. Though Kaplan claims he's a doctor and many articles list him as having a Ph.D., it has been nearly impossible to verify this promulgation. Roxanne Kaplan claimed that her husband "Earned a BA and an MA from City College of NY, another Masters degree from State University at Stony Brook, and a *non-traditional* Ph.D. from *Pacific College* of California."

Using this information, I contacted Pacific College of Oriental Medicine in San Diego. After being directed, I sent them a written request to verify whether Kaplan had in fact graduated from there. After about a week of phone-tag with a woman named, Cindy, she finally transferred me to the College's Registrar, Troy, who boldly stated that, "No one by the name of Stephen Kaplan graduated from this school." Troy was kind enough to point out that there was a Pacific College of Medical and Dental Assistants in San Diego in years past, but it had since closed down.

There was no information floating around about this mysterious school. So, I contacted the American Association of Medical Assistants (AAMA). They informed me that Pacific College was accredited through Commission on Accreditation of Allied Health Education Programs (CAAHEP) from 1972 to 1987. I also contacted the U.S. Department of Education to discuss "closed schools," and how to verify previous students. I spoke to woman by the name of Denise Hill who was very helpful. Denise claimed that the transcripts are destroyed after 5-years. I guess the more important question from these findings is, "Can one obtain a Ph.D. from a school for "Medical and Dental Assistants?" The answer to that question is an emphatic "No!" I located two former students of the school and they confirmed that Pacific College of Medical and Dental was just a 6 month course—not a regular college as in a 2-year or even 4-year type of college.

In her interview, Roxanne Kaplan says in regards to her claims that Stephen received a Ph.D., from Pacific College in California, "Although there has been much criticism of this last degree, it is very similar to degrees that are now available from colleges such as Empire State College, which is now accepted as a part of the NY State University system. Back in the 70's, it was quite a revolutionary idea, and Stephen took a lot of flak for it from people such as the Warrens, but he enjoyed being a pioneer in the field of alternative education." Notice how she couldn't resist taking a stab at the Warrens. Not only does Roxanne mention that her husband attended the college and received a Ph.D., but she also goes on to explain the legitimacy of the degree.

Coincidentally, she gives an almost identical answer in an interview with Ric Osuna. Ric asks her about Stephen's background, and Roxanne answers: "His doctorate was a non-traditional degree in sociology from *Pacific College* in California," She refers to it as a *"University without walls."* Roxanne goes on to say that the college her husband allegedly received his doctorate at was "a type of *correspondence school* that was popular during the mid to late 1970s. Stephen was always up front about how he wrote his thesis to get the Pacific College doctorate. Whenever anyone asked, he never tried to hide that it was non-traditional."

Many online sources on Kaplan say: [*Pacific College: Ph.D. in Sociology (1977). His thesis discussed the sociological implications of parapsychology*]. One reference of this claim is: http://en.wikipedia.org/wiki/Dr._Stephen_Kaplan. When the Pacific college link on the website is clicked, it leads to: http://en.wikipedia.org/wiki/Pacific_College; Or George Fox University's Wikipedia page.

George Fox University was at one time "Pacific College," but because of the many "Pacific" colleges, the school changed its name in 1949, in honor of the founder of the Friends, or Quaker, Church. I contacted Robert Felton, Public Relations Manager for George Fox University, he claimed that the college turned to George Fox University in 1996, but was George Fox College in 1977. Just to be sure, I contacted Dianna McIntyre from the registrar's office, and asked her if Mr. Kaplan received his doctorate there in 1977. Diana stated, *"George Fox University does not offer Ph.D. programs so I'm certain Stephen Kaplan did not earn a Ph.D. from George Fox University."* So, was there another mysterious Pacific College that was handing out doctorates in the 1970s? If there was another Pacific College of California during that time, it is almost impossible to confirm.

On the Long-John Nebel talk radio show in the late 1970's, Kaplan admitted that his doctorate was "strictly honorary." His credentials as a parapsychologist are also a debatable subject. What is known is that Kaplan was the founder of The *Vampire Research Center of America* in Elmhurst, New York. Part of Kaplan's research as a Vampirologist, included "sleeping in coffins and drinking blood," according to Ric Osuna's book proposal *The Amityville Horror: Discovering the Truth*, in which he describes the quote as coming from an article in the *Associated Press*.

In that same book proposal, Author Ric Osuna also wrote: "*The Amityville Horror Conspiracy* [Kaplan's book] is based on nothing more than misquoted newspaper articles, and of course the dramatic inaccuracies in Jay Anson's book." Coincidentally, it was Osuna that believed that the house was haunted, and has since teamed-up with the people that he had at one time been so strongly against (more on this later).

Kaplan finally had a chance to enter the house at 112 Ocean Avenue, when he attended a Halloween party on 31 October 1979, hosted by the Cromarty's (the family that owned the home following the Lutzes). Though not in an official investigative capacity, Kaplan still managed to take pictures and claim that he did an investigation of the house. Moreover, though he could not even state the instruments that he used during his quick investigation of the home, Kaplan claimed that "there was no haunting or paranormal phenomenon taking place at the time." Soon after his investigation, Kaplan became very ill. He died before his book, *The Amityville Horror Conspiracy*, was released.

Stephen Kaplan claimed that he was inside of the Amityville horror house three times. However, in a recent interview with Rick Osuna, Roxanne Kaplan appears to have fabricated the details of one of Stephen's visits. The first time was during the Lutzes' auction or yard sale. According to Roxanne, Stephen was accompanied—not by a "flock of witches," she jested, but by two members of his founding organization, the Parapsychology Institute of America (PIA). The auction was public, so Stephen and his employees stopped by. In his book, Kaplan told a story about the time that he tricked an auctioneer into letting him into the house for a 15-minute tour, which was during the Lutzes' auction. During their visit they had a chance to "walk through and tour the house." Of course, the Lutzes were not present. This is documented by Stephen on page 42 of his book.

Another time Stephen was allegedly at the horror house, he was invited by the Cromarty's house-sitter, Frank Burch. Frank invited Stephen to spend the night in the house. According to Roxanne; she, Stephen, two psychics, and several members of the PIA, spent the night. "We used methods mentioned above and found nothing even remotely in the house," says Roxanne." These methods, Roxanne had indicated, were an electronics expert and a professional photographer. In this new version, Roxanne seems to try and douse the criticism that her husband received for not being able to list any electronics equipment that he used to supposedly "debunk" the haunting. However, on pages 210 & 211 of Stephen's book he explains the night in the house with Frank Birch, but makes no mention of investigating the paranormal—as Roxanne claims in her quote. Rather, Stephen describes it more like just hanging-out with Frank, and listening to his stories.

Although Roxanne claims to have investigated the horror house that night with a photographer present, no photos have ever been released from this mysterious new investigation. The Halloween party investigation is well documented, and there are pictures to prove it, but no proof has been made public regarding these new claims. Moreover, no names are given as to the identity of the mysterious electronics expert, professional photographer, psychics, or the PIA members that may have accompanied them on their investigation. This story is almost impossible to verify, and is artfully vague. The only other person that she mentioned, Stephen, has passed, leaving us with more questions than when the interview began, and diminishes Kaplan's credibility even further. Kaplan claims that he can usually feel when a house is haunted and the horror house did not give off that feeling. This is the proof that he offers.

Many believe, from contradicting and vague interviews such as these, that Kaplan's claim of a hoax was clearly a life long vendetta against the Lutzes and the Warrens for shutting him out of the investigation; they did so for the simple fact that he was not qualified, among other things. Furthermore, Kaplan's hoax theory was based on the inconsistencies of Jay Anson's book and over-analyzing George Lutz to a fault. Even Lutz himself had said that the book had many inconsistencies and was a "fabrication" of the actual events. Nonetheless, Lutz still emphatically held his story to be true, and he made countless attempts publicly—several T.V. interviews included—dispelling the myths and inconsistencies of the book, and telling what really happened. This is not to say that George Lutzes' version of the story is true or not, but it proves that there are more inconsistencies from the other side.

***

On the same note, one should be very weary of the word of a man [William Weber] who claims that he helped create the Amityville horror story with the Lutzes over several bottles of wine. The Lutzes didn't drink, according to many people, including the Warrens. Lorraine says that the Lutzes had only one bottle of blessed wine in the house, given to them by Father Pecoraro, and it was never opened. Moreover, the fact that Weber was in the process of writing a book and giving a percentage of the proceeds to his client, whom he himself claimed was guilty of murdering his family, is sketchy in and of itself. Certainly we must not leave out the fact that even though Weber claimed that the Lutzes were lying; he still wanted to write the book, and claimed that it was a "true account," using the Lutzes' story to possibly get a retrial for his client on the basis that he was possessed by demons. Also add that Weber is the one who hired Hans Holzer and his transmedium-sidekick to investigate the house for "ghosts" after the Lutzes turned him down.

Weber later said (on the T.V. documentary *The Real Amityville Horror*), "Hans Holzer had been introduced to me as a man who had written about 50 books in the psychic arena, poltergeists, and ah, ghosts in the white house, ghosts in every house he's ever visited." What's odd is that Weber lets out a thunderous giggle after saying, "…ghosts in every house he's ever visited." Could this have been the reason why Weber had chosen Holzer; because he knew that Holzer would scream "Ghosts?" Weber does not even make an attempt to cover up his motives, in any way.

All this being said, it's fairly easy to rule out the two main sources in the hoax theory, Kaplan and Weber, as "credible" or "trustworthy" sources. As far as the bandwagon critics go, they pretty much follow suit with Weber and Kaplan's theories, adding in some hubbub of their own, including theories with major holes in them; reasonless skepticism; and that the Lutzes made a measly $300,000 dollars, which made others involved—and the final result of profits—ranging in the hundreds of millions of dollars. Let's also keep in mind the "lie detector test" that the Lutzes passed with "flying colors." None of the skeptics have ever commented on or acknowledged the polygraph tests, other than Kaplan's vague skepticism.

The book, *The Amityville Horror: A True Story,* was not written by the Lutzes; it was written by Jay Anson. Furthermore, though Anson did interview people for the book, he never interviewed the Lutzes; he used audio taped interviews of the Lutzes to piece together the story. The Lutzes' story has never changed throughout the years, except for a few skewed numbers, such as the number of flies that were in the room, etc., just as any story that anyone tells varies slightly throughout several years of rehashing. Try telling the same story over and over again, and tape record yourself each time. Many would bet that your story might change a bit, naturally.

The facts of their story have remained the same throughout the years. Could they have just been very good liars who conned the world, beat a lie detector test performed by one of the most prominent professionals in that field in all the world, and teamed up with a vast array of others—such as clergymen, psychics, parapsychologists, and *Channel 5 News*—to corroborate and perpetuate a hoax? Anything's possible! However, when dealing with things of this nature, one must take a closer look at the two opposing sides and try to determine what each individual was driven by in order to make a more accurate assessment.

Quoting again from *The Real Amityville Horror* documentary, Weber claimed that he was approached by Paul Hoffman, who indicated that the Lutzes would like to meet with him. "I said, I would like to meet with them to," Weber told Hoffman.

Weber continued, "Because, coincidentally, I had been given an oral commitment that we would get a large advance for a book and a movie." Weber already had a signed contract dated 14 February 1976, which was before he even met the Lutz family. A signed contract and an oral commitment are two very different things. "Weber never, in those first meetings, ever brought up the idea of that [a book]," claimed George. "He was very keen on helping his client get psychological help, or at least that's what we were led to believe." Weber first made the hoax claims in a *People magazine* interview in September of 1979.

Weber said that during that first meeting, George, he and Kathy met from "nine or ten in the evening until about three in the morning drinking wine." Weber continued, "And I can't tell ya how many bottles of wine we had, but it was many. I had photographs of the crime scene, and based upon the photographs and other facts I had related, we developed what ultimately turned out to be part of the Lutzes' version of the possession aspect of the case. They supplemented the facts that I was telling them about the case, and it all appeared in their book." Weber told journalist Marvin Scott more recently, on WPIX News (New York), "I think it was about three bottles of wine; yes, about three bottles of wine."

The following testimony by William Weber, on 12 March 1981, in a lawsuit against the Lutzes, Jay Anson, and Prentice Hall, are radically different statements made by Weber from those in more casual settings. Keep in mind that the statements he made in this deposition are while he was "under oath." The lawsuit was filed by the Cromarty's, citing that Anson's book was an invasion of privacy.

(Page 15)

Examiner: You just stated this afternoon that they [Lutzes] recounted some of their experiences to you at this first meeting at Mrs. Connor's house.

Weber: Yes.

Examiner: Could you recount any of those experiences as they were related to you as to what transpired in the house during the time they occupied it?

Weber: Basically, they were talking about the change in themselves and in their children and their relationships with each other during the period of time they lived in the house, and how they could offer no other excuse but to say there were certain forces acting upon them in the house. That was basically what they were talking about.

(Page 21)

Examiner: Did the Lutzes, on that occasion and during the course of those several hours, make any statement indicating that they had told of their experiences in that house at 112 Ocean Avenue to anyone prior to talking to you?

Weber: They told me they told the priest. They told me that their mother-in-law, Mrs. Connors, was there in the house one or two times when certain things happened to them, and that they told her the rest.

Examiner: What incidents had they told you had occurred while Mrs. Connors was present at 112 Ocean Avenue?

Weber: I specifically remember that when he was describing that Kathy had changed into an eighty-year-old woman, that Mrs. Connors had seen the after-effects. She was there the day or two afterwards, and she reiterated at her home that Kathy was improving, but she still looked very, very old and didn't look herself.

(Page 30)

Examiner: Did the Lutzes tell you at this first meeting what they wanted from you during this two and a half or three hour meeting?

Weber: They wanted as much information as possible about DeFeo and his family, because they wanted to see in what way their experiences in the house coincided with whatever information I could give them.

(Page 31 – 32)

Examiner: Did the subject of a commercial project ever get mentioned during the first meeting?

Weber: It did, but lightly.

Examiner: Who raised it?

Weber: I think I raised it.

Examiner: Could you recount what you said to them?

Weber: I think I told them we were about to retain someone—a writer who had an agent—who might look into the possibility of a book, and since they had been living in the house, maybe their story might be part of it as an epilogue.

Examiner: They had told you their story already?

Weber: No. They didn't really tell me any great story, other than the change in their living patterns, and the fact that Kathy had become an eighty-year-old lady, and they had heard voices there, and there were so many strange things going on. When they finally decided to go to the priest, the priest told them to get out of the house right away, and they didn't know at that point what was happening or what had happened. They said the priest was slowly going to educate them, because he felt that if he just came out and told them all at once, that he might adversely affect them.

Examiner: After you raised this possibility of a commercial project, what did they say to you?

Weber: They hedged. They did not say we want to participate; they did not say we don't want to participate. They said they will have to see.

Weber had hired an assistant by the name of Betty Carrington soon after the DeFeo conviction. Carrington wrote a book, published in 1994, entitled, *Judicial Carousel*. The book is touted as a semi-autobiographical exposé of the legal profession. In it, Carrington claims that she recalls the time that Weber had a warlock [Holzer] and a medium [Myers] hold a séance in his office. The result of the séance, according to Carrington, was that an evil force was present in the Amityville house. Carrington also wrote in her book, "I know I personally would not care to have resided at 112 Ocean Avenue if the place was given to me." Carrington also stated that Ronal DeFeo, Jr., told Weber at one point, that his family thought that "someone might be hiding in the house," and that he heard ghastly screams on different occasions. Carrington's book also reveals that Ronnie's father also thought that the devil resided in their house, and that Ronnie Sr. actually had a priest sleep at the house one night. The priest or the result of his stay have never been discussed or determined.

Would You Live In This House?

The original house at 112 Ocean Ave. has done a lot of traveling, according to the Amityville Historical Society. It was purchased by John & Catherine Moynahan from Annie Ireland in 1924. Within a year, the Moynahan's decided to build a new house on the property; apparently, the family outgrew the house. While the new house at 112 Ocean was being built, the family moved the house about 100-yards down the block. When the new home was finished the old 112 was sold. The original house is currently located on NW corner of South Ireland and Carmen Place in Amityville, NY. The new house stayed in the Moynahan family until 1960, when it was sold to the Riley's, who subsequently sold it to the DeFeo's in 1965.

Even before Anson's book hit the shelves, residents of Amityville were overwhelmed with thrill-seeking tourists who bombarded Ocean Avenue with hopes of getting a glimpse at the infamous home. In a town board meeting in 1976, town residents were aghast over the recent outburst of tourists who had been flooding the area.

On 22 July 1976, the *Amityville Record* published an article entitled *DeFeo House ghost vigil resumes*. In it was written, "At about 11:15 p.m., Sunday, while patrolling the Ocean Avenue area, Amityville Police Officer Ronald Kuhnia reported seeing Edward F. Lisa, 21 of Bethpage, walking around the grounds of the DeFeo home carrying a machete." Lisa was arrested at the house. That same article reported that people were seen by neighbors carrying flashlights and wandering around the home as late as 3:00 a.m. Neighbors reported that "groups of between 30 and 50 people were arriving at varying intervals throughout the day, beginning as early as 10 a.m."

On 26 August 1976, the Amityville Record released the article *Residents Blast DeFeo House Circus*. The article claimed that "About twenty-seven Ocean Avenue residents complained bitterly about massive trespassing, littering, and property destruction by hooligan curiosity seekers in their area at Monday night's village board meeting." Residents criticized the Amityville Police Department for only assigning one police officer to sit in the DeFeo driveway to watch the home. Residents complained that the surrounding areas were not protected. According to the article, Amityville police Chief reported that 12 persons had been arrested, there were 47 requests for police assistance, and 51 summonses were issued since July of 1976.

Ocean Avenue resident, Edmund O'Connor Jr., and South Ireland Place resident, Walter Saxton, were two of the more vocal residents in the meeting. O'Connor claimed that Rufus Ireland told him he found a butane torch on his property after the crowds had dispersed. O'Connor sarcastically stated that there should have been 551 summonses issued, instead of 51. Saxton told the board that he found "empty beer bottles, soft drink cans, coffee cups, pizza pie crusts and other litter in his yard, fences knocked down, petty thefts, and cars turned around on residents' lawns." If you know Ocean Avenue, you would know that the houses further-up on the opposite side of the horror house have no sidewalks, so the lawns are basically in the street. Though the residents of Ocean Avenue were outraged at the time; looking back, they must have thought it a vacation for what was coming next.

That's Incredible!

On 18 March 1977, Jim and Barbara Cromarty bought 112 Ocean Avenue for a measly $55,000, and moved in on 1 April 1977 with their three children: Meryl, Joyce, and David. The first big article appeared in the *New York Sunday News* on 18 July 1976, and was titled "*Life in a Haunted House.*" The second was in April 1977, *Good Housekeeping* published an article by Paul Hoffman (Weber's associate), which was the first to bring national attention to the horror house. Hoffman's article, *Our Dream House was Haunted*, captured the imagination of the national media and opened up the flood gates for an intense media frenzy that made the Cromarty's lives a living hell. Although Weber claimed the Lutzes' story to be a hoax, Hoffman released the article as a non-fiction piece. Litigation soon followed and the Lutzes were forced by Prentice Hall to sue Hoffman and Weber over the article—fearing that if they did not, more of its kind might surface.

The Cromarty's were vocal and firmly against the claims that the house was haunted. Regardless, once the book and movie were released, the house itself became an instant celebrity and an international phenomenon overnight! People traveled from all over the world, from every continent (in drones) to get a look at the ghostly Dutch Colonial home and its spooky quarter-moon-shaped windows, which looked like evil-peering eyes. The Cromarty's even changed the number of the house from 112 Ocean Avenue to 108 Ocean Avenue in order to confuse tourists. They also painted the house white, and added several panes of "mirrored glass" between the quarter-moon windows—connecting them—which gave the optical illusion of one long window. All of these were attempts to distract tourists from finding the house. Obviously, none of this worked. The house still remains 108 Ocean Avenue to this day.

Joe Nickell—who was a consultant working for the T.V. series *In Search of* at the time—spoke with the Cromarty's on three different occasions about their new home. The Cromarty's were adamant that no supernatural occurrences had taken place at the house since they had been there, and they wanted to go public with their story. Moreover, the Cromarty's also claimed that they had evidence to corroborate the hoax theory. Nickell put the Cromarty's in touch with a producer from the then forthcoming T.V. series, *That's Incredible*. The Cromarty's went on the show and pointed out several discrepancies with Anson's book, in regards to the damage claims in the book.

The Cromarty's went on the ABC television series *That's Incredible* in 1980 (hosted by Kathy Lee Crosby), to set the record straight about their new home and to bring to light several of the inconsistencies with Anson's book (a theme that has become common amongst hoax theorists). Jim Cromarty explained that he bought the home, because it was a good buy. Who can argue with that? Jim described that he had uncles and aunts who had played in the house as children. Cromarty even recalls playing in the house himself as a child. Barbara stated that she really thought "everything would just go away" (the attention on the house). If any family can be excused for moving into the house and expecting peace and quiet, it most certainly would have been Jim and Barbara Cromarty. There is no way that they could have predicted the onslaught of insanity that would follow. "We never dreamt what would take place here," Barbara explains.

Immediately after Anson's book, *The Amityville Horror: A True Story*, hit book shelves; the Cromarty's dream home was turned into a circus-like atmosphere that couldn't simply be ignored. Barbara remembered one evening when she and her family were trying to have a lovely Sunday dinner. Things were nice and quiet inside, and "insanity" outside; she protested. People all fought to get their pictures taken in front of the house, people casually walked on their lawn, and others peeked into windows as if they were going to get a glimpse of the devil himself.

Barbara seemed to be affected most by an incident that she described as occurring on Christmas Eve. "They literally attacked the house," she described. "Three cars: one car drove all over the front lawn; another one watched for the police; and the other one threw stuff at the house." There were different groups of people there that night, Barbara explained. Others "ran up onto the front porch and urinated all over it." In an attempt to dispel the rumors, different Amityville locals gave their testimonies on the show as well. Amityville Police Sgt., at the time, Pat Cammaroto, explained one particular instance when a man pulled up to the house in a van with six goats. Cammaroto asserted that the man told him that he was there to have the goats eat the grass to chase away the evil spirits.

The Cromarty's went on attempting to debunk several reported malevolent forces in Anson's book that supposedly caused severe property damage to the house, such as the front door being ripped off its hinges; windows being smashed; the banister being ripped from its setting; damage to the garage door; and water damage from hurricane-force winds, which local meteorological stations had no record of. Barbara Cromarty led the *That's Incredible* crew around the house, showing them the structures that Anson and the Lutzes claimed were destroyed. Barbara showed the camera crew the half-moon window that Anson's book claimed had been blown out. "This is the window," she said as she ran her hand across it. "And you can see that it's exactly the same as it has been in the last fifty-one-years, when the house was built in 1928."

One paranormal specialist that I spoke to—who asked to remain anonymous—told me, "That's what the evil forces do, they cause confusion. Just as Jodie was only seen by people 'she' wanted to be seen by. Likewise, storms and windows breaking might only have been an illusion perpetrated by these malevolent forces. If they wanted proof to be left behind, they would have left it, but it's in their best interest to remain latent." In the same respect, Hans Holzer claimed that the reason no one heard the gun shots the night of the DeFeo murders was because the spirits blocked the sound barrier. Although the weather doesn't indicate that there was a storm that night; in a 2003 interview with Tim Yancey, George proclaimed,

"There was a thunderstorm the last night in the house, I don't care what any weather man says."

Cammaroto's daughter, Patty, was even called in to discuss the infamous "Red Room." The Lutzes' claimed that one day, Kathy went into the basement and moved a book shelf, and a mysterious room appeared that was not on the original plans in the home. Anson wrote about the red room, "The stench of human excrement was heavy in the confined space; it formed a choking fog." Patty Cammaroto claimed that she was friends with Allison DeFeo, and they used to play in the room. Patty downplayed the room by entering it and claiming that it was just a room used for storage. Others say that the room was part of the old house that sat on the property, and the new home was just built around it. George claimed that even their dog, Harry, wouldn't go near the room, and ran when ever he was brought close to it.

Although Mrs. Cromarty shows no damage to front door, it's worth mentioning that George says it was the "pins" on the front door of the house that became loose; so the wood was not torn away. Also, Anson's book describes the window breaking in the "playroom," which is Dawn's old room and not the room with the eye windows. Early copies of Anson's book had those two rooms incorrectly switched on the diagram, which Mrs. Cromarty seems unaware of. Patty Cammaroto is also mistaken. She thinks Kathy discovered the whole area under the stairs. This is not so. The Lutzes knew about that area and the door that Patty opens, but the red room itself was closed and behind shelves when Kathy found it.

Though the Cromarty's claim that they were clearly convinced that the house was not haunted, one of their relatives tells a dramatically different story, as reported by Ric Osuna in his book proposal, *The Amityville Horror: Discovering the Truth.* Jim Cromarty's second cousin, Donna Cromarty, was 17-years old and attending Massapequa High School. For a school project, Donna decided to get Jim's cooperation to do a report on the house for Mr. O'Neill's class in 1978. "As part of a class assignment," Donna explains, "I chose to conduct an interview with my uncle Jim, thinking that it would be fascinating to hear his perspective on what it was like to live in the famous Amityville Horror house." Donna and her friend, Jaime, brought along a tape recorder and followed Jim around each room of the house, as he explained to them how the story of a haunting was nothing more than a hoax. After the interview, Donna and her friend returned to school without previewing the tape they had just recorded. "To complete our assignment, we played the interview in front of our class. It was a day that I will never forget, because a growling appeared on the tape, but it only appeared each time my uncle proclaimed the story a hoax. We were all horrified."

In a recent interview conducted by www.amityvillefiles.com, Donna has attempted to retract her story slightly. "There was indeed growling when I played the tape back during the class presentation," Donna says. "I was not aware it existed until the presentation." However, she identified the growling as coming from "the family poodle dogs." She does admit that the other students were scared and that the two poodles growled at her and her friend. During the interview, Donna defends Amityville and denies any claims of a haunting. "The inaccuracies in the film made me upset that my home town was being vilified by Hollywood. Amityville is a wonderful place, especially down by the bay where the home is." Although Donna protests that Hollywood's main goal was to "sell tickets," she does admit that, "The growling played nicely into my report and earned me an A plus. It was like a mini Hitchcock production." Regardless of where the growling came from, Donna admits that the children in the classroom were scared when they heard it. Although Donna finds the story "laughable," this story is none the less mysterious, as the dogs only growled each time that Jim declared the haunting a hoax.

Perhaps one of the strangest things to occur to the Cromarty's was the fact that their son, David, whose bedroom happened to be Ronnie DeFeo's old room, died suddenly. Since New York State's death certificates are not public record, the circumstances surrounding the death are unknown. In 2004, Scottie Gee (producer for the *History's Mysteries* documentary on the History Channel) reported that David Roskind (Barbara Cromarty's son from a previous marriage) died in 1986 and that neighbors recall seeing the ambulance arrive at the house; yet, the Cromarty's maintain that David died in 1987, one year after they moved out.

Moreover, in his book, *The Amityville Horror Conspiracy*, Stephen Kaplan writes, "They [the Cromartys] kept the house for a while longer, but eventually sold it after the tragic death of Barbara's oldest son [David] to an undisclosed illness." However, according to a *Newsday* article published on 11 June 1988 (entitled: *After living in THE horror house in Amityville Riverhead Is a Dream*), The Cromarty's claimed that David is said to have died of a heart attack in March of 1988 (at 29 years old), which would be 7 months after the Cromartys moved out of the horror house. Within the section titled on The *True History of 112 Ocean Avenue* on Ric Osuna's website it reads, "They [the Cromarty's] remained in the house happily until 1987 when David Roskin[d], Barbara's son from a previous marriage, reportedly passed away *in a hospital*." Again, reports say that neighbors saw an ambulance take him from the house and Osuna appears to make the distinction that David "died in a hospital" rather than in the house. Osuna was at one time a proponent of the haunting, and then he switched sides (more on that later). It has been reported that the Cromarty's moved out not because of any paranormal activity, but because the property tax in the area was very high and they wanted to save money for their children's college tuition.

Who's House?

On 17 August 1987, Peter and Jeanne O'Neill purchased 108 Ocean Avenue from the Cromarty's for an unspecified amount (Some sources indicate $325,000, but this has not been 100-percent confirmed). Things had died down considerably at the time that the O'Neill's finally moved in. Supposedly, they lived happily in the house until 1997. Had the property finally settled; had the spirits finally fled? The major contribution of the O'Neill's in regard to the house's aesthetic history is the fact that they are the one's who changed the Dutch Colonial style windows—the quarter moon windows—and replaced them with standard rectangular windows. Again, this was an effort to throw-off the tourists coming to visit the house. This was the biggest change to date, as the trade-marked windows were the main attraction that gave the house its spooky demeanor. With its current windows, the house now looks like it is looking at you half awake. However, even though the famous house has undergone a face lift, it's spooky none the less, knowing the history involved. Furthermore, isn't it fitting that the most famous house in Hollywood has had some work done on its face?

The O'Neill's moved in and out of the house unscathed and without any major incidents. That was until their son, Peter, died an awful death four-years later in the 11 September 2001 World Trade Center attacks. The strange thing, again, was that Peter's room while living in the house was Ronnie's old room. Oddly enough, two tragic deaths occurred to the next two residents of Ronald DeFeo's old room after the Lutzes moved out. Many say that they were cursed from sleeping in that room every night. On the contrary, Christopher and Danny Lutz both slept in Ronnie's old room, but no tragedies have ever been reported."

Former Long Island radio personality, Joel Martin, was the first reporter at the DeFeo crime scene on the night of the murders. In an interview on the *Lou Gentile Show* in 2009, Joel recalls the "eerie" feeling in the air that night. He also witnessed one of the DeFeo children falling off of the gurney while the workers from the medical examiner's office were carrying the body out of the house. He spent most of the night at the crime scene, he said. Joel was well-known in the area and he spoke with many of the spectators in an official capacity. Many people who spoke to him were saying, undoubtedly, that Ronnie did it. Joel also closely covered the Amityville story publicly and spoke to every major player in the case, some several times.

Even though Joel had covered many crimes up to that point, he remembers that there was just something particularly chilling about this crime scene. Joel could not put his finger on what this peculiar feeling was. Joel claims, in the interview, that when he returned home on the night of the murders he was sick to his stomach. He picked up his new kitten and began petting it. While petting the cat, Joel claims that—"for no reason, totally inexplicable even to this day"—the cat looked at him, made a choking sound, and died right there in his arms. Joel didn't make the connection between that incident and the house until later, when he realized all of the strange things that were happening to the people that were associated with this story. Joel openly admits that he was a skeptic of the haunting for many years. Early on—with the influence of Stephen Kaplan—Joel thought that the haunting story was made-up. However, his view has radically changed over the years.

On 10 June 1997, Brian Wilson—no relation to the Brian Wilson of the Beach Boys— purchased the house from the O'Neill's for $310,000. Brian Wilson is the one who was forced to live through the 2005 remake of *The Amityville Horror* movie. Wilson was the most private owner of 108 Ocean Avenue by far! Wilson refused to do any interviews or field any unannounced guests. In fact, Wilson appeared to get visibly angry if anyone got too close to the house. Do you blame him? Wilson was so private, that his neighbors—the one's that I've spoken to—claimed that he didn't associate with any of them and that he was rarely even home. Wilson spent quite a bit of money renovating the home, including adding a sunroom in the back of the home. He lived there with his son, who is in his 20's. He and his wife had split, and his wife lived somewhere in Massapequa. Wilson vehemently denied any rumors of paranormal activity occurring at the house.

In 2005, Wilson did an interview with *U-T San Diego* (story by Malcolm Mayhew) in which he claimed, "There are wackos out there who believe there are flying pigs in the house and bleeding walls. There's not a flesh eating fly around." Although Wilson has a bellicose attitude about the unwanted attention, he must realize that he has moved into one of the most famous houses in the world.

In May of 2010, Brian Wilson put the infamous Amityville horror house up for sale by owner at an asking price of $1.15 million dollars. Spending only 70 days on the market, the House went into contract in August of 2010. Joanne Mills of *Exit Realty Premier* found the buyers: David and Caroline D'Antonio. The D'Antonio family lived in the community prior to the purchase, formerly residing at 21 Hamilton St., in Amityville. When reached by phone that Thursday after the news broke, a man answered at the D'Antonio residence but refused to comment. Although it was put on the market with an asking price of $1.15 million, David and Caroline D'Antonio bought the home for $950,000 in September 2010. On 21 August 2010, Brian Wilson held a moving sale at the house. Cars lined Ocean Avenue and surrounding blocks and hundreds of people lined up outside 108 Ocean Avenue to get a look at the house. Caution tape and bodyguards helped to keep the sale under control, and it was announced that only 20 people at a time could enter the home. Although people were allowed to go inside, they were not allowed to go visit the upstairs rooms or the basement.

List of Owners of 112 Ocean Ave.

DATE	OWNER	PRICE
Jan 14, 1924 - ?	John & Catherine Moynahan	unknown
? - Oct 16, 1960	Eileen Fitzgerald	unknown (inheritance)
Oct 17, 1960 - June 27, 1965	John & Mary Riley	$35,000
June 28, 1965 - Nov 13, 1974	Ronald & Louise DeFeo	$30,000?
Nov 14, 1974 - Dec 17, 1975	(vacant — owned by DeFeo estate)	--
Dec 18, 1975 - Jan 14, 1976	George & Kathleen Lutz	$80,000
Jan 15, 1976 - Aug 29, 1976	(vacant — owned by Lutzes')	--
Aug 30, 1976 - March 17, 1977	(vacant — owned by bank)	--
March 18, 1977 - Aug 16, 1987	James & Barbara Cromarty	$55,000
Aug 17, 1987 - June 9, 1997	Peter & Jeanne O'Neill	$325,000?
June 10, 1997 – August 31, 2010	Brian Wilson	$310,000
September 1, 2010 - present	David & Caroline D'Antonio	$950,000

The Lutz Children Speak

What about the children who lived in the house, what do they have to say? Christopher Quarantino, the little boy who lived in the house, is now close to forty-years-old. Chris is Kathy's biological son, and was seven years old during the Lutzes' 28-day stay in Amityville. Chris broke his 30-year silence and did an interview with Jennifer Smith of *Newsday* in 2005. Chris "maintains the haunting was not a hoax. But he insists his stepfather at the time, George Lutz, brought the troubles on himself by dabbling in the occult and then amplified what paranormal incidents did occur to profit off books and movies about the house." Did Chris perhaps mistake the couples Transcendental Meditations or their blessing of the house as "dabbling in the occult?"

I've had to go through several intense therapy sessions just to uncover some traumatic events that happened to me only ten or so years ago; let alone when I was seven years old. Most of us have an air tight, cob-web covered vault of traumatic experiences that we keep locked away, forever unseen, even from ourselves. In the midst of the trauma people are perpetually terrified to feel certain emotions, perhaps, ever again. This goes for adults as well, and is even more prevalent in children.

Could a young boy at that age really conceive what was happening to him or his family? It was the famous Swiss Psychologist, Jean Piaget, who first introduced the theory that young children can only see things through their own perspective. Piaget once performed a study on several children who were in the *preoperational stage*—children between the ages of two and seven—that proves this theory. Piaget sat next to a child and placed an object in front of himself and the child. Piaget had a significantly different view of the object than the child. When the child was asked to indicate what Piaget saw, the child would always pick the view he/she saw themselves.

Christopher was obviously not very sensitive to the supernatural, however, he did say that he "he saw a menacing, shadowy figure approach him," and he "remembers the night his bedroom window kept banging open and shut." Christopher expressed his disgust over the 2005 remake. "I was absolutely disgusted with what I was seeing. The only thing they got right was that our family moved in that house and left." Chris said that both movies are far from accurate, but does claim to have witnessed paranormal things. He claims that he "saw a shadowy presence that looked as large as a man and it was headed towards him." When asked if he was scared while living in the home Chris said, "At times, for sure, yes, very!" Chris and George were estranged for many years before George Lutzes' death in May of 2006. George sued Chris in a Nevada court in 2003 for "trademark infringement." Chris did file a countersuit, but that was dismissed in January of 2005. George and Kathy divorced in 1988, and Kathy passed away in 2004.

Smith wrote that Quarantino's brother, Daniel Lutz, did not return a call seeking comment, and Missy could not be located. However, author Ric Osuna did report some years earlier (in his book proposal *The Amityville Horror: Discovering the Truth*), that Missy (now in her 40s) "laughs at the notion that Jodie was simply a cat." Missy described Jodie as an "evil entity trying to gain control over her actions." In the *Newsday* article, Chris never mentions Kathy's name, or that she may have been a co-conspirator. Kathy told the same stories as George, yet Christopher only pointed his finger at George. There was not even a mention of Missy and her experiences. I don't know how Chris and George's relationship withered, but I can't help but ask—was this someone with yet another axe to grind with good old George Lutz perhaps? I don't know the complete circumstances regarding the infringement case filed against Chris by George, but Chris does, however, have just as much right as George does to tell his story, in my opinion. After all, he did live in the house as well.

Chris told Diane McInerney, correspondent of *Inside Edition/CBS*, that "There were definitely a lot of flies, but nothing like how Hollywood is portraying it." Though Christopher disputes much of George Lutzes' claims of what went on during their 28-days of terror, he insisted that "he did have run-ins with the paranormal." Chris claims that he has his own documentary in the works, spelling out his version of what really happened in the house.

***

After moving to San Diego, George and Kathy Lutz eventually got divorced. Kathy moved to Arizona and George to Las Vegas in the late 1980s. Kathy Lutz became active in the Christian ministry, before her death in 2004 of a respiratory disease, which mysteriously caused her to age about 30-years! Witnesses say that Kathy looked very old, much older than her actual age, when she passed. George Lutz died of natural causes in Las Vegas, Nevada in the afternoon hours on Monday, 8 May 2006 at the age of 59, which the Clark County coroner listed as heart disease. A friend of George's by the name of Dan Farrands (Writer of the 1995 film *Halloween: The Curse of Michael Myers*) spoke to the Associated Press just after George's death. Farrands said, "Lutz was active in his Catholic church, volunteered at a homeless shelter and spent his time restoring old cars. Lutz was lighthearted, until the subject of Amityville came up, and then he'd turn sort of blank. It was a subject that was very troubling for him. Lutz always believed he had witnessed the supernatural in that home." Many believe that the truth died with him!

The great Ghostbuster, Ed Warren, passed away on Wednesday, 23 August 2006, at his Monroe, Connecticut home at the age of 79-years old. Lorraine Warren continues her work with the *New England Society for Psychic Research*—which her and her husband founded—to this day. Contrary to popular belief, the Warrens charge nothing for their investigations, and made no money from the Amityville movies, or books. They make their living by lecturing.

Jay Anson suffered another heart attack and died during the making of his next book (on 12 March 1980). Anson died at the age of 59. He was never able to enjoy the millions that he made off of his book, *The Amityville Horror*. Reportedly, Father Ray passed away in 1987. The circumstances or whereabouts of his death are not known.

Did Duke University Investigate Amityville?

It has been widely rumored, and many otherwise legitimate sources claim, that Duke Universities' prestigious Laboratories were actually present during the 6 May 1975, investigation, and that they were actively investigating the Amityville case. The fact is that Duke University never actually became officially involved in the investigation. I had the pleasure of speaking to Sally Rhine Feather, Ph.D., to get clarification on the matter. Sally is the Director of Development of *The Rhine Research Center* at Duke University. She also happens to be the daughter of the late Dr. Joseph Banks Rhine, who the center was named after, and who is widely considered to be the "father of modern parapsychology." The Rhine Research Center promotes research and investigation of paranormal science, actively seeking accounts of paranormal or psychic experiences. Dr. J. B. Rhine passed away in 1980, but he left a legacy of work on the paranormal and other forms of science behind that is unparalleled.

According to Sally, "Dr. Karlis Osis was for several years a member of the Duke Parapsychology Laboratories in the early 1950's (In fact I worked with him on animal psi studies), but he then moved sometime in the 1950s to NYC to work with the American Society for Psychical Research (ASPR). It was probably then that he investigated this case. I have no way of knowing the dates but he was not here in 1975." Sally also informed me that Alex Tanous, a well-known psychic from Maine, was never connected with the Duke Lab (Although in recent years the Foundation that he started has contributed to their center and there is a library there in his name). However, he would have been working with Dr. Osis through the ASPR. "So I think that you will have to go to them to see if they have any records about this matter," Sally suggested.

Sally was not very familiar with the Amityville case, but she knew somebody who was. She put me in contact with author, Stacy Horn, who is currently writing a commissioned book about the early Duke Parapsychology Lab. Stacy claimed that she did research into whether or not anyone from the lab investigated the Amityville case and found no evidence whatsoever that they did. However, she did find a vague comment made by Gaither Pratt (American psychologist who specialized in the field of parapsychology), who said it did not sound like a genuine case. Pratt was not part of Duke at the time; rather, he was working at the University of Virginia.

In fact, even the Parapsychology Lab was not part of Duke by that time. They separated from Duke in 1965. Although J.B. did a lot to assist the formation of the PRF (and his right hand man, Gaither Pratt, was the first President) it was still a completely separate organization with different research aims. Furthermore, by that time J. B. and the Lab had adopted what he called "a friendly detachment" with respect to Bill Roll (the head of the PRF) and his work at the Psychical Research Foundation. According to Roll, the PRF moved into two small houses on the Duke Campus. They had become "a sponsored program" within the Duke Department of Electrical Engineering. The PRF was a sort of a spin-off of J.B.'s lab (the FRNM as it was called then) in that J.B. helped the PRF's founder, Professor William Roll, in getting him connected with the PRF's backer, Mr. Charles Ozanne. Jerry Solfvin (who was at the first house investigation) is currently on the Advisory Board at J.B.'s lab. Osis would have been investigating on behalf of the Parapsychology Foundation and not the Parapsychology Lab. He was no longer a member of the Lab staff at that time.

Though the Amityville story received the backing of several top paranormal investigators, scientists at Duke University and the Association for Psychical Research in Manhattan—which were the top two paranormal investigative groups at the time—never went public with any of their findings. This basically means that they did not believe that it was a legitimate case. However, I decided to see if any written material existed that confirms this. I took Sally's suggestion and contacted the ASPR, and I also contacted the *Alex Tanous Foundation* (ATF). I did not receive a response from the ASPR, but my email request to the ATF was returned promptly. I maintained correspondence with a woman from the ATF, and she searched for any information that she could find for me. She informed me that Alex Tanous worked, and was affiliated with, the ASPR in New York City for 16-years. She said that he did much research and experimenting at the ASPR, and took his visit to Amityville during his time working there. When she found some information in regard to Tanous' findings, she was reluctant to share it with me, over concerns that the documents revealed sensitive information and that the ASPR in New York, who Alex was under contract with, owned all of the material and they were not willing to release any of it.

Finally she got the "clearance from a clerk from the Board who said it was fine, as it is not much and not the whole report." According to these documents, Tanous and the Warrens ideas clashed before they even stepped foot in the house, because Tanous did not believe in demonic possession. On 7 October 1979, Tanous sent a letter to Hartford, Connecticut radio station, KTIC, in regard to a program aired on 1 September 1979. Apparently, on the *Brian Dow Show* on that date, KTIC held a show entitled, *True Inside Story of Amityville*, with George Lutz, Rick Moran, Stephen Kaplan, and Ed Warren. Kaplan told Tanous that during that show, Ed Warren had made the claim that Tanous "levitated two feet off the ground when he was doing the research at the Amityville house." This angered Tanous and he wanted to set the record straight. Tanous clarified that the statement was "untrue" and that during his investigation he "witnessed nothing paranormal existing in the house."

In a letter to Barbara (no last name) in 1979, Tanous wrote, "I cannot make any statements on this [Amityville Case] since all my findings are property of the American Society for Psychic Research." Tanous also alludes to a private conversation that he had with Kaplan in regard to the house, which most likely proves that Tanous and Kaplan were allies of sorts, because they both believed the story to be a hoax. What the ASPR will do with Tanous' findings and when they will do it is yet to be determined. In an article from *Newsday* dated, 17 November 1977, the ASPR was quoted as saying that they bowed out of the Amityville investigation, because of "the commercial overtones." Tanous also wrote that if Dr. Osis wished to release the information on what happened during their Amityville investigation; it would be "OK" with him. However, Osis also went to the grave with his version of the story when he died on his 80th birthday, 26 December 1997.

Section III
A Closer Look

Destined for Amityville

I was excited for my impending trip to Amityville. For me, it would be my first visit; for Carl Ivan Allen, his second. Carl's mission was to get into the Amityville house and do a walk-through of the crime scene. Carl would try to estimate how much time it would have taken for Ronnie to commit the murders alone. I knew that there was little chance, if any, that Brian Wilson (the, then, owner of the home) would let us in. Still, Carl's overconfidence was inspiring. My itinerary was clear and noted. I had packed two video cameras, two digital cameras and a note pad. If all went well for me, I would not have to use my note pad at all. It was my intention to get everything on video and analyze the findings later. Carl's technique is far more primitive, using more aggressive techniques as opposed to more conventional methods. As eccentric as Carl is, his style can be very effective.

***

During Carl's first trip to Amityville, one month earlier, he rang the doorbell of the horror house, but no one answered. Observing that the next door neighbor was home, Carl decided to ask her a few questions and see if he could get some information.

Carl walked away from the front door of the horror house, crossing the driveway, over to the house next door. Reaching the side door of the house, which looked like it led to the kitchen, Carl knocked on the screen door three times. Not knowing it at the time; Carl was at the home where Rufus Ireland had once lived. This was the house that police used as a temporary command post just hours after the bodies of the DeFeo family were discovered. There were two doors: the first was a see-through screen door that led to a vestibule or foyer area; the second, approximately 5-feet beyond the first door, was an entrance directly into the house—apparently the kitchen, according to Carl.

As he waited at the side door, an older looking Caucasian woman, approximately 60-years old, opened the door leading into the house. Trying to put her at ease, Carl put his police badge up against the screen door. "Hello," he said. "I'm a criminologist, and I'm doing a criminal profile on Ronnie DeFeo, Jr. I'm also a college professor, and I'm doing the profile for my students. This is not official police business or anything." The woman looked somewhat enticed, though she didn't offer to let him in the house. "I just want to ask you a few questions about the people who live in the house next door." The woman was very cordial with Carl, but released little information.

When asked if she had personally experienced any paranormal activity while living in the house, the woman said, "No, but I try to ignore the house and all the hoopla. I pay it no mind." She informed Carl that she doesn't know much about the current owners of the horror house, "...they pretty much keep to themselves." The woman could not give any information on the owner's occupation, or much else.

When asked about the Lutz family and how long they lived in the house, she said, "Not long. They left in the middle of the night, leaving all their possessions." Carl tried to get a read on whether or not anyone was home next door, at the horror house. The woman was not sure, but she did say that it was not odd if they weren't home, because "The lights are always on there, all the time." With that, Carl gave her his card and asked her to pass it off to the owner of the horror house in case she runs into him. The woman said, "Will do," and closed the door.

Before leaving, Carl figured since he was there already, he'd take a walk down the driveway to the infamous "boathouse" and take a look around. Among the many odd things about the house is the fact that the driveway runs in a straight line past the front door of the house, straight back to the boathouse. Carl had somehow worked up the nerve to attempt to take the long walk down the pitch-black driveway of the horror house. The normally fearless Carl walked more than halfway down the driveway, stopping just past end of the house. He noticed that only a few feet ahead was almost complete darkness. Suddenly, he felt a tingling surge of fear running through his entire body. With goose bumps forming on his arms, Carl could not take another step. Completely overcome by terror, Carl turned and quickly headed back towards his car.

***

We set out for the sleepy town of Amityville, wide awake, on 30 December 2007; at 12:45 p.m. Carl hoped that we would attend 12:00 p.m. mass at St. Joseph's Church in Bogota, N.J. beforehand. We had talked about getting the backing of a higher power on our journey, but I was too anxious. I didn't think that I could sit through an hour-long-service, with the multitude of thoughts cascading through my mind. Plus, I had said my prayers! After a quick bite to eat and some coffee, we were on our way to Long Island. Getting to Amityville during daylight hours was imperative, and we had left early enough where time was not a factor. It was a fairly warm day for December, and we believed that there might be a fair share of residents perusing the neighborhood. I instructed Carl to approach only those that we believed might have known Butch or might have been living in Amityville during the time of the murders (older people).

We reached Amityville soon after 2:00 p.m. I conveniently tested my camera by taking a picture of the *Amityville exit sign* and the *Amityville Historical Society building*. In no time at all we made a right onto Ocean Avenue. My heart raced, and my journalistic instincts kicked-in. We both braced ourselves for the first glimpse of the home.

"It's coming up on the left," Carl said. Suddenly, we slowed down and soon we were in front of what many allege is the most famous haunted house in the world! A myriad of emotions ran through my mind-body as the house came into focus. My first impression of Ocean Avenue was that it is a side street, and not the main road that I was expecting. The traffic on this street was staggering, considering. I knew beforehand what type of street it was, but the visual adds a sense, *unequaled*. It was obvious that at least sixty-percent of the cars that drove by were not on any regular route; they were driving by intentionally to get a look at "THE" house. As we made a quick drive by the house, I noticed immediately that there was a black Range Rover sitting in the driveway; the truck sat five-feet from the front door of the house.

"They're home," I exclaimed. We made a right onto the block directly adjacent to the house, which is called Ireland Place. Once on Ireland Pl., Carl veered to the right, attempting to make a u-turn. Suddenly, the car felt as though it was being pulled forward, down the streets slope, and we slammed into the tree directly in front of the corner house labeled, *nine*. It had seemed as though the excitement had gotten to him a bit at that point. What was stranger to me was that Carl yelled at me for this, claiming that it was my fault for distracting him. We both couldn't have been more focused!

Carl composed himself and completed the u-turn, parking on the left side of Ireland Place near the tree we had just literally bounced off of. We were now parked on the left side of Ireland Place; the car facing the horror house. Without a plan, and without preparation, Carl said, "I'm going in!" He exited the car and made a B-line, straight for the house. I knew that we were in for a long day, and I didn't want to waste video. Carl walked confidently across Ocean Avenue, and for the second time in two months, he rang the doorbell of house number 108. The door suddenly swung open, Carl's body language shifted, and Carl was face to face with Brian Wilson's son. Carl introduced himself as a police officer and college professor. He went through every scenario of why he needed to gain access to the home; and though Mr. Wilson's son was cordial, he would not let Carl break the plane of the doorway. In any case, Carl came back to the car after a-good five or six minutes.

"No good," he said somberly. It was certainly not a confrontational standoff, but we knew that we were denied access and we weren't going to push it. We had previously read about the current residents of the home and we knew that they wanted to be left alone. The only reason we thought that we had a shot was the unique angle of "official business" that Carl was approaching with.

No Trespassing

Having unsuccessfully gained access to the grounds, our only next mission with the house was to take pictures and move on to phase two of our plan: which was to interview as many older residents as time would allow. Getting out of the car, it was a bit disorienting. There we were standing in front of a house whose reputation far preceded it! The traffic was so heavy that there was not a moment when a car was not passing. I had seen all the *YouTube* videos made by all the amateur thrill-seekers at the very spot that I was standing. In one video, a man said that the people in Amityville were not happy with him there; just when the man said that, a car rode by and screamed, "Get a life."During another amateur video, someone in a passing car screamed, "Leave them alone already!"

In any case, Carl was not as shy or as ruffled as I was. He walked directly onto the next door neighbor's lawn (formerly the home of *Rufus Ireland*) and began taking pictures with his digital camera. Carl served as a lead-blocker for me as I followed right behind him with my digital camera. We both quickly began snapping pictures. I tried to remain steady to get clear shots of the house. Carl couldn't have been more than forty-feet from the front door. I followed about ten-feet behind him.

Suddenly, and without warning, I saw the door of 108 Ocean Avenue swing open violently, and an angry man stepped halfway outside. He was an older gentleman, in good shape, with grey hair, jeans, and a long sleeve navy-blue sweatshirt on. It was Brian Wilson, the current owner of the house! He pointed at the neighbor's house and angrily said, "If they see you guys on their lawn they are going to call the police. Will you guys just get out of here and leave us alone!" Carl looked up and froze as if in shock. I snapped a picture, though it was a bit hard to remain steady. Immediately, I realized that I had the first known picture of the current owner of the house.

"Sorry Mr. Wilson," I squeaked out as I began retreating slowly back towards the car. Carl didn't move. In fact, Carl began moving forward and engaged Wilson in a non-confrontational manner.

"Mr. Wilson, I'm just here to do a criminal profile on Ronnie DeFeo for my class. I am a police officer and a college professor," Carl stated.

"I don't care who you are," he barked acrimoniously. "There is plenty of information on the internet. This is private property and you are trespassing."

I had my video camera in my pocket, but I just couldn't reach for it. I wanted to let Carl work his magic and see if he could possibly talk Mr. Wilson into letting us in the house. I didn't want to come off as paparazzi or show disrespect of any kind by snapping another photo. I believed that if I pulled out my video camera and began filming he would have gotten even angrier. I had continued to back up. I slowly inched my way to the car, stopping every few steps to see what was happening. Somehow I had wound up a spectator, standing on the sidewalk, about two-feet from Wilson's driveway. I knew that things could get ugly real quick, as Wilson was getting angrier as the conversation went on. He was obviously tired of all the hoopla and he had far more experience dealing with these situations than we did. Even more important, we were on his turf. Carl and I had previously had a conversation about this type of situation occurring. Carl had made a comment that he was probably going to go to jail, and in that event, he wanted to make sure that I got away so that I could get help. That plan was fine with me!

With our earlier conversation in mind, I began looking around for police. I had heard that police frequently drive by looking for people like us. First I looked to the right and there was nothing. Then I looked to the left, "Oh shit!" I said to myself. An unmarked white police car was coming up the block slowly in our direction. I couldn't pass up the opportunity, so I kept my composure and quickly snapped another picture of Wilson from the driveway. I knew that if I didn't take that picture, I would have kicked myself later. It was almost worth going to jail for.

Wilson had his left hand on his hip and was pointing in an aggressive manor. Under my breath I said, "Carl come on, let's get out of here." Wilson was not in position to see the police heading up the block, and I didn't want to alert him of their presence, because he might signal them. Carl ignored me and continued to converse with Wilson. I saw that Carl was fully engaged with Wilson at this point and was inching closer and closer, until he eventually ended up in his driveway—about ten-feet away from Wilson. I walked with urgency across the street and got back to the car just as the police drove very, very slowly past the house. There were two uniformed police officers [a black officer and a white officer] in the car. They looked and saw that Carl was talking to Wilson, and it was easy for any observer to see that Wilson was not happy. He was flailing his arms around, visibly frustrated with Carl's presence. The officers focused-in, eyeballing Carl as they slowly drove by.

I anxiously watched the police car as it continued past the house. Then, they abruptly made a left into the driveway just four houses up, on the same side as the house, and began making a u-turn. I immediately sensed the severity of the situation. I couldn't imagine the cops not stopping on their next drive by. I quickly opened the passenger door and stepped one foot out of the car.

"Carl," I shouted calmly. "Come on, police!" Carl looked back at me and I gave him a *head nod* in the direction of the police car. Carl then casually looked at the police car then turned back and resumed his conversation with Mr. Wilson. Knowing Carl, I knew what he was thinking, it was brilliant. He didn't panic or show any fear. He knew that if the police did stop, he would be able to talk his way out of the situation. He also knew that if he bailed at that moment, he would probably draw more attention to himself and look as if he was doing something wrong.

The police again drove by at a snails pace, looking at Carl—even eyeballing me as well. They must have noticed the government tags on the car, because they never stopped. They just kept on driving. I couldn't believe it! I breathed a brief sigh of relief, but I knew that they would soon return. Carl continued his conversation with Mr. Wilson. The conversation had now toned down to a mutual discussion. Mr. Wilson acknowledged that he was unhappy because people come and bother him frequently. The majority of the people that visit the house are "not professional type people," he said, "but people that want to come and do strange things to the house." Mr.

Wilson also expressed his dissatisfaction with the fact that his home had become a circus-type atmosphere.

"I mean this is the type of thing that I'm speaking of," Wilson said. "You guys come here and walk on the neighbor's lawn and it's just inappropriate behavior." Wilson had alluded to the fact that this type of thing happens all the time.

"I apologize, sir; I am not here to create any type of undue problems for you or anything like that," Carl said empathetically. "I'm just here to do a legitimate profile on Ronnie DeFeo."

"Well, there's plenty of stuff on the internet about what occurred and what didn't occur, as well as everything else about the house."

"It's not about what occurred or didn't occur," Carl retorted. "It's about what is true. I want to review the facts and the facts only of this case, and I would be better suited by seeing where the case itself took place. I'm not here to hunt ghosts or to prove or disprove whether this place is haunted or not. I am here for investigative purposes—to draw my own conclusions in regards to the DeFeo murders."

However good Carl made it sound; Wilson still would not budge on letting Carl enter the home. Carl then asked if he could have access to the back area, where the boat house is located, to review and take pictures. But again, Wilson declined. Oddly enough, Wilson did wish Carl luck in his investigation at the end of their conversation.

As soon as the police were out of site, I grabbed my video camera and began taping Carl conversing with Wilson. I was too far to get any type of audio, but it was still worth documenting. Cars continued to stream-by non-stop. Within two minutes of turning on the camera and doing some commentating of my own—for documentation purposes—Carl began walking back toward the car. I continued video-taping to get his reaction and a post-discussion interview with him. To my surprise, Carl had somehow managed to pull-off a ten-minute conversation with a hostile Mr. Wilson, and he had also seemed to calm him down a bit in the process.

"In my opinion," Carl said. "There's a little more going on here, because he did want to say something, because he kept talking to me." It did seem odd from my perspective as well that the conversation went on so long. Once Wilson knew that Carl was a law enforcement official, it seemed to ease his mind a bit and he had an unusually long conversation with him. Why was Wilson so adamant about explaining himself to Carl? If he wasn't going to give him access to the home anyway, why didn't he just say what he had to say and close the door? I realized that Carl could be quite aggressive and persuasive, and this could have been a good reason. In any case, this seemed to energize Carl even more. Already fearless and aggressive, this incident seemed to step his levels up even further.

The "Buddy" System

During our post-discussion interview, Carl spotted an older distinguished looking couple walking a dog about five-houses past 108. We cut the interview short and decided to head up the block and see if we could get an interview with them.

The couple was on our left, walking in the street, on the same side as 'the house.' Carl drove right up to them without any hesitation and introduced himself.

"Hi, my name is Carl. I'm a criminal profiler and professor and I am doing a profile on Ronnie DeFeo, and I was wondering if I could ask you a few questions?" The couple seemed hesitant and paused for a moment.

"What do you want to know," the gentleman asked.

"Let me pull over and I'll get out of the car and we can talk."

"Well, I don't have much time, I'm kind of in a hurry," the man said as he looked over at his female companion.

"It will only take a few minutes," Carl replied. "Do you have ten minutes?"

The man pondered the question, weighing his options by looking up and slowly swaying his head side to side.

"Ok," he said. We parked the car and Carl got out and greeted them. I stayed in the car until Carl got verbal confirmation from them to allow us to video tape the interview. The gentleman introduced himself on camera as Don Buddy, a current Amityville resident, born and raised. He was a soft spoken man, very polite and non-animated. We did not ask his age, but I assume he is in his early 50's. His attractive woman companion declined to be on camera, and she came over and stood next to me. Surprisingly enough however, she did participate frequently in the conversation, though she was reluctant in the beginning to even speak with us. Don claimed that he knew Ronnie DeFeo.

"Ronnie is a little older than me," Don said. "I didn't hang out with him; he wasn't really in my crowd; but I knew him; I talked to him." Don characterized Ronnie as "A little bit wacky; a little bit strange." Though Don said that Ronnie was not a very popular kid in town before the murders, he did have a lot of friends.

"I remember one time he showed me a big wad of money: thousands," Don recalled. "His family had a lot of money. I guess that's how he kept his friends."

Several people have made the claim that Ronnie always had a lot of money. It certainly seems odd that Ronnie had all this money at such a young age, because it couldn't have all come from his job at his family's car dealership. Some speculate that it is more realistic to assume that the money may have come from the family's alleged mob ties. Some claim that Ronnie's father gave him loads of cash to placate and pacify him. Others maintain that Ronnie regularly stole money from the dealership and was involved in other illegal activities.

When asked about his take on the murders—whether Ronnie committed them alone or not—Don brought up something very unexpected and unprovoked.

"Apparently, the truth is, the original foundation of the house is built over an Indian burial ground," Don stated, without any questions being asked about the paranormal. "*There are* and have been some weird things going on around here, but I think Ronnie was just kind of wacked in the head," Don went on to say. "Ronnie was a druggie and he used to hang out with other druggies such as, Bobby…"

"Bobby Kelske," Don's female friend said, finishing his sentence. She continued by saying, "…and others at the *Witches Brew*." [Another name for Henry's pub: the bar Ronnie drove to and first reported the murders]. Don's female friend was becoming more vocal and began to participate more in the conversation; adding regular commentary.

Suddenly, Don's expression changed, and he alluded to an old friend as if he sensed something strange had occurred. Out of nowhere, Don said, "...Oh, I had another friend of mine that was looking into it [the DeFeo murders]. He [his friend] thought that there were all kinds of cover-ups. He ended up dying, I don't know what happened."

"Can I ask what happened to your friend that was looking into it," Carl asked, as if he wanted Don to expound. "What did he die of?"

"He had a heart attack or something. I think!" Don replied.

"Young guy," asked Carl.

"Yea, he was young, yea. This is going back a long time ago."

"And he was researching the DeFeo case?" I asked.

"Yea, he was supposedly into it, he was ah, really into looking into the ah, ya know, cover-ups and stuff like that."

"What was his name," I asked, figuring I'd give it a shot.

"Rob Lennox," Don replied, without hesitation. "That was a long time ago," Don continued. "And he lived in the City [NYC]. Ya know, that's all he told me. I don't really know what he was looking at..."

We discussed the house and the legends associated for a few minutes. Don seemed to get as excited as his calm demeanor would allow when we spoke of the legends.

"I've never been in the house," Don said. "But my brother went to a Halloween party there years ago, and he painted a bullet hole on his forehead." We all chuckled for a second, although it seemed somewhat insensitive to the murdered DeFeos.

"Who ran the Halloween party there," Carl asked.

"It was other friends of mine." Don's lady friend continued to answer some of the questions with him.

"What were their names," I asked as, if I didn't know.

"Yea, tell me about them," Carl suggested.

"The O'Neill's," Don and his lady friend replied simultaneously. Don claimed that they were good friends with the O'Neill's, and that they were good people. Off camera, I asked Don more in-depth questions about the O'Neill family, since he was such good friends with them. He told us that the oldest son, Peter O'Neill, Jr., looked strikingly similar to his father, Peter O'Neill, Sr.

"They were known to those closest to them as "the twins." I asked Don if he knew of anything strange that had happened to the O'Neill's while living in the DeFeo home.

"No, not that I know of," he replied. However, Don claimed that Peter Jr., was working at his uncle's firm, Sandler O'Neill & Partners, at 2 World Trade Center in 2001. Don claimed that Peter Jr., was saving up for an apartment in Manhattan, but was still living in Amityville, not in the horror house though at that time. He informed me that Peter died an awful death in the September 11, 2001, *World Trade Center* attacks. Again, "rumors stirred up in town after the death," Don said, because Peter's room while living in the DeFeo home was the same room that Ronnie resided in 1974. Whether this was a chilling reminder or just a bizarre coincidence is unknown, but it is definitely noteworthy and adds to the list of strange occurrences and terrifying mystique surrounding the horror house.

Carl asked if they could possibly direct us to anyone who is still in the area who knew Ronnie. Don thought for a moment then suggested that we try to contact Beverly Nonnewitz. Don maintained that Beverly is someone "who has kept in contact with Ronnie" last he's heard. Although Don claimed he was unaware, Beverly is the daughter of Linnea Nonnewitz, who was the DeFeo's house keeper from 1969 up until the time of the murders in 1974. Don claimed that Beverly was "friendly with Ronnie and Dawn" and that she "might still be living in the Amityville area." Beverly was classmate of Dawn DeFeo's back in 1974. Beverly claimed, in a 1986 interview with *Newsday* (entitled: *A Convicts, Tale,* by Bob Keeler) that Dawn DeFeo had asked her [Beverly] to take her to Florida. "She asked me numerous times," Beverly stated. Dawn was apparently trying desperately to get to Florida to see her boyfriend, William Davidge. The Nonnewitzes were close enough to the DeFeo family that they knew the hidden secrets that others outside the circle did not.

Before we left, Don stated that Ronnie seemed like a pretty decent guy overall back in 1974. He referenced a T.V. interview with Ronnie that he saw recently and he noted the extreme difference in Ronnie now from back in 1974. Don acknowledged the difference that being in jail all this time has made on Ronnie's mental state.

The Needle in the Haystack

Our next tour of duty was to find out which house was the residence of Rufus Ireland at the time of the murders, and if we could somehow gain access. It was Carl's estimation that the Ireland home was the big white house on the corner of Ireland Place with the number *nine* clearly visible. The house is beautiful! It is truly an enormous piece of property that extended approximately fifty-yards from end to end. All five second floor windows had festive Christmas wreaths displayed. The land could easily fit three houses comfortably on the property. The front door of the home is about 70-yards from the horror house, and in plain view.

Without hesitation, Carl walked up the front door and rang the bell. A woman answered the door and the two began conversing. The woman was very pleasant and Carl ran down the list, from his introduction to his normal line of questioning. The conversation went smoothly, other than a hysterical dog that the woman fought back furiously without breaking concentration. Finally she closed the inside door and stepped out onto the stairs. She stood between the glass door and the inside door. The two conversed for more than seven-minutes; when to my surprise, she invited Carl in. As Carl followed her into the house he looked back at me and gave me the thumbs up. After about another ten-minutes had passed, Carl returned from the house.

"Is that the Ireland house," I asked anxiously.

"No," he replied. "It's (the Ireland house) the house across the street, on the corner." He pointed to a red house on the corner. I could only see the back yard of the house that he pointed to, because the front door of the home was actually facing Ocean Avenue. Carl had confirmed that the house was no longer occupied by Rufus Ireland. Little did we know at the time, but that was not the Ireland house, after all. The former Ireland house sits directly next door to the horror house, on the same side of the street. It is the house that Carl had visited during his first trip to Amityville, when he was trying to get information on Brian Wilson and his family.

Nevertheless, perhaps the best information that Carl received from the woman was sitting in his front pocket. All of a sudden, he reached in it and pulled out a yellow piece of paper.

"What's that," I again asked anxiously.

"I got two leads," Carl boasted. She gave me the names of two residents who live on Ocean Avenue that she believes will be willing to talk to us." He handed me the paper and I immediately saw the name, Ed Kangesier. "She said that this guy Ed is like eighty-years-old and has lived here forever. He lives on Ocean."

"Did she give you a house number?"

"She didn't know it. She said it's a yellow house and there is a large 'K' over the door. She said I couldn't miss it." Our next mission was to find the yellow house with the 'K' above the door.

"That's gotta be it," Carl said, pointing to an old yellow house that sat four houses from the home that we mistakenly thought at the time had once belonged to Rufus Ireland. We didn't see the large 'K' on the home, so we continued driving farther down the street. Another yellow house appeared only a few houses down from the last. This yellow house looked much newer than the previous one and there was no 'K' on this one either; so we figured that it was probably the first house. We drove all the way to the end of Ocean Avenue and saw no other yellow houses; so we made a u-turn, and headed back to re-observe our two prospects. We again past the newer yellow home and looked diligently for the 'K', but there was nothing. Then we pulled up to the older yellow house again.

"There's the 'K', you see it," Carl asked.

"Yea, I do!" I was excited, but I quickly calmed myself. I wasn't sure what to make of this lead at the moment.

"We should park directly in front of the house," I told Carl. "I'll be able to get the best video footage if you park right in front." I was thinking of the excellent angle that I had at the home on Ireland place, when he parked directly in front of the house on the same side. Carl made a quick u-turn and parked directly in line with the front door of the home. The spot was perfect! I couldn't have been more than twenty-feet from the front door of the house. What made it better was the fact that the opposite side of the street from the horror house had no sidewalk, and we parked where the grass met the street. I began the video feed as soon as Carl got out of the car. He rang the doorbell, and knocked on the door. Within minutes of no one answering, he opened the screen door to his left—which was a gazebo area connected to the home—and entered the porch, where there happened to be another door. He knocked on that door, but sill no answer. Carl walked back outside and over to the driveway, which was on the left side of the house.

Carl walked across the grass, which was approximately a foot incline above the unpaved-gravel driveway. He leaned forward and peeked around a six-foot high bush that stood in front of the house, in an attempt to get a look into the driveway area. Within seconds he leaned back quickly and looked at me. He made a fist and stuck out his thumb, thrusting his hand back and forth towards the driveway—indicating that there was someone present in the driveway. Suddenly, a white car appeared, driving very slowly in the driveway past the six-foot high shrubbery towards the street. The old man behind the wheel came to a halt at the direction of Carl. Carl leaned into the driver's side window and began speaking to the gentleman. He pulled out his ID and began conversing with the man. Within less than a minute, Carl turned, looked up at me, and made a beckoning gesture. I quickly shut the camera off and made my way over to the white Buick. As I approached the vehicle, I noticed an elderly gentleman in the driver's seat, and Carl standing at the driver's side window.

"Get in," Carl said. I wasted no time rolling with the punches. I followed Carl around the front of the car and entered through the right-rear door; Carl got in the front seat. Carl and the gentleman had been discussing the *for sale* sign on his lawn. We pulled out of the driveway slowly. I was still in shock that the man had let us into the car so freely and at his own suggestion, but I managed to stay focused.

The man was Edward J. Kangesier, a seventy-nine-year-old retired sailor and NYPD officer who lived alone. Ed was a very polite gentleman, who spoke very softly. It was apparent within the first minute or so that Ed was a lonely old timer who welcomed the company of such virile young men, who probably reminded him of himself in his youthful days. Ed and Carl hit it off immediately. Both men served in the armed forces of the United States—a similarity which has bonded millions of men throughout the years.

"You can leave your car here," Ed said in a soft voice. "I just need to stop by the grocery store and get a few cans of soup. We'll be right back." As Ed began to speak, it was apparent just how lonely he really was. Every word from his mouth seemed like an anecdote of a man whose better days were behind him. He was happy to tell us his story; he just wanted someone, anyone, to listen. Ed was a natural conversationalist, and he made his subjects feel at ease, as he reached into his large library of stories.

He began by telling us a story about the sale of his house. Apparently, Ed had a couple whom had recently attended an open house that Ed and his realtor held. The couple in question claimed that they loved the house and wanted to move in as soon as possible. The price was settled at $499,000. They had a "closing date of October 19th; it was a Friday," Ed explained. "It was all set with my lawyer here in the village. And, ah; they pulled out at the last minute; they never contacted us, nothing."

I didn't know it at the time, but Ed's house was very nice inside. However, the horror house was much bigger outside, had a bigger yard, and was also much bigger inside. The horror house has also had a tremendous amount of work done on the outside and the inside. It wasn't until after I viewed the inside of Ed's home that I began to ponder the thought of just what the horror house would be worth in comparison. My estimation is somewhere close to $100,000 more than Ed's home; which would land the price at close to $600,000 (history of the house-not included).

Ed knew everyone in Amityville. He dropped name after name— unpretentiously—as he told his stories. From Police officers, to building inspectors, to several generations of locals—including Ronnie DeFeo, Jr.—Ed knew them all. We pulled up to the supermarket, just a few blocks away from Ocean Avenue. Ed actually let Carl and I stay in his car, with the car running, while he slowly hobbled in to get his necessities. It was a token gesture—in my opinion—that he trusted us enough to leave us in his car with it running. Myself And Carl were buzzing as Ed entered the supermarket. We both knew that we had found the needle in the hay stack, and we planned to play it cool and let the information flow freely. Ed did not yet know our motive for approaching him.

Ed soon returned to the car, and immediately began speaking of his son, Gary, who had passed away recently. Gary was only 42-years-old when he died of AIDS, Ed would later tell us. His other son, Greg [47], is a truck driver who lives in Florida. His estranged son Greg didn't even visit his father during Christmas, and hadn't called him in months. During Ed's last attempt to contact Greg, he came up with a wrong number. The sentiment from Ed made my heart bleed. I just couldn't imagine how anyone would not be proud to have this man as a father, or grandfather for that matter. Ed's wife had also passed away some years back, and he was all alone. He was selling the house that he had lived in all his life, and moving to Florida to fade away like a lit match. It seemed that all the sorrowful talk, and excitement of company, had Ed in party mode.

"Though all my friends worry about me, and though my doctor advised against it," Ed said as he pointed to a liquor store. "…I'm going in there and buying myself a bottle of vodka!" The car suddenly filled with laughter, and the mood relaxed significantly.

"A man after my own heart," Carl shouted with jocundity. After Ed's vodka comment, the jokes began flying. Ed soon returned from the liquor store with a bottle of vodka and we were on our way.

"You know what they call this town?" Ed asked. We looked on in anticipation. "They call this place Calamityville." Ed pointed west of Ocean Avenue and said, "And they call that town down there, Swindlehurst." Again, we all laughed. Ed seemed happy that we enjoyed his comedy routines.

"What town is that?" I asked.

"That's Lindenhurst." Ed replied.

"Oh yea," I exclaimed. "That's where the First Precinct is?" It just shot out of my mouth; my research was paying off.

"Yea, somewhere around there, if that's what you're interested in?" Ed sounded a bit puzzled by my statement.

"Yea, we're interested," Carl said as he searched for the right words. "You know why we're here don't ya?" Carl asked. Ed looked up at him with an even more puzzled look.

"No," Ed answered sincerely.

"You don't know why we're here," Carl asked again.

"No," Ed said. He seemed a little bit nervous at that point. "Why are ya here?"

"We're here for the DeFeo murders," Carl said. Carl then identified himself as a college professor and explained the nature of his research.

"Ronnie DeFeo murders," Ed murmured. "Good old Ronnie DeFeo." At this point, I wasn't sure if Ed was willing to talk about this subject. I believed that it could have gone either way from here. It was very possible that Ed's pleasant demeanor could have changed drastically from here on out. It was a toss-up. It seemed likely; from all of the stories I've heard about the Amityville locals, that they didn't want to discuss this subject. However, Ed soon became even more vocal and enchanted with the conversation. On the tip of his tongue was information that, if true, would be unprecedented—for the first time adding information from a true Amityville insider.

"I'm doing a criminal profile for my students," Carl stated. "And I want as much information as I can get on that case."

"Well," Ed pondered. "You just missed out on some lady who I was with earlier, whose brother loaned the gun to Ronnie that killed his family."

"What?" I shouted in amazement. I was not sure if I heard him correctly.

"She loaned the gun to Ronnie DeFeo, the one that was used in the murders," Ed reiterated.

"The .35 caliber Marlin?" I asked.

"Yea, whatever it was," Ed responded. Ed was reluctant to give us her last name, but he did mention that her first name is Lynn. Carl and I were astonished at the admission from Ed. Up until that point we didn't really comprehend how small of a town Amityville really was.

"We were at the liquor store and she [Lynn] made those statements in this car; somebody else was also in the car," said Ed.

"This very vehicle that we are in now," Carl asked.

"Yea," Ed replied confidently. "That's what we were talking about at the liquor store, after the murder." Ed continued to talk about the murders and we continued to fire off questions.

"A well known journalist by the name of Rick Moran claimed that he was told by a friend in the DEA, that an unnamed DEA agent was stationed in front of the DeFeo home during the time of the murders, and actually saw Dawn [DeFeo] come out [of the house] with what looked like a rifle. He claimed that she went to the back of the house, by the water, and returned with nothing. Do you know anything about this," I asked.

"The night of the murders," Ed asked. "The DEA agent, what was he doing there?"

"Well, supposedly he [DEA Agent] was there doing an investigation on Ronnie, Sr. Moran claimed that Mr. DeFeo would take a boat out to meet up with another boat and bring back illegal drugs for distribution."

"Oh, ok, ok" Ed said. He seemed to understand the reasoning, as he shook his head in agreement.

"That's possible, because Ronnie DeFeo's father, [correction] Ronnie DeFeo's grandfather, did belong to the underground, somewhere in the City [NYC]." At just that moment, we drove past the Amityville horror house. Carl and I were a bit distracted. Within seconds we pulled into Mr. Kangesier's driveway. It was a slow walk from his garage to the back door of his home. Ed had to use a walker on the gravel-ridden driveway so he didn't fall. We entered his home, and I helped him put away his groceries. I also mixed him a *screw driver* (Vodka and Orange juice)—which is his favorite drink—while Carl went to the bathroom.

After getting settled and listening to a few more of Ed's war stories and nostalgic moments, Ed agreed to do an exclusive video interview with us. As I began rolling the tape, Ed stated that he had only once before done a brief video interview with what he believed was ABC, years ago, about the horror house; but other than that, he has kept his silence for all these years. Ed was now ready to tell his version of the story, and he claimed that he wanted nothing out of it other than to expose the truth.

"Ya know, whatever happens with this, however far it gets exposed, I really don't give a shit," Ed exclaimed. "Ya know why?" Ed continued. "I'm on my way out. What are they gonna do to me...oh, I mean, this town; they're such a bunch of fakes, phonies and frauds here." (Ed laughed sarcastically, and shook his head side to side) It's unbelievable! This, this has gone on long enough!"

Interviews with Edward J. Kangesier

Ed Kangesier was born in Amityville, NY. His father, Dr. Henry Michler, received his M.D. from Temple University at the tender age of eighteen. Ed has traveled the world, but still lives today in his first childhood home in Amityville, a house that was passed down to him from his mother. He's seen the ups, downs, growths, and setbacks of the sleepy seaside town. You would think that being third cousins to twenty-sixth President of the United States, Teddy Roosevelt—on his father's side—would be his most fascinating credential, but dive deeper in and you'll realize that Ed has lived a very interesting life. Unlike many others, Ed was born with a very special talent; he had the unique talent of being able to hand-draw anything that his eye came in contact with. Ed's drawings were very detailed; almost as vivid as actually seeing the picture first hand. Ed honed his talents with much practice, and he was soon able to legitimately call himself an artist.

At age fifteen, Ed quit Amityville High School and told his mother, "I'm going to join the Army!" His mother was adamantly against it; but Ed claims, "What was she gonna do? I was bigger than her." It's this type of sense of humor and charisma that makes Ed such a loveable and unforgettable character. Ed spent two-years in the National Guard before he was kicked out at age 17 for not being 18. The legal limit was 18 to join the military; but Ed claims, things were different back then. "When they kicked me out of the Army, I said 'screw you' and joined the Navy." Once in the Navy, Ed did not go into combat, as he claims, because he was a "Sacred Cow." By this, Ed meant that he was one of the military's elite, because of his inimitable drawing skills. Thus, began Ed's talented career as an artist for the United States Navy.

While in the Military, Ed received his associates degree in Engineering; a big accomplishment considering the college attendance rate was much lower sixty-years ago. With true artists like Ed being rare in the military, he quickly became a preferred resource for many top-flight individuals, even doing a personal job for the then president, Harry S. Truman. With an Engineering degree under his belt, paid for by the United States Navy, Ed left and got a job at the Grumman Aircraft Engineering Corporation on Long Island. It was there that Ed claims he went onto "bigger and better things." But not before he drew a picture of the plane and pilot of the plane that dropped the bomb on Hiroshima in WWII. That picture still sits in the Smithsonian Institute in NYC today. For Ed, bigger and better things meant television, motion pictures, voice-overs, etc. With the experience that he gained from Grumman, Ed left to pursue a career in producing and filming local documentaries. Ed's proudest T.V. moments were when he worked on T.V. series such as Defenders, with E. G. Marshal, and Car 54 in 1961 and 1994. To make extra cash, Ed worked as a private contractor; hand-drawing people's houses and other establishments.

In 1964, Ed became a NYC Police Officer, but he claimed that he only did it for fun. "I was just trying something out for my life," Ed claimed in regards to his brief stint as a NYC Police Officer. "Because, you're only here once my friend; once that's all," Ed stated. Once a member of Amityville's prestigious, Unqua-Corinthian Yacht Club, Ed hand-drew an amazing picture of their main headquarters.

Word got around about Ed's talents, and with his film contacts quickly spreading, Ed soon found himself in contact with Steven Spielberg. Ed's show business career got him in touch with some of the most powerful people in the business. Ed became a driver for some of Hollywood's most elite, including Tom Hanks, Julia Roberts and Steven Spielberg. With Ed's witty personality, charm, and the fact that he treated celebrities like regular people; he became an instant hit with them.

Steven Spielberg hired Ed to hand draw his mansion in New York, and Ed graciously accepted. Spielberg was so happy with the drawing that he asked Ed to paint his home in California, but Ed declined. Ed was particularly proud of his relationship with movie mogul, Julia Roberts. Ed describes Julia as a "wonderful human being" who is down to earth and sweet. After driving her around a few different times, the two became friends of sorts.

Ed: One time when I was driving Julia Roberts, she says to me, 'Where's the Amityville horror house?' And I said, 'Its right by me on Ocean Avenue. If you want to see the house, I can bring you down there. And then I'm gonna show you Amityville horror house two,' and she said 'Where's that?' and I said, 'My house.' [Laughs] So I brought her into my driveway, I drove all the way back to my garage, turned the car around, and came up to the side of my driveway. We both got out and came into this house and she took... well, my house was in better shape then, than it is now. It was a livable house then. And she came in and she walked all through the house and she thought it was a lovely, lovely, beautiful home. And I said, 'Anytime you want to stay here, you can.' [Laughs] 'You can have the whole upstairs if you want.' [Laughs] Then we stopped off at the Amityville horror house, I showed it to her. And she says, 'Well, it doesn't look like the movie?' And I said, 'Of course not, the owners wouldn't let them shoot it here.' And she said, 'Is it true?' And I says, 'Is Christ true?' (Pause) Is Christ true spreading the word, walking on water and dying on the cross? (Ed clarified this statement, saying that he meant "yes," it is true.)

Ed: Ronnie DeFeo, himself, had a problem with drugs. My oldest son—his name is Gary—he used to meet with Ronnie DeFeo and he thought Ronnie DeFeo was a nut. Ronnie DeFeo used to walk around with a .38 [caliber gun] in his belt, and ah was quite possible that he had done it. But, somebody around here in Amityville told me that when Ronnie DeFeo came home that night early in the morning [night of the murders] he found his oldest sister sitting with a rifle on her lap and she was totally dazed. And he asked her, 'What's going on, what happened?' And she didn't say anything, she just pointed upstairs (Ed points his index finger towards the ceiling, in an up and down motion). He runs upstairs and he finds the whole family shot in the back. So, he was so angry; so upset about that, that he came down, took the rifle off her lap and shot her and removed her *to her bedroom*. And then threw the rifle outside somewhere in the canal. And so that's another angle. Another angle is that Ronnie DeFeo owed so much money to the mafia—through his poor administrative system, his money—that every time he stole money from his father, taking receipts from the automobile store to the bank and come back and say, 'Guess what, I was heisted. The money's gone, somebody else got it.' And ah, that was all of course, a lie. What he was doing was trying to pay off his gambling debts. And, so, the mafia had to do something about it and they came out and wiped out the whole family. Now, that's weird because they generally don't wipe out kids, but who knows. No witnesses!

Will: Ed, can you tell us what you think happened on the night the DeFeos were murdered; or what you might have heard had happened?

Ed: It seems that when Ronnie first came home on the night of the incident, from wherever he was, it was during the early evening; he climbed through the window. He [Ronnie] goes through the house and finds everybody dead, and he goes outside the house, and immediately goes up to the bar up here [Henry's Pub] and he told them what had happened. Those people that he told [at the bar] came down with him to the house to see what he was talking about. The door was now of course unlocked, and they went inside and they went from room, to room, to room, and 'oh my God; oh my God; oh my God.' Now everybody was scared shitless. That's when somebody picked up the phone and called the police [Joey Yeswoit]. When the police arrived, only a couple of cars came down.

Will: Was it Amityville police that came down first, or was it Suffolk County Police?

Ed: Amityville came down first and when they saw the mess, they saw that it was over and beyond their jurisdiction, they called Suffolk County. Amityville Police cannot go into felonies, so they called Suffolk to come in. And of course, they [Suffolk County Police] took over completely; with the assistance of the Amityville Police. And then they brought in a big crime truck that sat in the drive way of the horror house for the next 30 days. (The "Crime Truck" served as a portable police headquarters).

Will: Now let me ask you? You said that Amityville [Police] were there and kinda 'hung around.' Did Suffolk County show up on scene and cordon off the area? (Ed shakes his head up and down) Was Amityville allowed access to the area anymore, or did Suffolk County take over and Amityville were just stragglers hanging out?

Ed: I would say the latter. Amityville Police's job was then to do menial things like keeping the crowd back, traffic duty, and things of that nature. On the night of the DeFeo murders I drove by the house, because you couldn't stop and stare; cops kept moving you on.

Will: And when you passed by, what did you see?

Ed: Big crime truck in the driveway

Will: In whose driveway?

Ed: I think the driveway belonged to ah, to the Ireland house. And people were driving by and taking pictures. And ya know, here it is 2007 and people are still coming by and taking pictures. They still come down here" (Ed puts his left hand on his head and smiles. He pauses, in deep thought over the years of publicity that the house, just four houses from his, has received).

Will: So, did you see the point in time when they removed the bodies from the house?

Ed: No, no. That was done I think sometime between midnight and early morning. You couldn't go down there anyway, even if you wanted to. First of all, people said, 'Well did ya hear the dog barking [on the night of the murders]?' (Ed is speaking of the DeFeo's dog, Shaggy). No, I never heard the dog barking. I remember the mutt, big fluffy dog with hair over the eyes. I wouldn't have been able to hear it anyway from here. Cause, people have their windows closed, it was winter. I never heard gunshots either, never heard them. And, my bedroom is right upstairs facing that house (Ed points upstairs). I can see the horror house from my bedroom, especially in the winter when there's no foliage obstructing. From my front porch you can see the front door of their house a lot better than from upstairs though. When I first heard about it, I went onto my front porch to see what was going on. When I first went outside, It was daybreak, about 5-6 in the morning. I said, 'Holy Cow!' I saw police everywhere, the front door of the house was closed, and the crime truck had not arrived yet.

Phone Call from Lynn

During a short break, Ed decided to contact his friend, Lynn Tewksbury, to speak to us. Ed said that she could help us out with some of the details that we were searching for. He put her on speaker phone after informing her of the situation .We introduced ourselves and explained our intentions. Ed continued small talk with Lynn briefly, then...

Ed: (Ed says to Lynn while on speaker phone) Wait; let me put you over to them.

Will: Ed told us about the weapon that Ronnie had allegedly killed his family with. Ed claimed that you told him that the weapon was loaned to him. (At the time I didn't know Lynn's last name).

Lynn: The Marlin? That was my brother-in-laws rifle. I think Ronnie had either bought it from my brother-in-law or my brother-in-law just gave it to him. *This was like the night before.* It was owned originally by my brother-in-law. Now the police [Suffolk County Police] went to him [Chuck] to find out, ya know, of course they had to interview him about how Ronnie got his gun.

In an affidavit written on 8 October 1975, Ronnie's best friend, Barry Springer, told police that he was with Ronnie about three or four years earlier and they went over to their other friend's house, Chuck Tewksbury. The reason for the visit to Chuck was to purchase a rifle that Ronnie and Chuck had previously discussed. Chuck sold the .35 caliber Marlin rifle to Ronnie that day for $40.00, handing it to him in a long, rectangular shaped cardboard box. Ronnie claimed that he was going to use it for deer hunting. After Ronnie purchased the gun, Barry claimed that he and Ronnie went over to their other friend's house, Steven Hicks.

While in the Hicks' living room, Ronnie asked Barry to show him how to use the gun. Barry put one shell into the chamber and attempted to eject the bullet, but the gun accidentally went off. Luckily it was pointed at the floor at the time it was fired and no one was hurt. The bullet 'ripped' through the floor somewhere in the middle of the room. Lynn was reluctant to give us his name, but Carl pressed her.

"See, he won't be happy with me giving his name," Lynn said. "Does the last name 'Tewksbury' ring a bell?" Lynn asked. She also mentioned Barry Springer, Steven Hicks. "Those were all friends of Ronnie's," she stated. Barry Springer was Ronnie's best friend. "My brother-in-laws' name is Chuck Tewksbury," Lynn said.

Lynn: Ronnie was the first person I met when I moved out to Amityville. When Ronnie committed the crimes I was a Tewksbury, but when I had first moved to Amityville, I was a Krauser.

Carl: How long prior to the incident did the .35 caliber marlin get surrendered from your brother-in-law to Ronnie DeFeo, Jr.?

Lynn: I have no idea!

Carl: Can you give me any approximate time on it?

Lynn: *Nope, don't have any idea.* I don't think it was like ah, I don't think Ronnie borrowed it to go kill his family. *I don't even think he killed them all anyway.* All I know is from what my brother-in-law told me, cause right after it happened [DeFeo murders] my brother-in-law of course went to see Ronnie [in jail], he's [Chuck] gone a couple of times to visit Ronnie in jail. A couple of the other guys visited Ronnie in jail also. I don't talk to my brother-in-law any longer; I'm the outcast of the family. My husband and I are not together any longer. I know I can't call my brother-in-law, we don't speak. Now what my brother-in-law was told was that his sister [Dawn] shot everybody, and he [Ronnie] shot his sister.

I was reviewing the tape later on the next day, and what struck me as odd was when Lynn first said, "*This was like the night before,*" talking about Chuck giving the gun to Ronnie. Then, later in the conversation, Lynn said that she had "*no idea*" when Chuck relinquished the gun. The former statement was probably just made by accident and had no relevance, but it still got my attention. If Lynn's earlier statement—about Chuck loaning the gun to Ronnie the night before—was true, then a whole new can of worms would be opened. Regardless, we continued to press, but Lynn was adamant that she had no idea when the transaction took place.

Lynn: Ronnie's father was a terrible person too! God, he used to beat Ronnie up all the time. We all just knew that he [Ronnie, Sr.,] beat the mother and we just knew he was like that. It was just common knowledge in the neighborhood. Some of Ronnie's friends witnessed these incidences with Ronnie, Sr. Barry Springer witnessed it as well, but he's passed away now.

Lynn was very helpful. She was trying to lead us to someone who could give us more information about the case. She seemed to really be digging into her thinking cap to find us someone, but the only person that she really had info on was her brother-in-law, Chuck Tewksbury, but she didn't feel comfortable about giving us his phone number.

Lynn: Unfortunately, Barry has passed away, I don't know where you can find Steven Hicks, and my brother-in-law, Chuck, lives in Florida. We all kinda grew up together. You can probably get Chuck's phone number in Florida and speak to him (Lynn would not give out Chuck's number). I believe Chuck lives around Tampa... St. Pete [Florida], but I'm not sure.

Will: Did you hang out much with Ronnie around the time of the murders?

Lynn: After Ronnie graduated in 1969, we didn't really hang out much after that.

Will: Would you describe Ronnie as a ladies man or womanizer, from what you knew about him?

Lynn: Ronnie had a lot of money, so he had a lot of girlfriends. I wouldn't call him a womanizer, but if girls were interested in him, it was probably because he had money. Ronnie was pretty quiet in High school. It wasn't until after high school that Ronnie got messed up with drugs. I didn't get involved with him after that, because I knew he was on drugs. (Lynn declined to come over to Ed's house that night for an interview, but she gave us her number and said that we could call her if we had any other questions.)

Ed & the Gang

Ed: When I first talked to someone who was a part of the investigation, former Captain of the Suffolk County Police Department—I'd rather not mention his name—and he said, as far as he was concerned, it was a gang-land killing rather than just a straight murder case.

When asked to briefly describe his definition of a "gangland" killing, Ed replied, "Well, there could be two people in a gang; there could be twenty-five people in a gang. You do something wrong, that is against their particular way of doing business—if you owe them money, or you walk out on them, or you cheated on them, or you turn them in or something, or whatever—then they're gonna get even."

Will: So, it's your opinion, when he mentioned this, you feel that this is what he was trying to tell you, from his professional police opinion?

Ed: That was his opinion, yea! Well, you find bodies on their stomachs with their hands along their sides; shot in the backs or in the back of the head; that doesn't look like that's something a single handed person could do. How do ya kill six people in the house without anyone jumping up or anyone getting out of bed? At least without somebody else keeping em down! There could have been five or six people there holding them down while the sixth guy goes around shooting the gun that belongs to the family.

When asked how he thinks that one person could have killed all six family members without any of the six getting out of their beds, Ed's response was, "Because it was more than one person doing the killing. It was a gangland killing, that's what it really was! It wasn't just Ronnie going around with a rifle shooting each person while they were waiting around in bed to be shot!"

Amityville Revisited

After analyzing the first interview with Ed Kangesier, many questions came to mind. I remembered during our first visit that Carl had mentioned something to the effect that he wanted to make sure that the questioning was thorough, because we might not have another chance to talk with Ed again. Ed sat up in his chair and said, "We will talk again! You guys can call me anytime." The sentiment stuck with me, and I knew that I was welcome to visit Ed again, but I knew that we had to do so. Realizing this, I decided to give Ed a call. It had already been two weeks since my last visit, and I believed that time was of the essence. I knew that the best time to contact him would be during the day, so I decided to phone him the following weekend.

I called Ed at 1:00 p.m. that day after preparing seventeen detailed questions. When Ed realized who I was, he was once again happy to speak to me. Ed wasn't doing so well. His health was deteriorating rapidly, he believed that he was in jeopardy of losing his house, and he was still very lonely. Ed had a realtor, but he feared that they were not going to be able to sell the home. I offered to put him in touch with a friend of mine who was a successful realtor. I had just set my friend up with another person in a situation similar to Ed's, but even worse. My friend was currently in the process of doing a "short-sell" of the other home, and I believed that he might be able to assist Ed with his "prime real estate" home. Ed appreciated the sentiment and said that he would at least hear what my friend had to offer.

We talked for nearly a half-an-hour before I advised Ed that I was going to be in the area the following Saturday, and that I would like to stop by and ask him a few more questions. Ed graciously accepted my offer and said that it would be his pleasure. He began calling me "friend," to which I felt honored. I didn't know much about this interesting gentleman and I wanted to know more. Moreover, I was curious myself to know if Ed had more to tell; I believed that he did.

On Saturday, 19 January 2008, I took my female assistant up to Amityville to do another interview with Ed Kangesier. On 26 January 2008, I again traveled up to Amityville to do yet another interview with Ed. This time I brought a different female assistant with me. Ed loved the fact that I had brought along two beautiful women on two different occasions. He was quite the romantic, and charmed the socks off both of them. Though Ed was in good spirits during my last visit, he was not doing so well. Ed hadn't eaten in three days and his will to live was fading. On January 26th, Melanie and I went and got some food for Ed, and we coaxed him into eating it. I had vowed to keep in touch with this old-timer and make sure that he was doing ok. The more Ed and I talked, the more he revealed about himself and the incidents involving the Amityville horror house. Ed told me that after all these years he was very excited to tell his version of the Amityville story.

Gary gets spooked!

On my third trip to Amityville, Ed told me a riveting story about a time that his son Gary had his own bizarre encounter with the horror house. Ed emphasized twice that the police officer in the story, who was a patrolman at the time, is currently the Amityville Chief of Police (who happens to be Woodrow Cromarty).

Ed: Gary was truckin' up the street one day and he stopped off to see the Amityville police officer who was sitting in the driveway of the Amityville horror house. Gary and the police officer were high school pals. The cop that was sitting in there is now the Chief of the Amityville Police Department [Woodrow Cromarty]. The cop was a big jerk; his hat was always cockeyed (Laughter). And the only reason that he became chief was because it was a political thing. The guy that should have become chief, who was a lieutenant, never made it. Every time I see this lieutenant, he's retired, and he comes up from the South; I always call him chief (Laughter). So, he was sitting in the driveway of the Amityville horror house guarding it. Gary goes inside with the cop and sits in the car with the, chief of police… [Correction] who is today the chief of police, at that time he was a patrolman. As they sat there together, all of a sudden, all of the lights in the house started going on and off; on and off; on and off.

"In order for all those lights to go on and off all at the same time, that meant that someone would have to be in each room pushing each switch up and down simultaneously. My own mother, who lived with me at the time, was up stairs in what used to be my art studio. She happened to notice the lights going on and off while Gary was sitting in the car with the patrolman. My mother had asked a few days later, 'Who the hell was in the Amityville horror house?'

I have no idea (Ed shakes his head and puts his arms up, palms facing in). Well, Gary told me that he got out of the car with this cop, and they went in there. The cop had the key to open up the front door. And they went into the house for what the hell was causing that. All of a sudden, all that stopped [Lights stop going on and off] when they got in the house! And Gary, being an eighth degree karate instructor—he could kick the crap out of anybody—he was scared stiff and very concerned about going upstairs. When they entered the house it was cold. It was summer time, but for some reason it was cold. Even though it was summer time, the house was cold! It was about thirty degrees inside and they could see their breaths [mist] as they breathed. They went all through the house looking for who might be causing this problem, couldn't find anything. And of course, Gary was constantly looking around, protecting his back. Gary went all the way upstairs to the attic, third floor, there was nothing there. So the cop called into Amityville headquarters, for back up, and I guess the backup came, whatever."

"So, Gary went back out to the car with his cop friend, and they couldn't understand what the hell was going on. Gary and the cop went around to the back of the house wherever the gas meter was. When they got to the meter, they realized that it was going (Ed begins moving his hand quickly in a circular motion and making the sound "chica-chica-chica-chica"). It was going like crazy! It was going chica-chica-chica-chica, like there was tons of heat and electricity being used; and there was nothing on, no lights, no nothing! So, more Amityville cops came, and they checked all over, there were no lights on or anything going on at this time. Who the hell knows what was going on, but why would there be power on, if nobody lived in the house?"

In an article by Carolyn James of the Amityville Record (entitled: *Why Hollywood's Version of DeFeo Murders Isn't Amityville's,* 2000), Chief Cromarty explained that he went to school with Ronald DeFeo and Gary Kangesier, said that "every time something new is written or filmed about the case, or when the old movie is in re-runs, the area becomes a tourist attraction for the curious and weird. The last time they showed a new film, we had a break in to a house next door. The guy was dressed in a white gown and hood...We don't need more of that."

In an article by Carolyn James of the Amityville Record (entitled: *The Amityville Horror Seekers Begin to Come Around,* 2005), Chief Cromarty reports that the first weekend after the 2005 movie was released, between 400 and 500 vehicles went through Ocean Avenue. "Many of the residents living there lived there during the first wave when the movie first came out," said Cromarty. "But there are some new families who are going through this for the first time. We are doing all we can to make it as easy as possible for them." Has Chief Cromarty ever publicly commented about whether he believes that the haunting occurred or not? Oddly enough, it seems as though Chief Cromarty has evaded this question all these years. Although Cromarty has made several comments regarding what measures the village will take to avoid curiosity seekers, and he certainly appears to be annoyed by the curiosity-seekers, he has not been as outspoken as others in denouncing the haunting.

Ed: Everyone knew that my son Gary was a black-belt in karate. One time, my son Gary walked into Henry's Pub and Ronnie grabbed my son around his neck with his arm (Ed takes his left arm and holds it up as if he is holding someone by the throat) and said, 'Now what are ya gonna do karate Joe?' Ronnie knew that Gary was an 8th-degree karate instructor. So, Gary knew he [Ronnie] carried a gun inside his belt. And Gary would humor him by saying, 'You got me, you got me; you can do whatever you want.' And then that pacified him [Ronnie], and he would go mess with somebody else. And Gary thought that this guy [Ronnie] was a little bit of a nut.

Gary and the Horror house

Shortly after the DeFeo murders, before the Lutzes moved in, Ed's son Gary was notified by a friend of his that he [the friend] had a problem involving the horror house. The gentleman who called used to work for his father's gardening service in South Amityville at the time. Ed could not recall the friend's name, but he remembers that the man called on the telephone one night. Ed answered the phone and the man sounded a bit frazzled, upset, and nervous—asking to speak to Gary, who lived with Ed in his present house at the time.

This friend [we'll call him "Scott"] said that he needed Gary's help, regarding something very fishy and bad in connection with the horror house. Knowing that Gary was an eighth-degree black belt and Karate instructor, Scott needed Gary for protection. Ed claims that Gary advised him that Scott needed his help and that they were going into Queens, where he [Gary] was going in a body guard-type capacity.

"This guy wants me to go into Queens with him. He needs somebody to protect him."

"Protect for what?" Ed asked

"This guy has something going on in the City, which has something to do with the horror house," Gary replied.

"Holy shit," Ed said in amazement. Ed and his family were now caught in the middle of the whirlwind.

Ed notes that the DeFeo house was called "The horror house" (by locals) right after the DeFeo murders. Ed was adamant that the Amityville locals all called it the horror house before the Lutzes' moved in. "People would say, what a horror, what a horror, and that's how it caught on," Ed recalls.

Ed explained, Gary picked Scott up in his car and the two hit the highway. When Gary and Scott arrived in Queens, Scott took Gary down some stairs to the bottom floor of a seedy establishment, which doubled as a bar and pool room. Gary quickly noticed that the place was not open to the general public, and all of the people in the room seemed to be of Italian discent. People were walking by and looking them up and down, trying to size them up. Suddenly, a man came and took Scott into a private room.

Gary followed, but hung back, because he was not allowed into the room. He walked up to the door where Scott had entered, and got a glimpse of Scott talking to four guys. Gary told Ed that there were two other white gentlemen dressed in black eyeing him and prevented him from entering the room. Gary waited outside the door of the back room with his arms folded waiting patiently for Scott to return.

"As far as I know, it was a gangster place." Ed proclaimed. "I know exactly what it is," Ed continued. "It's a hang out for unscrupulous people." Scott came out moments later looking pale and visibly shaken. Frantically, Scott said to Gary, "Lets get out of here!" A fight ensued and Gary used his "lethal karate skills" to fight off a few of the men and break free and out the front door. As they ran out and up the stairs, two shady-looking characters gave chase "looking for trouble," Ed said. Gary and Scott turned their fast-walking into a full sprint to Gary's car, with the two thugs behind them keeping pace. The men were forced to pull back, however, when they noticed that there were a number of police officers on a robbery call right near Gary's car. Scott and Gary thought that they were in the clear, and they took off in Gary's Pontiac.

The Italians were far from done with the men, though. Soon after they began driving; Gary and Scott noticed that they were being tailed. A high speed chase ensued. Gary began speeding through the streets of Queens trying to lose the tail. He also needed to get a grasp on their location and find the direction home. Somehow, they were able to locate the Hempstead Turnpike, but they still had company. Every so often the car chasing them would come up along side their car and ram into them, in an attempt to run them off the road.

Suddenly, shots were fired. Bullets ricocheted off of Gary's car. Panic-stricken, Gary sped up. The men were followed all the way back to Long Island until they finally lost them. Once back in Amityville, the two stopped at a bar [Henry's Pub, a.k.a. The Witches Brew] on the corner of Merrick & Ocean and discussed the traumatic events that had just taken place. After Gary dropped his friend Scott off at his house, south of Merrick Road, he returned home. Ed noticed that Gary was in his room and he wanted him to expound on everything that he had just been through. Ed and Gary had a very open father/son relationship. They kept no secrets, according to Ed.

"I wasn't scared or anything," Ed remembers. "Just as long as they didn't follow him home."

"I was very proud of Gary, that he punched a couple of them out, and nothing more ever came of that," Ed said. "But it had something to do with the horror house," Ed said as he swayed his head back and forth. Scott was so scared and terrified after that experience that he left his father's business; left Amityville; left Long Island; and neither Ed nor Gary ever saw him again. He just skipped town.

"Supposedly there were unscrupulous people involved with the horror house and what had happened," said Ed. "I seem to think that this guy [Scott] that Gary was helping knew something or had some information about something pertaining to what had happened the night of the DeFeo Murders." Startlingly, Ed claims that this guy [Scott] was one of the men who followed Ronnie DeFeo, Jr., back to the house and discovered the bodies. If this were accurate, then Scott would have to be either, William Scordamaglia, John Altieri, Joseph Yeswoit, Al Saxton, or Robert "Bobby" Kelske. It was unlikely that it was Scordamaglia, as he was a bar owner and Kelske's father reportedly owned a stone mason company.

Ed recalls witnessing the damage and bullet holes in Gary's car after the incident. He also recalls getting the damage fixed on Gary's car "real cheap-o-cheap" from a mechanic he knew in town at the time.

Merv Griffin

Soon after the Lutz family appeared on the Merv Griffin show, Merv became curious and wanted to see the house for himself. Merv rented a car from the *Chrysler Corporation* one Saturday afternoon and decided to take a drive out to see the house. The *Amityville Horror* movie was being filmed at the time over in Toms River, NJ, because the current owners of the home [The Cromarty's] would not let the movie be filmed in the actual home. Moreover, the town of Amityville would not permit the movie to be filmed anywhere in town. The Cromarty's later filed a law suit against the Lutz family, and others, for invasion of privacy.

Merv was so spooked after interviewing the Lutzes, that he was determined to see the house for himself. According to Ed, Merv claimed on television that once he got onto Ocean Avenue and pulled up by the Amityville horror house, his rent-a-car died directly in front of the house. Merv walked to a neighbor's house right by the horror house, and asked the resident if he could use their phone to call the rental company and inform them what had happened. Merv told the rental company where he was, and they told him that they would send someone out to take a look at the car. About an hour later, two representatives from the rental company showed up. They looked over the car, tried to start it, but had no luck. They decided to push the car onto Ireland Place, moving west, directly adjacent to the horror house. They tried starting-up the car, and this time the car started on the first attempt. Now, thoroughly spooked, Merv decided to investigate further. He wanted to speak to some of the residents on Ocean Avenue and see what they had to say about the house. Merv began ringing on door bells on both sides of the street. During his investigation, Merv came upon Ed's house. Ed was a big fan of Merv's at the time, and he was shocked to see him standing at his doorstep.

Ed let Merv in and the two had a brief conversation. Merv explained to Ed the bizarre story of his rent-a-car experience. According to Ed, Merv appeared fairly shaken up. Merv asked Ed if there had been any paranormal activity occurring in his house. Ed said "No," and Merv replied, "There's something wrong here in this neighborhood! Why would my car blank out on Ocean Avenue at approximately where the horror house is?"

Miles Curran

Will: You told us the story about your neighbor who used to live directly across the street from you, by the name of Miles Curran, being pulled into a tree right next to the horror house. I believe that you said that he passed away, God rest his soul!

Ed: My neighbor next door, who's no longer alive, was coming home from Long Island Railroad where he worked; he had 4 guys in the car with him. They were all going to stop and watch the ball game and drink beer at his house. One of the guys asked, 'Isn't this the Amityville horror house?' And Miles said, 'Yes it is.' When he got up approximately where the horror house is, his car pulled to the far left and hit a tree, directly in front of the horror house. So, Miles pulled the car back, noticed that there was damage to the front of his car, and he continued to drive down Ocean Avenue back to his house across the street from me. And they all went in there and they were talking about what had happened at the Amityville horror house.

"I went next door to ask where he got the damage on the front of his car, and Miles told me what had happened. Miles said, 'Alls we were doing is talking about the horror house, and the God damned car pulled right into a tree in front of the house, and damaged my grill and bumper.' So, they said and believed that it had something to do with the horror house. This is all the kind of crap that was going on at that time. It seemed like all hell had broken loose, in regard to ghosts, or whatever you call them. Miles never forgot that! He always repeated it to me—about how he was pulled into that tree by the Amityville horror house. After Miles pulled back from the tree and went on home to his house next door, they all got drunk and talked about the Amityville horror house. And, at one point, they walked out onto the front lawn of Miles' house and began looking at the house and laughing and talking loud about it, cursing it and what not."

Ed explained that at one point he heard Miles scream at the house, "That house is crippled, there's something wrong with it," or words to that effect. I turned the tape off so that Ed could take a phone call; I began recording immediately after he disconnected the call. I began to explain to Ed that we had hit a tree on Ireland Ave, no less than two-hours before, while making a U-turn directly in front of the Amityville horror house. I was not driving, so I could not explain what actually occurred, or if any force pulled us into the tree, but Carl blamed it on me for distracting him. All I was doing at the time was telling him to make a U-turn and park facing the house so that we could survey the area and take pictures.

The bizarre thing was that it felt like to me, that we were pulled into that tree. There was no explanation for it. There was no driveway there to actually pull into and back out of to make a routine-type U-turn. Carl is one of the best drivers that I have ever seen controlling a vehicle, and yet we hit that tree pretty hard, considering the low rate of speed that we were traveling. Ed did not seem shocked by our story. He responded by finishing the story about his neighbor Miles. Some months later, Ed explained to me that Miles had problems with alcohol and hung himself not too long after this incident.

Ed: Now here's a strange thing. Way back, in the…I don't know, early 1800s, a man by the name of John Ketcham; he was a warlock up in Massachusetts—warlock, meaning 'Man-witch.' He escaped from that town and came down to Long Island where he knew there was a bunch of Ketcham's [people with the same last name as he had]. He was looking for a place to hide. He came across this house up here (Ed points in the direction of the Amityville horror house). But it wasn't the house that's there now. Supposedly, shortly after this Ketcham moved into the house, it was burned down by the warlocks of Massachusetts. Now, I wasn't there, and I wasn't born, but that's the information I've picked up from the old timers here. And they said that the warlocks from Massachusetts came and burned down the house, Ketcham escaped, and found another house where he could hide. In the mean time, when the second house was built on the same property; somehow, someway, Ketcham got back in there, and that's when all the crap started again. Obviously that's all hear say.

Ed claims that he didn't know the Lutz family personally, but from what he remembers, "They were pretty genuine." Ed also claims that, "The book that was written about them, best seller, [*Amityville Horror: A True Story*] couldn't have been that far off. They did the best they could to explain the truth as they knew it. And I believe that they had two of the children talk about it, while under that medicine that makes you *tell the truth,* out in California; and the kids did tell the truth, to the police; that's what started this whole thing." (Ed clarified that by "the kids telling the truth," he meant that they explained all the bizarre and ghostly things that happened to them in the house).

Ed then explains how "hoaky-folky" that the neighbors on Ocean Avenue thought the DeFeo house was, with all the religious statues that they had surrounding their property. Ed said that the general consensus of the neighbors was that it was overkill to have had so many religious statues on the property. He claimed that it was as if they were trying to "override religion." The overall consensus—Ed explains—of the Ocean Ave. residents, was that something was strange with all the statues on their [the DeFeo's] property.

"See, here on Ocean Avenue, we didn't push things like that; ya know, too many religious things; too much this; too much that. It's kind of a neutered town: *Neuter-Village*. And, his place just stood out; it was loaded with all kinds of statues." Ed tells a funny story about an encounter that he had with Ronald DeFeo Sr.

"One day I was driving by the house and I saw him [Mr. DeFeo] out on the front lawn. I rolled down my window and I said to him, 'How much do you want for that?' and I pointed to one of the statues. He cantankerously replied, 'Not for sale.' And Ed replied sarcastically, 'Oh, I thought you were selling it,' and Ed chuckled to himself as he drove off.

Incest: Motive for Murder

During the very last interview that I did with Ed, he revealed some startling and shocking things about this case that have never before been mentioned or even speculated about publically. After digging and digging for a motive in this case, Ed handed it to me on a silver platter, unexpectedly.

Ed: Do you remember the story that I told you? When I said that Ronnie DeFeo came home [the night of the murders] and he walked into his house and found his sister sitting in a chair with a shotgun on her lap and she was supposed to have shot everybody, because of ah, incest.

Will: Because of what? [I was taken aback, and I wasn't sure exactly what Ed had just said].

Ed: Incest [Ed repeated quickly]. The father was sleeping with her [Dawn], did you know that? That's what I was told by three people on Ocean Avenue.

Will: [in amazement] Ed, the autopsy report shows that Dawn had sex sometime prior to the murders, and her boyfriend [William Davidge] was in Florida. Many have speculated that Butch had been having an incestuous relationship with her, but you're saying it was her father who was…?

Ed: Her Father! [Ed promulgates] Her father, the pig, was having sex with the oldest daughter [Dawn].

Will: How do you know this?

Ed: Because I've been told this by three or four people here in Amityville!

Will: No one has ever come forward and reported this, you understand?

Ed: Well, I'm reporting it to you now, my friend. And if you want to hear that from Lynn Tewksbury, she'll tell you that; if you want to hear that from her MOTHER [Lynn's mother], who lives south of me here in Amityville, she'll tell you that too.

Will: Was the [incest] only happening with the oldest daughter, or any of the other children?

Ed: No, only with the oldest daughter; the oldest daughter.

Will: That is sick!

Ed: Of course it's sick!

Will: No wonder…

Ed: Yea, of course…So she shot the whole fucking bunch of them.

Will: So why did Ronnie shoot her then?

Ed: Because when he finally realized what had happened, when he came into the house, he took the shotgun from her and shot her. And he was on alcohol and drugs at the time, too.

As I sat there completely awe struck, Ed stared at me with a very serious face. I was speechless, just saying, "Holy shit," and things of that nature—just above a whisper. "Uh huh, yup, I know," Ed uttered, as if he was literally seeing the wheels in my head turning.

Will: How come you never told me this before, during our other interviews?

Ed: Well, I don't remember…I had so much to tell you at the time.

Ed lets me ponder this newly discovered evidence. He watches me closely as I am in complete awe of what he has just revealed to me. The biggest thing about this revelation is that it establishes a reasonable motive! People do not just randomly murder their families, or do some drugs and slaughter their parents, brothers, and sisters. That was another thing that made this case so intriguing. Originally Ronnie's motive was established as being on drugs and trying to steal jewelry out of the house. When it was determined publicly that the jewelry was not in the house, but in a safety deposit box elsewhere, the motive was then switched to insurance money. It was believed that Ronnie killed his family to get the insurance money on their deaths. Being the oldest child, Ronnie was due to inherit the estate anyway.

Moreover, Ronnie always had wads of money, according to just about everyone who knew him. The fact that he was on drugs raises speculation, but people don't just do drugs and kill their entire family. Ronnie's home life was never that bad; it is actually a dream of many Americans to live as well as Butch did. Plus, Ronnie was twenty-four years old and could have moved out if he wanted. The circumstance that tips the scale, however, would be incest. Incest can and has destroyed many families. Incest has been a motive in countless crimes throughout history. If this were to be true, it would seem to have something to do with the heinous acts committed. I contacted Lynn—as Ed requested—and she acknowledged that she heard these rumors as well, but could not confirm this for sure.

All things considered, it makes much more sense that, if Dawn DeFeo was being consistently molested by her father, she had more of a motive to kill than Ronnie did. Many in the media tried to play up the turbulent relationship between Ronnie and his father, but in reality, it was not that unusual of a relationship between father and son, unfortunately. Taking a closer look at Dawn's situation, we see that she was desperately trying to get away from the family and move to Florida "by any means necessary," as indicated by her then boyfriend, William Davidge, and even Beverly Nonnewitz. Moreover, a vaginal wipe conducted during Dawn's autopsy revealed that she did have sex sometime right before the murders, possibly even that night. Had she just had enough?

I have seen the affects of what incest can do to a young female, and the detrimental affects that it can have on them mentally and emotionally. Many would agree that if it had been occurring then it is highly likely that it played a key role in the tragedy. Incest and molestation are more common in our society than we are willing to admit or examine. The song, *"Janie's Got a Gun,"* by one of my favorite bands, *Aerosmith*, immediately came to mind when Ed revealed this to me; because the lyrics in the song could hypothetically be an indirect indication of what allegedly occurred that very night.

Amityville's Hang-Ups with the Curious

The Amityville Horribles

"It is absolutely amazing how this hoax seems to be continuously perpetuated," Amityville Mayor, Peter T. Imbert, told *The Amityville Record* on 27 April 2005 (in an article by Carolyn James entitled, *The Amityville Horror Seekers Begin to Come Around*). "Now with the release of the latest film, we have a whole new generation of kids who weren't even born when the first film came out. We continue to be upset and angry about it, and the image it gives our community," Imbert promulgated. Sergeant Pat Commarato has always been a vocal adversary to the notion that the house was ever haunted. In an article entitled, *Haunted House Murder – Attorney: Evil Spirit Pushed Killer*; Sgt. Commarato told the Chicago Tribune, "The story is a great rip-off," says Commarato. "I knew two families who lived there before the DeFeos and they had great experiences." Commarato added, "It is just an ordinary, charming house, and the sightseers are killing us."

What is absolutely amazing is the fact that Amityville refuses to capitalize on this phenomenon! It's hard to believe that the people in Amityville don't look at this as a good thing. I would be thrilled to have a blockbuster movie made about my hometown. Just look at what the 1979 movie did for Toms River, NJ (the site of the movie house, which could have been in the real house). Filmmakers originally wanted to use a home in Amityville, but were denied. So, they settled on the Fragoso's home, 60 miles away in Toms River, NJ. They paid the then owners of the home $15,000 to use it for the movie. Producers pumped approximately $250,000 into the local economy and cast local residents as extras. And, in March 1979, eight-hundred locals attended the screening of "The Amityville Horror."

Like the old adage goes, 'any publicity is good publicity.' I certainly don't look down on the town for the DeFeo murders or the bizarre things that happened in the house, and I believe that most would agree. I don't think that the civilians of Amityville, who believe that this has been a black mark on their little town, are too in touch with reality or the outside world. Amityville is a beautiful town! Ocean Avenue is one of the nicest suburban blocks that I've ever seen. It's homey, quaint, and of course the even-numbered houses sit on the edge of the Amityville River; which includes the horror house.

In a *Newsday* article (by Samson Mulugeta entitled, *The Fame Demon: in Amityville, Legacy is a Horror in Itself,* 1998), Amityville village trustee, Peter Casserly said, "Wherever you go, it's the first thing people ask" What a conversation piece that would be, huh? Could you imagine living on Ocean Avenue? I asked a good friend of mine, Thomas Perri, this question. He said, "All the girls I could pick up with that line! I could ace any job interview, because I could have the interviewer so enthralled in ghost and haunting stories, they would forget that I wasn't qualified for the job." The fact of the matter is that tourism adds to any community.

Current Mayor of Amityville, Peter Imbert, has lived in Amityville his entire life. Along with being mayor, Imbert helps run his family's multimillion-dollar insurance business in Amityville. At a village meeting in 1997, a master planner and consultant of Imbert's told the villagers he was from Massachusetts, where the town of Salem has turned its sordid history of witch-burning into a multimillion-dollar tourist industry.

Although Imbert believes the story to be a hoax, he suggested moving the house to downtown Amityville and making it into a bed and breakfast or a museum. "Could you imagine what kind of attraction it would be?" said Imbert, in the same article mentioned above. "People could come from all over the world to stay in the house or see it. From a business point of view, it would be a tremendous draw." The town residents, however, shouted down the idea, claiming that it would exploit the murders of the DeFeo family. The fact is that people are not visiting the house because of the DeFeo murders. I'm sure people have compassion in regard to the fatalities. In fact, most people who know about Amityville don't even know the story of the DeFeo murders. Still, people visit the

Lizzie Borden House in Fall River, Massachusetts all the time for a tour price of just $12.50 a ticket and they make a killing, no pun intended.

People go to the house because they believe that the house might be haunted. In fact, the movie, *The Amityville Horror,* doesn't even discuss the DeFeo murders—apart from the opening scene of the first movie and a few brief flashbacks. The original movie chronicles the Lutzes' experiences. This story did not gain international prominence because of the DeFeo murders; it gained its real notoriety once the Lutzes' story became popular. So, if any type of event is being perceived as celebrated, it would be the story of the Lutz family, not the DeFeo murders. Whether the Lutz family's story is true or not is not the issue. Professor, Carl Ivan Allen, said, "If these people are so concerned about remembering the family members [DeFeos] and the sacredness of life, then why don't they use the house as a tourist attraction and dedicate a certain percentage of the money to cancer research or something?" The issue here is that people are interested, and for the town not to capitalize on the mass marketability of this story is proof of its own vanity and insecurities. Surely the town and its tax payers could figure out how to put tourist money to good use!

If anything was a 'black mark' on the town of Amityville, it was the illegal drug activity occurring in the North Amityville Community. "It affected Amityville because many people saw the two communities as one," said former Mayor, Emil Pavlik, Jr. "Again, it wasn't just people in other parts of the country, but Long Islanders' as well who perceived Amityville as a drug infested village."

There are some locals in Amityville, however, who have the wherewithal and vision to understand the value of tourism in their community. Philip Gandiosi, 46, who runs the S&P Used Furniture shop with his brothers, Steve, Scott and Frank, told *The San Diego Union-Tribune* in May of 2005 that he has no problems with tourists coming to the area to view the horror house. In fact, Phil says that he is even happy to point them in the right direction. "Why not?" Phil asks. "The one good thing that's come out of all this is that it brings in people from out of town and helps out everyone's business. The tourists are harmless. They usually just want to see the house, then go shop and get something to eat." And the good thing about this is that it raises awareness about the murdered DeFeo's; and that is the whole point, isn't it?

The Amityville residents have matured a lot over the years. Certainly Amityville had their share of actual disturbing incidents back when the first movie came out, but times have changed. When the 2005 remake was released, Amityville residents once again braced themselves for a perceived nightmare that never materialized. The staggering reports after the first movie: of a man bringing goats to eat the grass; people urinating on the stairs of the house; and even nuns visiting to bless the house—didn't occur as expected with the 2005 release. The Amityville house is a part of our culture, like it or not. Like a hit song that plays over and over, burning into our memories; we remember the first time we saw the movie and how it made us feel. It's a story that stirs up certain emotions that are collective in all of us. It bonds us! With the power of these human factors, it should not surprise anyone that the name "Amityville" still evokes certain feelings every time it is heard, all around the world! Perhaps the most ironic part about this is an odd cause and effect of Amityville's residents: the refusal of the Amityville community to accept the fact that people are intrigued by this story and the community's adamant denial of anything paranormal, and the fact that this conjures up feelings in many outsiders that Amityville residents might have something to hide, and it only perpetuates the thrill-seeking mentality.

Former Suffolk County Detective, Ed Miller has been through it all in Amityville. He was one of the many officers who investigated the DeFeo murders back in 1974. Ed is convinced that "it's just a matter of time before somebody tries to transform the house into a cash cow." Ed's prediction is a testament to the staying power of this story. "...whoever does this is going to make a whole lot of money on it, I guarantee it," Ed stated in a *Newsday* article (by Samson Mulugeta entitled, *The Fame Demon: in Amityville, Legacy is a Horror in Itself,* 1998). When asked about turning the house into a tourist attraction, then owner, Brian Wilson, said jokingly, "Only if they offer me a million dollars." Apparently, even Wilson has his price.

Ed: People in Amityville are strange; they don't want any notoriety about this, what-so-ever. It's a black-spot on their background. I say, there's a lot worse here to hide here than that. (Ed chuckles).

Ed & the Thrill-Seekers

Ed claims that there were numerous occasions, after the first movie, when several cars were parked by his home and further down the block. During these occasions, there were times when he witnessed people drinking beer on his lawn, beer cans scattered across his property, and people talking loudly with no regard for the residents of the neighborhood. Still, Ed smiles when he says that he can't believe that people still come down to get a look at the Amityville house after all these years. It truly is amazing, even to Ed, and he looks back on the memories with fondness.

Soon after the Lutzes' story went public, hordes of thrill seekers flocked to the small town of Amityville to get a glimpse of the infamous horror house. Most just wanted to see the house for themselves; others were there to wreak havoc on the town and it's residents. Ed's Police training came in handy when some rowdy thrill seekers came down to the horror house to cause trouble.

Ed: There was one instance when a bunch of hooligans were ganging up on the Amityville horror house out on the street, causing all kinds of trouble. I was driving down Ocean Avenue, on my way home, with my son Gary and I saw one of the Amityville cops—nice guy; he's not with them anymore—he was having trouble trying to lock these bozos up. So I pulled the car over and said to my son, 'Stand-By.' I got out of the car and I went after these guys that were causing this cop trouble. I was kind of like, mean to them, very mean. Apparently, they kept locking the police car on him [the cop]. Every time he'd open the police car and put one of them in the car, they would lock the doors. And I said, 'Open these God damned doors or I will destroy this car to get to you if I have to.' And I helped this cop get these guys into the car and followed him and the perpetrators up to the Amityville police station. Cause, this was my street; and these were people from out of town. Later on, he thanked me very much for helping him. I said to him, 'Well, ya know, I'm a little older than you, I've been on the police department, and I know what it takes to corral these bozos.

Ed & Mrs. Wilson

Will: I heard through the rumor mill that Brian Wilson is not the actual owner, but it's owned by a non-profit organization. Do you know anything about that Ed?

Ed: Really? (Ed sits back in his chair contemplating. He folds his hands).

Will: I don't know this for a fact, like I said, I'm investigating this. Something strange is going on there!

Ed: I think the whole damn house is strange.

Will: Yea, there's obviously more going on than people in Amityville are willing to accept.

Ed: Well, I told you that I met the wife of the guy [Brian Wilson] who lives in the house now.

Will: Right! Where did you meet her?

Ed: At a drug store over in Massapequa.

Will: You didn't know it was her at the time right?

Ed: No, no.

Will: If I recall correctly, she was just a pretty woman and you randomly approached her.

Ed: Well, she was a very pretty woman; she was just well organized, and I approached her and told her so. And then she told me that she used to live on Ocean Avenue. Her son and her husband lived on Ocean Avenue. And I said, 'Why don't you live on Ocean Avenue now?' And she said, 'Well, because my husband is very controlling. I can't handle him.'

Will: Right, which is Brian Wilson [home owner]! So, she told you that she lived at the horror house?

Ed: She said that she didn't live there.

Will: So how did you know she was with Brian Wilson, what exactly happened?

Ed: Well, when we were talking she said, 'Where do you live on ocean Avenue?' I said, 'right by the Amityville horror house.' And she said, 'Oh yea, my husband and my son live in that house.'

Will: Oh, you must have been in shock!

Ed: Nah, no I wasn't. I don't get shocked very easily.

Will: Well, it was a big coincidence to run into someone who lived in the house?

Ed: I know, I know. We talked for another half an hour-forty five minutes! And she said that ah, the only reason that she couldn't be with her husband anymore, was because he was too controlling.

Will: So they are separated?

Ed: oh yea! He was too controlling…too controlling, which is typical for the Amityville horror house.

Will: You think he's controlling like that, because he's in the house?

Ed: I don't know what the hells going on over there! That house is so spooked! Ya know; I don't know what's going on in that house.

Will: It's the most famous, alleged, haunted house in the world and what I don't understand is; why are there so many secrets?

Ed: People that live around here don't want to know anything about it. They won't cooperate with anybody, because then it brings people to it.

Will: Which means more business; which means more money being spent in the area.

Ed: Well, Judge Walter Saxon was a friend of mine; he died a couple of years ago. I used to talk to him about it, and he wanted to know why I had a CBS tripod on the corner of the property of the old Buckley house, the white house across the street from the horror house, shooting the horror house. He stopped the car, he says, 'Ed, what the hell are you doing with this camera crew here?' I says, 'Because I'm helping them get shots of the Amityville horror house.' He said, 'You're on private property, you're not allowed to do that.' (Ed puts his right hand under his chin and throws it forward, meaning "fuck you"). [Laughter]…

Will: So nobody wants to acknowledge it; nobody wants to talk about it?

Ed: No, they're all a bunch of babies here! They are all sissies.

Will: They want everyone to know about, ya know, how great the town is, and it does have a very deep, rich history; but no one knew about this town before the murders and haunting, and they feel that there's a negative stigma attached, which there's not!

Ed: Right, right. (In agreement)

Will: I mean, so, so, there's the Amityville horror house here as well, that doesn't take away the fact that this is a beautiful town. I would have never heard of or seen this town if I didn't know [About DeFeo murders and the alleged haunting]. I have only good things to say about the town and the people that I've met [thus far]! If you drive down this block, I mean, the houses are gorgeous and so is the area!

Ed: I know, I know! (Again, in agreement) I know it's a gorgeous house; I'm selling this gorgeous little old house. I'm getting rid of it, because I can't afford it anymore, and it's too big for me. This is an 18-room-house, what the hell do I need an 18-room-house for?

Section IV
Aftermath and Analysis
DeFeo Appeals

Crooked Cops

Ronnie has always maintained that he did not receive a fair trial. Immediately after the guilty verdict was handed down, DeFeo and Weber went right to work on the appeal. The two had a lot to work with, as there were several key mistakes made by the police and by the courts. As far as the investigation and trial, much was left to be desired. Suffolk County law enforcement officials came under heavy scrutiny in the years following the DeFeo murders. Many other complaints against these officials started piling up, and an independent commission was assigned in April of 1989 to investigate the Suffolk County District Attorney's Office and Police Department.

Among the many areas under investigation was misconduct and deficiencies in homicide investigations and prosecutions, the unlawful gaining of confessions by over zealous police officers, and police brutality. Once again, Detective Rafferty's confession tactics were in question. James Diaz was charged with the murder of Maureen Negus, a 35-year-old nurse and mother of two. According to the evidence, Diaz broke into Negus' home and brutally raped and murdered her. In the case of People v. Diaz (Indictment no. 1102-84), the NY investigation commission stated the confession was made out in Rafferty's handwriting, and only signed by Diaz on the first page.

Furthermore, the estranged husband of Negus had moved into the house after his wife's death, in order to take care of their two children. Ten-months after the murder, the estranged husband found the murder weapon (knife) just 15-feet from where the body was found. According to the report, Suffolk County had a 94 percent confession or oral admissions rate. This is staggeringly high for any police department, and certainly suggested that some type of corruption was occurring. As a result of the Commission's damning findings, one senior police officer committed suicide and dozens of other ranks retired. Rafferty had been a 17-year veteran in the Homicide Department; but soon after the investigation, he was transferred to the Robbery Squad.

The Appeal

In reality, testimonies of police officers in charge during the arrest and investigation appear to have as many inconsistencies in their stories as does DeFeo. In the pages of DeFeo's 1975 appeal to the New York Supreme Court, Weber made a detailed list of complaints, explaining what he believed to be illegal acts committed by police during their initial twenty-one-hour custodial interrogation period. The appeal also detailed the failure of the Court to recognize the illegalities that took place during that time. As per Arthur, 22 N.Y. 2d, 325, 329: "Once an attorney enters the proceeding, the police may not question the Defendant in the absence of council unless there is an affirmative waiver, in the presence of the attorney, of the defendant's right to counsel" (*People v. Vella* 21 N.Y. 2d 249). Detective Randazzo testified that he personally called the First Precinct and told them that an attorney [Richard Wyssling] for the defendant wanted to speak to him [Ronnie]. R47; A106

Still, Wyssling—an attorney by law, friend of the DeFeo family, and appointed attorney of DeFeo at the time (by his grandfather)— identified himself as such to police, and testified that he was given the run around all night long. Weber contended that Wyssling had officially entered the proceedings at 11:00 p.m. on the night of 13 November 1974, but was still denied access to DeFeo. However, Mindy Weiss (DeFeo's girlfriend at the time) testified that she encountered Wyssling in the Ireland house while she was talking to Detective Grieco. Mindy claims that Wyssling identified himself as Ronnie's lawyer and provided her with his business card (which was later entered into evidence and labeled: "Exhibit C"). Estimates of this time range from between 8:00 p.m. - 8:30 p.m. Weber may have been quite generous by offering that Wyssling joined the proceedings at 11:00 p.m.

It states in *People v. Ramos* 40 N.Y. 2d 610, the Court emphasizes there is no specific manner required for an attorney to "enter the proceedings." If the police have physical control of a *person* and an attorney informs the police that he wishes to speak to that *person*, that *person* has a constitutional right to the assistance of an attorney. Also in *Ramos*, the Court observed: "If in fact the prosecution was in doubt whether an attorney has entered the proceedings, the burden should rest squarely on it to ensure that the defendant's right to counsel be protected. The ambiguity of the lawyer's statement or the manner in which the defendant's attorney went about representing his client cannot be seized upon as a license to play 'fast and loose' with this precious right." (*Ramos*, supra, pgs. 617-618).

SCPD got around this by determining that Ronnie was not considered a suspect until 3:00 a.m., on 14 November 1974. Many find it hard to believe, that Ronnie was not viewed as a suspect until 3:00 a.m. He was certainly no stranger to the SCPD; he appeared drunk and on drugs, he was the only surviving member of the family, and he presented a severely disheveled appearance to police. First, Kelske testified that when Ronnie was leaving the Ireland house at approximately 8:00 p.m., he asked Detective's Randazzo and Napolitano where they were taking him, and they "waived him off." Second, Ronnie was not permitted to drive in his own car from the scene of the crime to the First Precinct. Instead he was escorted in a police car. According to witness testimony, Weber determined that Ronnie had signed the written statement at approximately 10:00 p.m., at which time Sgt. Barylski ordered that he then be taken to headquarters in Hauppauge—where questioning continued for several hours. At 12:00 p.m., Randazzo checked Ronnie's criminal record. Ronnie was denied access to his attorney, family, and friends for more than fourteen hours before the first "Miranda" warnings were given.

DeFeo was interrogated for more than 21 hours, ending at 4:30p.m., on 14 November 1974. Moreover, for the final 7½ hours of the interrogation, Ronnie was questioned without interruption by two teams of police officers in the same small 8x10 "file room" in which he was placed in at 3:00 a.m. Ronnie testified that he was not given any food or drink during the 21 hour period. Police testified that they gave him some food, but none could recollect what he was given. Also in his appeal, Weber contends that police set up an atmosphere that was not conducive to clear thinking, and they deprived Ronnie of several basics rights afforded under the laws of the Constitution of the United States of America. Furthermore, Weber claims, "If the Defendant truly insisted on cooperating with police after they told him 'he was their man,' what right of society or of justice would have been prejudiced, if at that point he were permitted to speak with his family or an attorney?" Weber adds, "Because the police denied him [Ronnie] access to his attorney and family, the Defendant's chances of refuting the Police version of the events of 14 November 1974, are miniscule, because he must rely solely on his own testimony."

Two prior cases that support the appeal speak of the circumstances in which a confession is made. "On the 'totality of the circumstances' in this case, the confession cannot be held to have been voluntary, and its use as evidence against petitioner deprived him of due process of law" *Cf. Davis v. North Carolina,* 384 U. S. 737 (1966). "The 'totality of the circumstances' that preceded the confessions in this case goes beyond the allowable limits…The use of the confessions secured in this setting was a denial of due process" (*Cf. Johnson v. Pennsylvania,* 340 U.S. 881; U.S. Supreme Court - *Fikes v. Alabama,* 352 U.S. 191, 197).

Weber also made a case that his client was denied fair preparation for trial, stating that the "defendant's right to adequately prepare council" was not afforded by the court. Weber was nettled that the court allowed extensive testimony by three officers regarding a burglary of a house next-door to the DeFeo's, and the Brigante-Karl Buick robbery; both of which Ronnie was a suspect in. Weber claimed that these crimes were irrelevant to the murder case, and yet the court allowed extensive testimony on these crimes, "for the sole purpose of leading the jury to believe that DeFeo was a criminal, likely to commit other crimes."

Although Weber makes several good points in the appeal, his insanity defense severely backfired. After studying the various testimonies in this case, it's clear how one-sided the court was in regards to the trial. It appears as though the defense was not afforded the rights dictated under the laws of the United States of America. However, police lucked out, because DeFeo and Weber showed complete incompetency in their approach. Weber was determined to ride-out the insanity plea to the end. He even tried to put a spin on it.

Soon after the appeal, an article appeared in the Chicago Tribune (entitled, *Haunted House Murder - Attorney: Evil Spirit Pushed Killer*) reporting that Weber said that he researched the history of the property and concluded that the land was a "forbidden Indian burial ground." Weber also mentioned that many of the families that lived on the land had also experienced tragedies. He claimed that he intended to move for a new trial for DeFeo, bolstering the insanity argument with the demonic possession theory. It's no wonder why he retracted these statements later and screamed hoax.

"We would respond and oppose such a motion on the grounds that Mr. Weber is commercializing and prostituting these events which resulted in the deaths of the DeFeo family," said Gerald Sullivan in the same article. "His grandiose accounts are good copy, but bad law." Sullivan concluded that, "Satanic possession would not come under the category of mental disease or defect." It's clear that Ronnie DeFeo was involved heavily in the murders in one way or another. It's quite possible that Ronnie did kill all six of his family members. However, it is not society's right to pick and choose who gets a fair trial and who doesn't. Many believe that the investigation was compromised to make sure that Ronnie took the fall for all of the murders. However, from the evidence of this case, it's very likely that there was at least one other accomplice. This theory is corroborated by several officers and medical professionals originally involved. Some of them even believe that there was more than one gun used. Although Ronnie has told several stories, he did mention Dawn as being part of the murders at the 1975 trial. In addition, Ronnie has said (in a Newsday article by Bob Keller entitled, *A Convict's Tale* - 1986), "There's another gun involved. That's a fact!" Coincidentally, the .38 caliber handgun that Ronnie was known to carry around was never recovered.

DNA Testing

Butch still protests the verdict in his case, claiming that Dawn killed everyone, and that he killed only Dawn. One of the original investigators of the house, and then *Channel 5 News* Anchorman, Marvin Scott—now senior correspondent of WB11—recently communicated with Butch. In the WPIX interview (entitled, *Amityville: Horror or Hoax?*), Butch again insisted that it was his sister Dawn DeFeo who killed everyone and that he killed her in self defense while wrestling for the gun. Butch wrote Marvin Scott from jail.

"Really, I need to find a real criminal lawyer, get the DNA testing done, and I am out the door; because the truth speaks for itself," Ronnie stated confidently. DNA testing has been Ronnie's main grouse over the years. According to Ronnie, during the initial custodial interrogation period, he was beaten to a pulp by officers Rafferty and Dunn, and he bled all over his clothes as a result.

Detective George Harrison testified that after Ronnie's oral confession of guilt, he began processing him at 7:00 p.m., on 14 November 1974, at which time Harrison ordered Ronnie to remove his clothing. Ronnie turned over a pair of Brown boots, dungaree trousers, a blue shirt, and a dungaree jacket, which were all collectively labeled "Exhibit 101." The clothes were then turned over to the Suffolk County Lab. Detective Nicholas Severino—the serologist employed by the people—testified that he found blood stains "inside the right and left cuffs of the dungaree jacket." The physical configuration of the DNA—deoxyribonucleic acid—molecule was unearthed in 1953, but the forensic application of DNA fingerprinting was not introduced until 1986. In 1974 ABO (H) typing (or blood-type testing) was the best offered by the system at the time. Severino testified that although he could determine the blood to be *type-A,* all of the DeFeo's except for Louise had *type-A* blood. Severino concluded from this, that he could NOT determine whose blood appeared on appellant's dungarees.

Ronnie claimed that the blood on his clothes was his own, as a result of physical beatings handed down by the interrogating officers. Detective Rafferty testified that Ronnie confessed to him that while he was cleaning up after the murders, he picked up a shell casing that was lying in a pool of Allison's blood, and wiped it on his "pants leg." After retrieving the clothing that Ronnie was wearing at the time of his arrest, police later recovered the contents of the storm drain. The contents in the drain included a pair of blue jeans, and a blue work shirt. Blood was found on the "Pants leg" of the blue jeans; also *Type-A*. These set of clothes were labeled "Exhibit 110." Although it was Detective Harrison who entered the dungaree jacket into evidence and Severino who examined it, neither was questioned by Weber or Sullivan as to the source of the blood stains.

During Sullivan's summation to the jury, he argued that the blood from *Exhibit 101* and *Exhibit 110* were that of the murdered victims. What Sullivan was basing this assumption on is unclear. Lacking proof, Sullivan's statement was pure conjecture. The defense claimed that Ronnie was wearing both the blue jeans and the dungaree jacket at the time of his interrogation, and that the police had somehow switched the blue jeans, placing them in the storm drain so that it appeared as though Ronnie had put them there himself. Once DNA was introduced, in the late 80s, Ronnie immediately filed a 440 motion to vacate judgment. His argument was based on paragraph *(g)* in the motion:

> *"New evidence has been discovered since the entry of a judgment based upon a verdict of guilty after trial, which could not have been produced by the defendant at the trial even with due diligence on his part and which is of such character as to create a probability that had such evidence been received at the trial the verdict would have been more favorable to the defendant; provided that a motion based upon such*

ground must be made with due diligence after the discovery of such alleged new evidence."

In 1990 Ronnie filed suit in the Supreme Court of New York for DNA testing. He received a letter from Suffolk County saying that the "Evidence" (clothing) was "Destroyed." Yet, in August of 1992, attorney, Dennis O'Doherty, discovered the clothing in question. Immediately after that, Suffolk County sent Ronnie a letter of apology, and Judge Stark followed up with his own letter to Ronald DeFeo stating, "If you want the DNA testing, you will have to obtain the monies for the DNA."

Ronnie's grandmother, Angela Brigante, gave Ronnie's then lawyer, Gerald Lotto, $10,000 for DNA testing. Angela Brigante, through her attorney, Gregory Hesterberg, provided Lotto with the $10,000, which was to be used specifically for the forensic investigation (the DNA testing was main purpose). Lotto took the money and deposited it into his personal IOLA Escrow Account (#0144332488) at the Bank of New York, Ronkonkoma, New York. Although Ronnie seemed to meet all of the criteria for DNA testing, the court still denied him.

There were three reasons for the denial—as indicated by Judge Thomas Stark: (1) "The defendant [Ronnie] failed to state 'When and where' his arrest took place." (2) "The clothing in question has been held for 17 years and not suited for DNA testing." (3) "He [Ronnie] has failed to demonstrate the relevancy of any evidence he hopes to produce after the examination of the clothing." Lotto and DeFeo maintain that Ronnie was "beaten upon during his arrest and a confession was coerced from him." Lotto makes mention of Weber several times in his 10 June 1992, Affirmation to the Suffolk County Supreme Court, and is puzzled as to why Weber did not expound upon several pieces of key-evidence that could have helped his client. Lotto claims that "for reasons unknown," Weber did not effectually press the matter of a forced confession at the trial.

In the Affirmation, Lotto criticizes Weber several times for sticking with the "fabricated insanity defense rather than a defense on merits." Lotto seems to accuse Weber, in not so many words, of not using readily available credible evidence that would have helped his client "for reasons only known to him [Weber]." According to Lotto, Weber had demonstrated complete ineffectiveness in the assistance of his client. Lotto also brings up the matter of Reverend McNamara. According to the testimony of Bobby Kelske; while he and Ronnie were being interrogated together at the Ireland home, there was a priest present. Ronnie claims that the priest that Bobby was referring to was Father McNamara. Lotto states that Reverend McNamara "saw the defendant [Ronnie] immediately before his arrest without any injury and subsequent to the arrest with substantial injury." For reasons unknown, Judge Stark would not allow the Reverend to testify at the original trial.

If DeFeo were granted DNA testing on the pants he allegedly wiped his sister Allison's blood on and this proved to be his own blood and not his sister's; this would be proof that Detective Dennis Rafferty perjured himself at the 1975 trial. This may be why Christopher Berry Dee reported that Rafferty said, "Not a chance in hell this stuff [the clothing] will ever be looked at again. We'll make sure of that." It could also prove that a confession was coerced through a beating, and that Ronnie was deprived of effective representation of counsel. On the other hand, if Ronnie was once again "pulling everyone's leg," and the blood was his sister's, then at the very least Ronnie would only be discrediting himself further. Ronnie is well within his rights in this respect. The fact that Ronnie is so adamant about having the testing done and the police are so against it certainly makes one wonder about the motives of police—especially since Ronnie's grandmother has already put up the money for the testing.

After Dawn

Many mysteries still remain in the way that the DeFeo's were murdered. It is likely that we will never get the full story of exactly what happened in the early morning hours of 13 November 1974, at 112 Ocean Avenue in Amityville. But, so many questions remain! Dawn was found dead in the third-floor bedroom. She was allegedly killed in that room as well. What's unusual about this is that many claim that Dawn shared a bedroom with her sister Allison on the second floor. It's been said by some that it was odd that Dawn was sleeping in the third-floor "guest bedroom" when she normally slept in her own bed, which was reportedly on the second-floor with her sister. Many things can be deduced from this, but nothing definitively. Coincidentally she was sleeping in the "guest bedroom" on the night that her whole family was massacred. Is this just another strange coincidence, or is it further evidence of a truth yet told? Did she hear the gunshots and run up to the third floor to hide? Was she involved in the murders in some way? Whatever the conclusion, it stands as another unusual circumstance surrounding one of the most controversial figures in this case: Dawn DeFeo.

Surely, the Paraffin test that was allegedly done on Dawn's hands is a very significant piece of evidence in this case. During Bobby Kelske's cross examination (on pgs. 549 & 550), Gerald Sullivan acknowledges that there were Paraffin tests done on "all six of the deceased bodies, and about a half-a-dozen other people that night." Dr. Adelman also states that there was a paraffin test done on Dawn's hands. However, a request to the Suffolk County P.D. for the tests & results claimed to have been done on Dawn DeFeo's hands came back empty. Police claimed that "After a diligent search, the record cannot be found." This huge mishap by police opens up the door for serious speculation as to the credibility of the SCPD's investigation. Without this evidence, one now has the right to speculate on the accuracy of scientific statements made by Adelman and Sullivan, for lack of proof. Did the results come back negative, or was there evidence in the test that suggests Dawn perhaps fired a gun that night? Lack of receipt, in the form of test results, leads some to consider that there may have been some type of cover-up involved.

Could Dawn have been involved in the murders somehow? The mounting evidence against her—although not conclusive—still suggests a second look at her as a possible suspect in the murders. The fact that Ronnie is not a credible witness should not deter the need to use his words to help decode this mystery. Could allegations of incest between Dawn and her father have played a part in this sinister plot? Neighbor, Ed Kangesier, thinks so! Moreover, Ed believes that others that knew the family were also aware of the possibility of an incestuous relationship. Yet, Ed does not offer that as the only motive; he simply offered that as additional information on the family dynamic that made up the DeFeos from what he knew of them. What Ed believes is that it was a "gang-land killing." Ed claims that he was told this by the Amityville Chief of Police at the time.

Exploring the Possibilities

Unfortunately, it's very difficult to believe anything that Ronnie says, because he has changed his story so many times. During the 1975 trial, Ronnie testified that there were no lights on in the rooms that he fired the shots into. This would mean that he fired the shots into dark rooms and still remained extremely accurate. Couple that with heroine and booze and we see just how spectacular all of these shots had to have been. All eight shots hit their targets precisely. The shooter(s) never missed. Again, under the circumstances that Ronnie described in his testimony at the trial, it seems almost impossible—in more ways than one. According to the testimony of Ronnie's aunt, Mrs. Phyllis Procita—and a discussion that she had with Ronnie's mother, Louise—Ronnie's eye site was horrible. His eye site was so bad, that "Louise was having a hard time filling his prescription." As Phyllis described, "Ronnie never wore his glasses."

Ronnie, himself, said (in a Newsday article by Bob Keller entitled, *A Convict's Tale* - 1986) that after the Amityville movie came out he was sick of being looked at by the other prisoners as being possessed or demonic. It was at that point that Ronnie broke his eighteen-year silence by claiming that he lied about any demons being involved. However, Ronnie acknowledged that he thought that his mind was "playing tricks on him." He said this several times, including under oath at his 1999 Parole Hearing. Does he even have a clear recollection of the night's events; or was he too drugged-up to recall?

"Very often, that is the general consensus when it comes to witnessing paranormal activity," I was told by several paranormal specialists. "You feel like your mind is playing tricks on you." As time goes on, one questions whether the incident was true or just a figment of their imagination. Other widely reported aspects of the paranormal experience are confusion and disorientation. At his 1999 Parole Hearing, Ronnie said, "Exactly what happened in my house [that night], I am not really sure to this day." Ronnie claimed to have black-outs and acknowledged the fact that he had a "serious drug problem" at the time. Ronnie testified that he saw someone, or something, run down the stairs and out the front door after he killed Dawn.

Hans Holzer, author of three Amityville books, claimed that the sound barrier is blocked when there is heavy paranormal activity occurring. Ronnie asserts that there was complete silence in the house and that he never even heard any of the shots being fired. In fact, no one in the neighborhood came forward saying that they heard any shots either. William Weber had a test conducted before the trial on the sound that a .35 caliber Marlin rifle makes. The test results proved that the firing of that particular weapon could be heard some 5-blocks away. However, all the neighbors interviewed claimed that they did not hear any gunshots. Furthermore, Suffolk County Ballistics expert, Detective Alfred DellaPenna, testified that, from his analysis, no silencer was used, make-shift or otherwise.

Former Deputy Head of New Scotland Yard's Forensic Firearms Laboratory, Brian J. Heard, who has over 35-years experience in ballistics said, [25] "The rifle used was designed for deer or black bear hunting, it had a six round tubular magazine which meant he had to reload at least once. It fires a projectile of 200 grains with a velocity of about 2100 feet per second with a kinetic energy of about 1970 ft. lbs. This is an extremely noisy combination and if fired in a house would result in probable hearing loss for anyone in close proximity. An effective silencer could have been fitted considerably reducing the noise of the discharge but as the bullet is still traveling well above the speed of sound the noise of the bullet breaking the sound barrier would still be extremely noisy, well above that caused by a car back firing as a benchmark."

On 1 May 2000, Ronnie wrote a letter to a producer who was going to pay him for an interview. In the letter Ronnie Wrote, "...it was cold-blooded murder, Period! No ghosts; No demons, just three people in which I was one." In the letter, Ronnie corroborates that he and two others committed the murders.

Ric Osuna, author of *The night the DeFeos Died*, claimed [13] that Butch's alleged first wife, Geraldine DeFeo, told him, "Butch felt insulted that his insanity could be questioned. Weber had to convince him by alternative means. He promised Butch that he'd get out in two to three years, and that he'd be rich from the book's success." The plot thickens! In a 1992 article by the Associated Press (entitled, *'Amityville' Killer Says Sister Did It*), Ronnie says that he would have told the truth at the 1975 trial, but Weber coerced him into entering an insanity plea in order to up the price of the book and movie offers. "The whole thing was about money," DeFeo announced. "Weber told me we would get a lot of money from the book rights," DeFeo asserts. "He said I would go to a nut house, I would get out, and get my family's entire estate."

On 23 July 1988, Butch's best friend, Barry Springer, said (in his affidavit to Suffolk County Police) that William Weber had told him that he was approached about a book deal even before Butch's trial had started. Somehow, Weber was able to convince Butch to plead not guilty by reason of insanity, and the game had begun. According to other signed affidavits [50], Weber went around to every defense witness attempting to coerce them into testifying that Butch was insane. Others who testified for the defense declared, later in sworn affidavits, that not only did Weber coerce them into testifying that Ronnie was insane, but also that Weber would not let them say what they really believed.

According to both Mr. and Mrs. Nonnewitzes' statements (in sworn affidavits) in November of 1989, both claimed that Ronnie's court appointed lawyer, William Weber, rehearsed them to testify only about the things that were consistent with his insanity defense. "My testimony," both Mr. and Mrs. Nonnewitz wrote, "if it would have been allowed by William Weber, would have shed an entirely different light on the jury and the court and changed the verdict in this case." In each of the affidavits, they also explained that they both informed Weber before the trial that Suffolk County Detective, Dennis Rafferty, and another officer—presumably Detective Lt. Robert Dunn—both visited their Amityville home to ask them if they knew whether Ronnie had a .38 Caliber hand gun and if they knew where it was. William Weber never pursued this very important issue at the trial. Linnea Nonnewitz did not believe that Ronnie was insane. In her affidavit she stated, "Being high and drunk on liquor or drugs does not constitute insanity or an insane person."

In an interview with Ric Osuna [79], well-known criminologist, Christopher Berry-Dee, gives his opinion of the DeFeo trial in brutally honest fashion, explaining how it was mishandled terribly by Suffolk County Law enforcement. In response to Suffolk County's investigation of the case, Berry-Dee explains, "I believe that Gerald Sullivan knows more about the true facts of the DeFeo case than he says he does. However, the entire prosecution case is linked together in a most incestuous manner from top to bottom. We have a cast of crooked cops, bungling and dishonorable attorneys, and a judge whose behavior borders on criminal."

When asked to describe Ronnie DeFeo, Berry-Dee said, "He is arrogant, self-opinionated, and self-serving. He is a man who actually believes that he is an important character when he is no more than a bullying thug. His only claim to fame being that he is serving a handful of life sentences for the murder of his family and a number of motion pictures and books have contrived to keep his black-name in the public domain ever since." When asked to describe Judge Stark's actions in the DeFeo case, Berry-Dee said, "I am happy to state for the record that this judge's behavior from the outset is a damning indictment of the American Justice System when it is allowed to go wrong. I would have great difficulty in finding another example to match Judge Stark's outrageous behavior anywhere in the world." Berry-Dee does not believe that Ronnie acted alone in the murders. "With the evidence that is available, I believe that it is highly likely that Dawn DeFeo committed the murders and Ronald DeFeo shot her," Berry-Dee offers.

Kicking up dust

On 30 November 2000, Ronald DeFeo, Jr., met with Ric Osuna, the author of *The Night the DeFeos Died*, which was published in 2002. According to Osuna, DeFeo claimed that he had committed the murders "out of desperation," and that his sister Dawn and two unnamed friends assisted in the murders. Osuna claims that, "Attempts to contact the two alleged accomplices have failed." Osuna also writes that one is in the witness protection program and the other died in January of 2001. It's not hard to figure out who Osuna was alluding to in regard to one of the alleged assailants, considering Ronnie's running mate, Bobby Kelske, died of cancer on 1 January 2001 at the age of 50-years old. Even the first officer on the scene, Kenneth Greguski, finds it hard to believe that Ronnie was the sole killer. Greguski—who later became Amityville's Police Chief—said [G], "How could one guy do all this damage, kill six people with a .35 caliber Marlin rifle? It makes a lot of noise! How could he [Ronnie] do this and nobody was able to get up and get away? It was ah, hard to believe."

Bobby Kelske took the stand in 1975 at Ronnie's trial. During cross examination, Suffolk County's Assistant District Attorney and Prosecutor, Gerald Sullivan, grilled Kelske about a death that happened a year prior to the DeFeo murders. Sullivan pressed Kelske, implying that he and Ronnie had an argument inside Henry's bar with an unnamed man, and then followed him outside after the dispute and drowned him in the Amityville creek. Did Bobby Kelske have a secret side that was never made public? The following is an excerpt from Kelske's testimony while on the stand in the 1975 DeFeo trial.

> ***Sullivan:*** *I take you back to November of 1973, and ask you if on that occasion during that month in that year you, in the presence of Ronald DeFeo, followed a patron out of the bar, took him to the Amityville River and drowned him?*
>
> ***Kelske:*** *No Sir.*

Sullivan: Did you not take money from his wallet before throwing him into the Amityville River?

Kelske: No Sir.

Sullivan: Was this not a patron who had gotten drunk and boisterous inside the bar?

Kelske: Excuse me? Am I supposed to have drowned this person? Is that what you are accusing me of?

Sullivan: Would you answer the question Mr. Kelske?

Kelske: No Sir.[I did not]

Gates, Osuna, and the FLIP-FLOP

Ric Osuna's opinion on the haunting has changed dramatically from one extreme to the other a couple of times over the years. Osuna's "Flip-Flop" is well documented. According to emails from Osuna, obtained by Amityville enthusiast, Jason Pyke [48], Ric operated an Amityville website back in 1999, which was a pro-haunting website. The evidence that Osuna presented was so convincing that the *History Channel* asked him to assist them in the making of their upcoming Amityville documentary.

[85] On his original website Ric said, *"My name is Ric Osuna, and I have been following the Amityville case since I was six years old. It all started when I saw my mother and sister scared silly from reading Jay Anson's The Amityville Horror."* Osuna later read Kaplan's Conspiracy book when it came out, and believed it. Therefore, when he began his website he thought it was all a hoax!"

"In March 1999, horror writer Daniel Farrands contacted me because he was quite impressed with my extensive research." This was true, even though Ric didn't believe in the story. When he joined the *Histories Mysteries* show (on the History Channel) he found out that George Lutz was living just ten-minutes away. So, the

two of them met up in a local Starbucks. George showed him the black and white Warrens' photos (including *Ghost Boy*) and Ric came away a believer, after just one meeting. In the early 1980s George decided to publish the photos that he showed Osuna, along with other photos, as *The Amityville Horror Picture Book*. This book would be a visual compilation which would serve as an accompaniment to Anson's book.

However, for one reason or another, it never happened. When George's interest in Amityville was rekindled in 1999 he decided to finally publish the picture-book, but he needed someone to write the text. Ric put himself forward, and a contract was signed soon after. Ric, however, had other ideas. Osuna decided that he was going to write the ultimate "tell-all" book, despite this not being what he had signed up for. Osuna submitted a book proposal entitled, *The Amityville Horror: Discovering the Truth,* but it was rejected for various reasons, not to mention that it wasn't what was ordered. Ric agreed to go back to the Picture-Book project (this time as a CD-ROM) while it was suggested he work on his writing skills.

In a *Long Island Voice* article back in October of 1999 [10], Ric Osuna claimed (on pg. 3) that he had new information that "is gonna blow everyone away."

"It's "proof," he says, that the house "truly is haunted." A short time after Osuna wrote the book proposal; he and George reportedly had a falling out. In an article by Carolyn James of the Amityville Record (entitled: *Why Hollywood's Version of DeFeo Murders Isn't Amityville's,* 2000), Osuna said the reason for his departure was because "The History Channel was more interested in ratings than at getting the truth." In fact, this was not the case. Instead, Osuna decided to write his own book, not about the Lutzes, but about the DeFeo murders instead. Osuna wrote a letter to George Lutz, denouncing the rights to the 44-page book proposal that he had written. Osuna went on a few message boards claiming that he now had proof that the haunting was a hoax, and that he'd show proof in his upcoming book.

Apparently, a large percentage of this 'so called' proof came from a woman who called herself "Geraldine Gates DeFeo." Geraldine claimed that she was married to Ronnie DeFeo, Jr., prior to the murders, and that she knew the DeFeo family well. Geraldine claimed to have insight and information on Weber and the Lutzes, and also that the haunting was a hoax. Almost immediately after Osuna met Geraldine Gates "DeFeo," he somehow teamed up with her, and flipped over to the Amityville hoax theorists. How did this happen? Osuna claims that Geraldine contacted him when she found out that Osuna was part of an Amityville documentary that was in the works. But what really happened was that some guy, calling himself Michael, was posting on the net claiming he was Ronald DeFeo Jr.'s son! He also put letters on EBay[1] claiming that, "These letters were written to his first wife who was married to him from July 1970 to sometime in 1978." He would write "I have recently found out I am the son of Ronald DeFeo," and he claimed that Geraldine was his mother. One of these posts was spotted by Kevin Wagner of the Amityville Hoax site, who alerted Osuna. Soon after, Osuna posted a cryptic message to Kevin on his board - *"I have contacted this person and yes he is the son of you know-who."*

After Ric met Geraldine, Michael began posting on Osuna's board saying how they missed him and joked about uncooked chicken. Osuna joked back, but he never introduced him as DeFeo's son. However, it was quite clear that's what he was saying on other boards. At this point – mid 2000 – the 1986 Keeler *Newsday* interview was undiscovered, which was the article where Geraldine claims that Butch and her had a daughter. When it surfaced, Osuna dismissed it as garbage. And then, on his first *Lou Gentile* interview, Osuna mentions them having a daughter! By this time, Osuna had deleted his 2000 forum, so all evidence of Michael was gone. Later on, after this fiasco, Geraldine told Amityville expert, Jason Pyke, that Michael was her adopted son, and that he was deluded[2]. Is Geraldine the real deal or a fraud?

According to Osuna's book, Geraldine was married to Butch back in the early 1970s, before the murders took place. The book

---

[1] EBAY http://amityvilletruth.freeservers.com/ebay.htm

[2] Michael's posts can be read here:
(http://amityvilletruth.freeservers.com/michael.htm).

also claims that Geraldine was present when William Weber and the Lutzes met and were concocting the hoax story. Geraldine claims that the meeting took place in a local bar in 1975. Geraldine also said that Father Ray told her that the voice that said "Get out," was George Lutzes' voice on a tape recorder. In the 1986 interview with *Newsday* (entitled: *A Convict's Tale* by Bob Keeler), Geraldine said that the two [her and Ronnie] met just before thanksgiving, 1973, at a bar in Manhattan called, *The Ninth Circle*. Geraldine and Ronnie both claimed, at one point, that they began dating at that time and had a child on 21 August 1974. Butch corroborated this story for several years; but now says adamantly that he met Geraldine Gates in 1985, and not before that. Although Butch is proven to be a compulsive liar, this happens to be true.

Ric Osuna currently runs a website called, *The Amityville Murders*, where he has an article written about Geraldine and his perception of her involvement. There, Osuna writes [53]: *"Butch's two friends, Barry Springer and Chuck Tewksbury, wrote affidavits attesting to the fact that Geraldine was Butch's wife prior to the murders and the mother of Butch's daughter."* These two affidavits were written in 1989 by two of Ronnie's closest friends. Their reasoning was obvious: they were going along with the story that Ronnie and Geraldine had made-up in order to help Ronnie, however wrong it was. Osuna fails to acknowledge that Springer has written a handful of affidavits following his 1989 affidavit, and all of them give detailed reasons why he lied in 1989. Moreover, when Springer was interviewed by the Suffolk County District Attorney's office in 1990, he told them that when he received the affidavit, it was already prepared, and all he did was sign it [X].

In an affidavit dated 14 August 2004, Ronnie's best friend, Barry Springer, stated that "Geraldine Gates was in fact NOT Ronnie's wife, and that Ronnie had only first met her in March of 1985." Springer writes that Geraldine came to Ronnie at the *Auburn Correctional facility* "with a message from the MOB." According to Springer, the MOB was asking Ronnie to date Geraldine to help out a fellow prisoner in some way. The prisoner's name on the affidavit was doused with white-out, other than the first letter of his first name "*J.*" In that same affidavit, Barry Springer wrote, "I, Barry Springer,

Chuck Tewksbury, John Carswell, Frank Davidge, Steve Hicks, John Bello, Rod Hicks, Grace Fagan, Mindy Weiss, etc., were with Ronald all of the time. As I, Barry Springer, spoke to all of the above, they will verify in a court of law that there was no wife or Geraldine Gates or a daughter in 1974, or any time of Ronald's life."

In another affidavit (dated 21 September 2004), Springer wrote: "At no time was Ronnie DeFeo married nor did he have any children. There was no Geraldine Gates, or whatever name she used. All Ronnie's friends along with George Brigante (Ronnie's cousin) and Phyllis DeFeo Procita (Ronnie's aunt) will all verify the above to be true and correct."

Geraldine and Butch were both using each other for various reasons. At Butch's 1992 appeal hearing, he stated that Geraldine's brother, Richard Romondoe, was with him during the murders and could verify that he [Ronnie] only killed Dawn. All attempts by police to locate Romondoe, or even verify his existence, came up empty. What police were not told was that Romondoe came from Geraldine and Ronnie's imagination. It was a poor attempt by them to try and exonerate Ronnie from committing any of the murders, except for Dawn. Geraldine said that her bother Richard accompanied Ronnie to 112 Ocean Avenue that night, and was there to witness that Ronnie only killed Dawn in self-defense (in two separate 1989 affidavits (one signed by Geraldine Gates & the other by Richard Romondoe [s]).

According to Osuna [53], "Geraldine and her daughters only denied the relationship with the DeFeos out of fear." Geraldine's daughter, Stacy, claimed: "The cops persecuted my mother for information." Geraldine claims she was a suspect in the murders after she came forward in the early 1980s. However, no proof exists that she knew Ronnie DeFeo Jr., before 1985, except for the bogus affidavits that Springer and Tewksbury wrote in 1989.

According to Barry Springer's (25 August 2003) affidavit, Geraldine contacted him and his wife [Tracy Balk Springer] and said that she was going to retain Mr. Barry Scheck (Attorney at law) for Ronnie's pending DNA appeal. Geraldine claimed that she needed to obtain some of Ronnie's legal materials that Barry had been holding for safe keeping. Geraldine entered the Springer household on 4

August 2000, with two men that she introduced as "investigators." One of these so called investigators was Ric Osuna; "Scheck" was not present. Barry Springer remembers falling asleep at some point during the encounter. When he awoke, his wife Tracy informed him that they had gone, but they had taken some of Ronnie's stuff with them. At the request of Barry's wife, Geraldine made a list of the stuff that she took. This included, legal transcripts, videos, photos, and so on.

Springer didn't feel that they had the right to take most of the things that they took, and he notified Ronnie a few days later. Ronnie was furious and ordered Springer to contact Geraldine and have her bring back his property immediately! Geraldine returned some of Ronnie's property, but not all of it. Apparently, they took this stuff for Osuna and his book. Weeks later it was reported that Osuna used some of the information for his website. Geraldine scheduled to visit Ronnie and bring along Mr. Scheck with her. In November of 2000, Geraldine arrived at the prison—not with Mr. Scheck, but with Ric Osuna. The two met with Ronnie for about ninety-minutes, not the six-hours that Osuna claims in his book. Apparently, Ronnie was so infuriated with Geraldine that he stormed back into the prison, after only meeting for a short time.

Joseph Poette, an inmate at the Green Haven Correctional Facility at the time, stated (in his affidavit, 2003 [T]) that Ronnie was "complaining that he'd been 'suckered' by his ex-wife, because she brought a writer, not a lawyer. Ronnie was very upset." Poette also remembers Ronnie saying, "I'm not telling them anything." Poette says that this was Ronnie's way of telling everyone that this [Osuna's story] was going to be "another fairy tale, not the truth."

Another inmate, Hasson Zarif, said (in his affidavit, 2003 [U]) he remembers that Ronnie wasn't gone for very long, which Zarif claimed was unusual for prison visits. Zarif recalls that Ronnie was "angry" and "frustrated" after the visit. He remembers Ronnie complaining that he'd been "suckered" by his ex-wife into a meeting with a writer. Ronnie was complaining about "another book of lies," according to Zarif, and he heard Ronnie say, "I'm not telling them anything."

Inmate, Jeffrey Satless, remembers (in his affidavit, 2003 [V]) Ronnie being upset. Ronnie first got angry when his ex-wife was late, he says. The meeting was scheduled for early morning, and when they didn't show by 11:00 a.m., the prison locked down morning visitations, forcing Ronnie to wait longer. The prison resumed visitations at 11:30 p.m., at which time Ronnie was sent to the visiting room. All three prisoners said that Ronnie returned at 1:00 p.m., just after lunch. Satless recalls Ronnie being "visibly agitated" upon his return. All three stories from each of the men were nearly identical. Satless remembers trying to calm Ronnie down, but Ronnie kept repeating, "She was supposed to bring Barry Scheck, not some writer." These incidents sparked a feud between Osuna, Gates, and DeFeo that still resonates to this day. Ronnie has filed criminal complaints and lawsuits against Gates and Osuna for their actions. The verdict on these charges is still pending.

So, what's the real story?

Geraldine's life plays out like a classic con-artist movie. She has more names than you can count, infamous MOB ties, and a laundry list of criminal offenses. The fact is that Geraldine and Ronnie were never legally married, and the two never had a child together. Prior to 1974, Geraldine was married to Fredrick Cory. After they divorced, Geraldine married her second husband, Joseph Pisani, in April of 1974. Later that same year they had a daughter, Stephanie Pisani. Stephanie is the child that Geraldine claims is Ronnie's, but Stephanie's birth certificate clearly states Joseph Pisani as the father.

In 1978, Geraldine married her third husband, Gerald H. Gates, in New Jersey. In 1980, both Gerald and Geraldine were convicted of grand larceny in New York State. Geraldine served fourteen-months in Bedford Hills Correctional Facility, and Gerald served the same in Attica State Prison. However, in Keeler's 1986 article (mentioned above), Geraldine said that Ronnie had sent her away to keep her and their child safe. For years she claimed she couldn't see Ronnie. This led to her writing $78,000 in bad checks, she stated. As a result, Geraldine said that she spent fourteen-months in prison. This was all part of the elaborate scheme that the two had devised. Geraldine covered her past by changing details and stating that her maiden name was Rullo.

As Barry Springer explained, Ronnie and Geraldine met for the first time in Auburn Correctional Facility in 1985. The couple ran into problems shortly after, when the prison made an announcement that they were going to ban her visits. This was because she was an ex-con on parole, and New York State Law prohibits ex-cons on parole from visiting prison facilities, unless they're an immediate family member. It was at this point that Ronnie reportedly paid a Corrections Officer of the prison $200.00 to get Geraldine an ID with the last name "DeFeo" written on it. In a lawsuit DeFeo filed against Osuna in 2003, Ronnie claimed that Corrections Officer, Mark Stagwall, told him that his mother was an employee of the Cayuga County Sherriff's Department, and she could obtain a fake ID for Geraldine. Geraldine allegedly paid Stagwall's mother $200.00 to print up the fake ID for her with the name Geraldine DeFeo on it. The picture-ID was issued on 16 July 1985, by NY's Cayuga County Sheriff's Department.

The visits to Ronnie continued, unabated. During this time, Ronnie was still fighting over his mother and father's estate. One stipulation of the court said, "The only way to accommodate the settlement is if Ronnie was married and had a child at the time of his incarceration." The two devised a plan: they decided to pass-off Ronnie as the legal father of Geraldine's daughter, Stephanie. Taking the plan a step further, the two got married on 5 July 1989. Since Geraldine was already married to Gerald Gates at the time, she singed the marriage certificate as Geraldine Romondoe—another one of her many aliases.

Their lies grew bigger and bigger as time went on. With Ronnie's 1992 appeal hearing coming up, Geraldine and Ronnie decided to concoct another enormous lie. They both made-up a fictional character that they named, Richard Romondoe. This made up character, they'd say, was Geraldine's brother. Their aim was to say that Richard was with Ronnie during the murders and a witness that Dawn killed everyone, and then Ronnie killed Dawn. This is also stated in Richard Romondoe's affidavit. Richard, they said, had disappeared soon after. In a voluntary statement made by Geraldine to Detective Allen Watterson of the Suffolk County PD (1990 [Z]), she claimed that they both [her and Ronnie] created two homemade affidavits attesting to the Richard Romondoe story that they had just fabricated. Geraldine took the two affidavits—one signed Geraldine DeFeo and the other that Ronnie had signed, "Richard Romondoe"—to a notary in Pennsylvania.

The notary was a friend of Geraldine's by the name of, Donald Brink, located in Great Bend, PA. Brink notarized the affidavits without question, even though he knew that Geraldine's last name was Gates; and even though Richard Romondoe did not appear before him and swear to the validity of the affidavit with his signature on it. Osuna claims that Geraldine refused to testify for Ronnie at his 1992 appeals hearing [53], but he again fails to acknowledge that Geraldine not only filled out an affidavit detailing the fabricated story of Richard Romondoe in her own words; she also had the affidavits illegally notarized by one of her friends.

Moreover, Osuna fails to acknowledge the letter written by Ronnie's then lawyer, Gerald Lotto, addressed to Ronnie regarding the fabricated story. In the letter (dated 10 September 1992), Lotto writes: "You will recall that although she [Geraldine] originally informed investigators that Richard Romondoe did exist, she later telephoned me [Lotto] and stated that if called to testify, she [Geraldine] would be required to tell the truth, which was that you [Ronnie] and she [Geraldine] made up that story." Lotto goes on to say, "You [Ronnie] told me not to seek her testimony…" So, it was Ronnie that informed his lawyer that he did not want Geraldine to testify, and Geraldine would have testified, but she would have been compelled to tell the truth out of fear of perjury.

In a letter to the Dutchess County Courthouse (5 September 2003), Linnea Nonnewitz (the DeFeo's housekeeper at the time of the murders) debunked Geraldine's claims in Osuna's book. The following is an excerpt from the letter written by Linnea Nonnewitz.

"Please be advised Ms. Geraldine Gates and I never met at the home of the DeFeo's. In the book, 'The Night the DeFeos Died,' Ms. Gates stated that I, Linnea Nonnewitz met her at

John DeFeo's communion party, which is not true. I first met Ms. Gates in 1985...I truly hope this will help clear up some of the lies that were told in the book, 'The Night the DeFeos Died,' that pertained to me."

All of their lying efforts were in vain when then Suffolk County Assistant District Attorney (SCDA), Karen Peterson, exposed Geraldine and Ronnie's lies in a thirteen page affidavit in 1990. The SCDA's staff did more than a thorough job debunking Gates and DeFeo's scams. Peterson says:

"The affidavit of Geraldine DeFeo a/k/a Geraldine Gates must be dismissed as it is totally untrue and lacks any factual support. Initially, Geraldine Gates married Fred Cory, not Ronald DeFeo at the Garfield Grant Hotel in Long Branch, N.J., and it is that marriage license that Ronald DeFeo altered to establish that he and Geraldine were married. Secondly, the daughter that Geraldine speaks of is not Ronald DeFeo's daughter, but is Joseph Pisani's daughter, as is evidence by her birth certificate."

Peterson and the SCDA staff interviewed a number of people regarding the existence of Richard Romondoe. Some of those interviewed include Geraldine's adopted father, Ralph Rullo, her next door neighbor, her landlady (The address provided on Richard's affidavit was Geraldine's), her two real brothers Peter and James Striano, her adoptive mother, Barry Springer, Chuck Tewksbury, Gerald Gates, and a slew of others. Peterson and her staff also ran checks for a driver's license, criminal history, criminal complaints in NY, NJ, and PA, telephone records, and a nationwide credit search. Everyone interviewed denied the existence of a Richard Romondoe, and there were no records of him anywhere.

All of these and other lies only hurt Ronnie further, and certainly played a part in the denial of his appeal for DNA testing, as well as hurt all of his other appeals. Fast forward to the year 2000, when Geraldine and Osuna met. After all was said and done, Osuna wrote the book, *The Night the DeFeos Died,* passing Geraldine's story off as true. It's hard to believe that Osuna has not read these prior documents, each clearly discrediting Geraldine beyond a shadow of a doubt.

Who let the dogs out?

[3]In May of 2002, Gerald and Geraldine Gates were visited at their home of 18-years in Deposit, NY, by Animal Control Officer, George Zandt, after the town conducted a census of the dog population. From this census, they uncovered several unlicensed dogs that led them to the Gates residence on Beebe Hill Road. What they found was not a pleasant site! Zandt entered the home, and after a brief search, he uncovered close to 100 dogs in the Gates household, most were sickly. Eighty-eight dogs were seized initially from the Gates home and brought to *Delaware Valley Humane Society* in Sidney, NY. A large percentage of the dogs that were seized had medical problems such as, eye infections, tumors, as well as not being sprayed or neutered. To make matters worse, the couple had already been involved in a similar case a few years earlier, said President of the shelter, Julie Byrnes. "We are very upset that this could happen again," Byrnes said in disgust. "These people have to be dealt with." Charges were brought against the couple for animal cruelty and being unlicensed.

Gerald Gates claimed that he didn't know how many dogs he and his wife had until they were taken away. The charges were only brought up against Gerald, who was charged with 69 counts of having unlicensed dogs. Geraldine said she realized the number of animals was "beyond her control," but she disputed any cruelty charges. Although Gerald (a local construction worker) pled not guilty to the charges, he was eventually fined $1,725 in August of 2002. The town left the couple with five dogs that had been sprayed and neutered prior to the inspection. The court also ordered that the couple is not permitted to accept or buy any more dogs.

Some neighbors interviewed showed their anger over the situation. Local Deposit resident, Robert Briggs, said, "Finally the

---

[3] Daily Star articles (see end note 57)

town took action! During the summers, the smell from the house was unbearable," Briggs commented. He also said that there was "constant barking" coming from the house and it was very disturbing. More problems arose when the dogs were taken to the shelter. Overcrowded conditions made it almost impossible to treat the dogs adequately. Furthermore, of the 88 dogs taken from the couple, 25 puppies were born in the shelter. This made it even harder for the dogs to receive the necessary care. The Sidney shelter eventually contacted other shelters for help boarding the animals after they had been seen by the veterinarian. "People have to be more responsible," Byrnes said. "Pets are not a throw-away item!"

Mr. Postman

Recently, radio host, Lou Gentile, sent Ronnie a letter in jail concerning the murders and to get his take on Ric Osuna's claims. Ronnie wrote Gentile back and seemed very agitated that his own lies were once again coming back to haunt him. The following is Ronnie DeFeo's written response to Gentile's questions:

Dear Mr. Gentile,

Let me begin by introducing myself. I am Ronald DeFeo Junior, the only person who has actual knowledge of what actually occurred on the night the DeFeos died and I have not collaborated with Ric Osuna or any other person or entity on this matter. Mr. Osuna is a fraud perpetrating yet another hoax on the public using my name as his source, a lie as you will soon find out.

To begin with, Geraldine Gates was never legally my wife nor have we ever had relations that could of led to her child. I met Geraldine while I was incarcerated in 1985 and therefore she never knew my family or been to my family's home. Her conception of our "married life" stems from a never consummated ceremony that took place at the time she was still married to her first husband, Mr. Gates. The marriage, if you wish to call it such, was dissolved by court order on the grounds that she could not be married twice at one time. This was prior to be allowed a "family reunion visit" whereby we could have had relations. As for her daughter Stephanie, the fact is that she is 28 and I first met her mother in

1985. That should cast extreme doubt on my fathering her unless you think that I am capable of siring a child years before even meeting the mother. Prison records will confirm that Mrs. Gates and I never were legally married and that we never had any relationship that could of let to any child except in Geraldine's imagination, as was her idea of marriage, for which any male would have been arrested on the grounds of bigamy.

As for Ric Osuna, he is nothing but a fraud and a liar. He came to visit me with Geraldine and once I found out the nature of his visit, I left the visiting room, which can be attested to by the records and people present. I never helped him with his book, nor did I ever authorize him to use my name as one of the sources or as a co-author. In fact, I wrote the District Attorney of Suffolk County as a criminal complaint against both him and Geraldine Gates charging one, criminal impersonation, two, solicitation without a license and three, misrepresentation with the intent to commit the act of fraud. If this sounds like aiding in the writing of his book then something is wrong with the English language I learned. Mr. Osuna visited a number of my friends stating that he was an investigator for Mr. Barry Sheck and was helping in an action that was pending before the court. He took my legal papers from one couple and I have been fighting for their return ever since. Some were returned but I fear that all the documents were not. That is theft by deception as it was accomplished without my consent or knowledge. Mr. Sheck has never represented me and he can attest to that fact. Mr. Osuna's only concern was the writing of his novel and how he could obtain information for it. All he cares about is the money that he can and will make off me and my family.

To prove this, he has turned my family gravesite into a tourist attraction. He has set up his own "charity fund" to collect money, ostensibly, for the upkeep of graves, soliciting on the internet for that purpose, again without my consent, knowledge or permission. He continues to perpetrate this fraud even after I have repeatedly asked him to stop. There is no limit to his ego and his lies continue to pile up as each new day passes. He has even taken it upon himself to write the division of parole on my behalf, but his letter falls far short of wanting my release and is more in the nature of keeping me here to I will not have access to areas such as the internet to purposely protest his invasion of my privacy and impeach his "story" or for that matter the police or courts where I could seek prosecution in an action in appropriate manner. As long as I am behind a 40 foot wall, he feels safe and secure to perpetuate his lies without fear of being found out for what he is, a liar and a fraud. His actions are those of a criminal and as I live totally surrounded by the criminal element, I should know. It takes on to know one as the saying goes. And since I have been behind bars for almost 28 years, I think I fit the bill.

At the moment, I have been unable to obtain a copy of his book so I can not accurately comment on his editions or rendition of the event. I do know that he has made mention that Donald kelske was one of the killers. I learned that from his son Brian, who also gave me your name and address. A copy of his letter to me is enclosed. Why he used Donald's name is obvious, we were friends and he is now dead so he can't refute the lie. Never did I mention Donald's name in connection with that evening, so there is no basis of this alleged fact from Mr. Osuna. Brian has heard these allegations before but has never heard them from me and I am the only person capable of telling the actual accounting of the event of that evening. Mr. Osuna can not, Geraldine Gates can't. Neither were present. I am the only person alive who knows the story and I have never told it, not to the police, the district attorney, the court, the parole board or any writer. Thus, Mr. Osuna is only capable of writing fiction. Unfortunately, he reports his fiction as a true accounting and the public is again the brunt of yet another hoax.

I am enclosing a few of the letters and internet messages that have been forwarded to me, so you can see for yourself a little of the events leading up to this. Mr. Osuna is not what he claims to be. He wrote a Novel, nothing more than the Lutzes did in having their "true story" written, The Amityville Horror. No matter what Mr. Osuna claims, this is about money and a lot of it. He has no interest in me other than using my name to make his fortune. The events of the night are "his facts" written from reports by police and alleged interviews with others, however, the only true accounting of that night could ever come from me and I have not spoken of it to him or anyone else. And until I write a book the true accounting will always be solely with me. However, I have no desire to write or even aid in writing any story thus the true account of the night will never come. At the moment you are the only media source I have contacted and that is due to Brian's letter to me. As you are urging him to speak I felt it necessary that you know that he knows nothing of that evening. He wasn't present, nor anyone else that is capable of telling the story. Like Mr. Osuna, he can only give his opinion or his thoughts of what might have occurred, not what actually did occur. Only I can do that, so until then, then night will remain one of speculation and surmise.

However, Mr. Osuna's claim is for reality and truth, but his real motive is the sale of his Novel and I would imagine the movie rights when they are offered. Yes, his motive is money, nothing more. My problem now is obtaining a copy in order to lodge a federal criminal complaint to the proper magistrate. My intention is to put the record straight, Mr. Osuna is not working with or for me. He can not speak for me, nor can the events of the night in question be accurate because "his facts" are just that, his. Unless he has added forgery to his criminal agenda, he cannot produce one document signed by me to prove his claim that I helped him author his book or that I even aided him in his fact-finding. Mr. Osunas only interest is money and how he can make it off of me at the moment. I can only hope that this is helpful in your search for the true facts about Mr. Osuna's claims and accuracy. If your search was for the truth, you now have it. I am available if you need any more information to address this slander and fraud publicly in your forum. Thank you for your interest.

Ronald DeFeo, Jr.

Osuna's expertise research on the case has been compromised by his belief in a proven con-artist. But, Perhaps a more worthy discovery made by Osuna was the location of the DeFeo's dog, Shaggy, during the time of the murders. Several sources claim that the Shaggy was tied up out by the boathouse and was barking violently in reaction to the brutality occurring in the house. Among some of these sources are Gerald Sullivan in his book *High Hopes*, and *The Real Life Amityville Horror* article at tru.tv.com. However, police reports reveal that the dog was inside the house during the murders. Osuna claims that "the house was quiet, except for the barking of Shaggy…who was tied up to the inside of the kitchen's back door" [P]. Osuna explains that the family routinely tied the animal there, because he was not completely housebroken. However, earlier reports indicate that the dog was not tied to anything, and was roaming the house freely during the murders; this led to speculation that the intruder was "someone the family had known" [E].

If the dog was inside of the house at the time of the murders, which it was in all likelihood, this adds another quandary to a story already shrouded in mystery. If the dog was tied-up on the inside of the house during the murders; how could neighbors have heard the dog barking, but not the gun shots? Since it was winter, and late at night, it would be safe to assume that the back door (that the dog was tied-up to) was closed and locked. This being the case makes it harder to believe that eight shots from a .35 caliber Marlin rifle could not be heard, yet, a wildly barking dog inside the house could be identified by several neighbors. Police claimed that the house muffled the sound of the shots. However, many people who have been in the house reported that "street noise" could be heard from inside. Others reported that sounds from the second floor could be easily heard on the third. Butch himself testified that he heard his sister and father fighting on the first floor while he was on the second. The noise was so loud that Butch "couldn't take it anymore."

Using a .35 caliber Marlin rifle, DeFeo's defense team performed sound tests. The result was that the rifle could be heard from "five-blocks away." Moreover, a sound of that nature is more likely to catch people's attention. Ronnie testified that he "didn't hear the shots as he was firing the gun." All neighbors questioned said that they never heard any gun-fire. Allegedly, the murdered DeFeo's pretty much slept through the blasts. The only common factor here is that no one reports hearing the shots, even the killer. Was the sound barrier blocked by evil spirits, as theorized by Hans Holzer? Or could this be easily explained had we received more information? Lorraine Warren contends that the DeFeo family was "in a state of phantomania" during the time of the murders and that the family was unable to move, because of "psychic paralyzation brought on by spirit activity" [G].

Affidavit Fraud

Piecing together the story of the DeFeo murders is certainly not an easy task. There are many unsolved portions of this story that leave empty spaces, forming an incomplete puzzle. The majority of the speculation revolves around the allegations that Dawn DeFeo may have been involved in the murders. We have looked at just about every scenario that could have involved Dawn DeFeo in the murders. However, most of these scenarios revolve around a key piece of evidence: the 24 July 1990 affidavit of Dawn's boyfriend at the time, William Davidge. When we do this, we find some bizarre things that seem to hurt the credibility of this document, making it hard to believe that it is legitimate.

First and foremost we must consider the affidavit fraud and other types of fraud committed by Ronnie DeFeo and Geraldine Gates. Both individuals have been caught and have confessed to doctoring affidavits and creating a fictional character that witnessed the murders. However, it's the Davidge affidavit that I have personally found the most controversial. First, the fact that this affidavit was signed almost sixteen years after the murders is speculative. Why this evidence was not brought to light sooner raises an eyebrow, at least. Yet, it's when we take a closer look at the document itself that we begin to question its veracity.

The affidavit originated from Florida, as indicated on the top left corner, but was notarized in Suffolk County, NY. Why would Davidge take the affidavit from Florida to NY to sign it and have it notarized? Note: The notary is supposed to witness and ID the person signing the document. This seems far too fishy to be taken at face value, especially since William's brother, Frank Davidge, also wrote an affidavit on the matter two years earlier and it had originated and was notarized in Florida. Theodore Yurack is the man who notarized the William Davidge affidavit. Unfortunately, he was not available for comment on this matter. Yet, the seemingly fraudulent activity does not end there.

Both Davidge affidavits appear to have been prepared ahead of time by Ronnie. Frank Davidge wrote Ronnie a letter, wherein he wrote, "I have read the affidavit you sent me and the problem I have with it is I just don't remember; some of it rings a bell…" From this, it appears that Ronnie prepared the affidavit and sent it to Frank, requesting his signature. Also interesting to note is the fact that, at the top of the William Davidge affidavit, it lists the county as "*Volousia*." Edgewater is in *Volusia County*, so the county name on the affidavit is spelled wrong. One would assume that if it was written by William or someone from the county, that they would most likely know how to spell it.

Back in 2009, I retrieved William Davidge's home phone number in Edgewater, FL. I called and a man answered; I asked for William. The gentleman paused for a second and asked me what it was in reference to. I explained that I wanted to clear up questions regarding the affidavits that were written. At that point the man introduced himself as William's brother, Robert Davidge, who was a boat mechanic in Amityville when they lived there. He claimed that William was away on business. Although he claimed that he knew nothing about his brother's involvement or the affidavit—when I told him that I believed the affidavit to be a fraud that was alledgedly prepared in advance and sent to William for him to sign in Edgewater, FL and return to Geraldine Gates (who then had it notarized in Brooklyn)—he said, "That's probably true." He also laughed when I asked him if Dawn was on drugs and responded with, "Drugs? No, she was just a kid…" He informed me that Ronnie was on drugs and that, in his opinion, Ronnie killed the whole family. He also revealed that Dawn was a "nice girl." I asked him if she hated her parents, as stated in the affidavit. He said, "No." The gentleman that I spoke to (claiming he was Robert) was very engaged in the conversation, and appeared to enjoy talking about it after all these years. It is my firm belief that I was speaking to William, himself. In any event, all of this evidence together appears to show that both of these affidavits were fraudulent and should be discounted, which basically diminishes further the theory of Dawn's involvement in the murders.

Domestic Abuse

No matter how bad things seemed between the DeFeos, things would get dramatically worse towards the end. The insanity that was going on in the DeFeo house just weeks, even days, leading up to the murders was unbearable, according to Ronnie and others. The confrontations had been growing more frequent and more violent each time. Threats of murder became more prevalent, and fights escalated dangerously close to attempted murder. It became commonplace for Dawn and her mother to run and grab knives to defend themselves against Ronald Sr., and his violent outbursts, according to Ronnie's testimony. On more than one occasion, Ronnie had to get in between his father and sister while his sister was waving a knife. Ronnie would hold his father back just long enough so that Dawn could get out of the house and come back when Big Ronnie cooled down.

Many neighbors in the area knew the DeFeos as a very loving and close knit family. Only few saw what went on behind closed doors of the home. Friend of the DeFeo family and Police Officer, Burt Borkan, testified that he was at the DeFeo home on 8 November 1974 (just five-days before the murders) and witnessed Ronald Sr., throwing a chair at Butch. According to Ronnie, Borkan and Big-Ronnie were friends for 17-years. However, they had a falling out at one time. Borkan used to have an office in the back of the Brigante-Karl dealership. They had an altercation once, and Big-Ronnie threw Borkan and all his stuff out into the street. The two then got into a fist fight. Later on they became friends again, Ronnie said.

Weber asks Ronnie on the stand to recount some of the fights that his father has gotten into. Ronnie described a fight that broke out between his father and his grandfather that he calls, "the best one." In 1974, the family went to Phyllis Procita's house in West Islip for a family get together. Ronnie witnessed a conversation that Big-Ronnie was having with his father, Rocky DeFeo. Ronnie says that his father was having some problems with law enforcement and he was discussing it with Rocco. Somehow Ronnie's uncle, Peter DeFeo, was mentioned, and the two started arguing. Suddenly, Big-

Ronnie hauled-off and punched Rocco in the face. The whole family rushed in and attempted to break up the fight. Ronnie said that they had to get out of there fast, because Big-Ronnie wanted to kill his father.

Did Ronnie snap; or was he seriously considering the family's insurance policy as an easy way out? Was Ronnie being set-up by his sister, as he claimed, so that she could pin the murders on him and walk away scot-free with all of the money? In a 1986 interview with *Newsday* (entitled: *A Convicts, Tale,* by Bob Keeler) Ronnie tells his most bizarre tale: he claims that Dawn killed their father and that their mother killed everyone else. Ronnie said that he took the rap because he was afraid that his mob uncle, Peter DeFeo, and his grandfather, Mr. Brigante, would have surely killed him. He claimed that since they were both dead, he can now speak the truth. On September of 1986, Ronnie wrote a letter addressed to the Suffolk County Surrogate Court (which he also addressed to several others) regarding Estate Fraud. In the letter, Ronnie alleges that Rocco and Peter DeFeo had a mob contract out on him, and that if he signed Michael Brigante, Sr., as the administrator of the DeFeo estate, Michael would stop the contract.

The one resounding fact of this case is that it was well known that Ronnie DeFeo Senior was an abusive brute. In the same *Newsday* article mentioned above, Linnea's husband, Roger Nonnewitz, said, "It must have been hell for the people living there with this man [Ronald DeFeo, Sr.]." In a 1999 *Long Island Voice* article (entitled, *Resident Evil,* by Bill Jensen), retired Amityville police sergeant, Pat Cammaroto spoke of Ronnie and his father. "The guy was a scumbag," Cammaroto eloquently described Butch. "Anybody who can kill his family, brothers and sisters is. The father, I can understand, cause he was a scumbag, too."

Linnea Nonnewitz, the DeFeo's maid at the time of the murders, was a close friend of Ronnie's mother Louise. In her testimony, she said that the two of them frequently had "girl talk." She loved the DeFeos and would do anything for them. Linnea knew the problems that Louise was having with her difficult husband. On more than one occasion Ronnie Sr., had made Linnea cry. One time, Ronnie Sr., had gotten into an altercation with Linnea's husband,

Roger, which almost halted her employment with the DeFeos. Just before the grisly murders, Louise spoke to Linnea about a terrifying premonition she had. "She wanted to die," Linnea told the court. "She wanted to put her head in the oven. She said to me, 'Linn, I'm preparing you. Something so tragic is going to happen.'" The domestic abuse in the DeFeo house was out of control. According to William Weber, "It was the craziest family you could imagine."

Many believe that Ronnie just did not have it in him to kill all six family members. Many attest to the fact that Ronnie acted tough, but was not a fighter at all. Lynn Tewksbury told me that Ronnie would never fight his own battles. She said that if Ronnie wanted someone beat up, he would pay someone else to do it. As for his brother Marc, Lynn says that she could not see Ronnie killing Marc. "He loved Marc! Ronnie used to carry him around when he got hurt, and he always bragged about how proud he was of him playing sports." Lynn claims that her ex-brother-in-law, Chuck Tewksbury, used to visit Ronnie in jail all the time. She claims that Ronnie told Chuck that Dawn killed the family and that he killed her out of anger for what she had done. Lynn was adamant that the Amityville police hated Ronnie and made sure that he took the fall for all of the murders.

Another bar that Ronnie used to frequent was the Chatter Box Bar, which was located at 114 Merrick Road. In a *New York Times* article (in 1974 [82]), Patron, Glenn Hoffman, claimed that he used to drink there with Ronnie on occasion. "I can't believe it," Glenn said. "I was talking to Ronnie recently about how proud he was of his brother playing football. He'd never kill his brother." Hoffman said that Ronnie was "not a good fighter." Hoffman recalls that Ronnie paid several older boys to take care of him back in junior high school.

That's my story, but I'm not sticking to it: 26 Tales of a convict

Ultimately, it was Ronnie who discredited himself by telling numerous tall-tales about what happened on the night his family was murdered. Although the practices of the Suffolk County Police department were less than adequate, Ronnie did not help things by fabricating a myriad of stories.

1. First, Ronnie said that he didn't know what was going on. At 4:00 a.m., he reported walking past the upstairs bathroom, and that his brother's wheelchair was in front of the door. He also claimed to have heard the toilet flush. He said that he could not go back to sleep, so he went to work early. He said that he called home all day, but strangely, no one answered. He had no idea who, when or why the murders were committed. He did offer police a possible lead, though. Butch told investigators that known mafia hit man, Tony Mazzeo, must have done it, because he had a gripe with his family.

2. Next, he told his interrogators that he was awoken by Tony Mazzeo at 3:30 a.m. He claimed Mazzeo put a revolver to his head and ordered him out of bed. "Another man was present in the room," Butch said, but upon further questioning, he could not provide any kind of physical description for the police. According to Butch's new version of events, Mazzeo and his companion led Butch from room to room, murdering each one of his family members. The police let Butch keep talking, and he eventually implicated himself as he described how he gathered and then discarded evidence from the crime scene.

3. 1974 - Ronnie confesses (to police) to killing all six members of his family.

4. 1974 – Ronnie told Chuck Tewksbury that Dawn killed the family and that he killed Dawn in a fit of rage.

5. 1975 - Ronnie tells a jailer that he was in the house with Bobby Kelske, Mindy Weiss, and another man and woman. In this version, Ronnie claims that the other four people were responsible for murdering the family.

6. 1975 - Ronnie tells a fellow inmate that he killed his entire family.

7. 1975 - Ronnie tells his aunt (Phyllis Procita) that he was awakened by gunshots, hid in a crawl space until perpetrators were gone. Later, he found his family dead.

8. 1975 - Ronnie tells his aunt (Phyllis Procita) that a friend of his came to the house, got high and fell asleep. Ronnie tried to wake the friend up, but he remained asleep. Ronnie then told Dawn to wake him up, and rushed out of the house. Upon his return home, Ronnie found his family murdered.

9. 1975 - Ronnie tells his aunt (Phyllis Procita) that Tony Mazzeo committed the murders.

10. 1975 - Ronnie tells his aunt (Phyllis Procita) that Bobby Kelske killed the family.

11. 1975 - Ronnie tells his aunt (Phyllis Procita) that a Mr. DeGennaro killed the family.

12. 1975 - Ronnie tells his aunt (Phyllis Procita) that Dawn killed the family, and he's protecting her by admitting to the crime.

13. Then, one year later, at the 1975 trial, DeFeo admits to killing his entire family. He claimed that he was influenced by a demonic force.

14. 1979 - Ronnie gives an audio interview to Hans Holzer in which he admits to acting alone. (Holzer believes that Ronnie was possessed by the spirit of the angry Indian Chief who inhabits the property).

15. 1986 - Ronnie tells Bob Keeler of *Newsday* that Dawn killed their father, and then his mother finally went crazy from the years of abuse and killed Dawn, Allison, Marc, and John. Then, in dramatic fashion, Louise DeFeo turned the gun on herself. In this version, Ronnie admits to accidentally firing one shot into his mother. Ronnie says he was with his fictional brother-in-law, Richard Romondoe.

16. 1989 - ABC contacted Ronnie in jail to get his take on the haunting. Ronnie said that his "parents were abusive," and that on the night of the murders he was "drunk and high on heroine" and that there were no voices commanding him to kill. [38]

17. 1992 – At his 440 hearing, Ronnie stated that his fictional brother-in-law, Richard Romondoe, can confirm that Dawn shot everyone, and he only shot Dawn in self-defense. He said that Romondoe disappeared immediately after the shooting.

18. 1992 – DeFeo tells a prison interviewer that he was down in the basement playing pool with a friend when he heard a loud roar. When he and his friend got upstairs, they found five dead. Ronnie said that he then went up to Dawn's room and she was surprised that he was home. He claims that she then reached for the rifle to fire it at him. A wrestling for the gun ensued, and Ronnie got control of it. "I was like a madman," DeFeo said, after he realized that she killed the whole family. He fired one shot into her head, killing her instantly. [76]

19. 1993 - Ronnie gives an audio interview where he claims that he was in the basement with a fictional brother-in-law, and they both raced upstairs after hearing the shots. Ronnie got angry when he saw that Dawn had killed everyone, so he went "berserk," and shot her in the head. In this version, after Ronnie kills Dawn, he and his "brother-in-law" are passed in the hallway by an unknown person who "Zoomed down the stairs and out the front door."

20. 1994 - Ronnie gives an on-camera interview to Christopher Berry-Dee and only speaks about killing Dawn.

21. After nearly two decades of silence, Butch told another story at his 1999 Parole Hearing. This time, he claimed only to have killed his sister. Butch claimed that he was in the basement with one of his friends and another friend of his was upstairs. He heard shots ring out—although he didn't realize they were gunshots at the time—and he went to see what was going on. When he got upstairs, he saw that everyone was dead, and his friends had run out of the house. He went up to his sister Dawn's room and saw blood on her and on the rug. Dawn looked at him surprised and said, "Oh my God, Butch, you're not supposed to be here!" As she said this, she went for the gun. Butch had a wrestling match with her. He wrestled the gun away from her, pushed her back onto the bed, and shot her in the head.
[B]

22. Again, one year later, DeFeo reconstructs the story. In a letter dated, May 1, 2000, a tainted and compromised DeFeo wrote, "As for Amityville, the only thing that's real is the murders...it was cold-blooded murder. Period. No ghosts. No demons. Just three people in which I was one."
[26]

23. 2002 - Ronnie tells the *New York Post* that only he and Dawn were responsible for the murders.

24. 2005 - Ronnie tells the parole board that he killed his parents, left the house, returned to find that Dawn had killed Allison, Marc, and John. Then, he admits to killing Dawn.

25. 2005 – In an interview with Marvin Scott of the WB11, Butch insisted that it was Allison DeFeo who killed everyone and that he killed her in self defense, while wrestling for the gun. [J]

26. On March 9, 2005, The New Criminologist (*Ronald DeFeo: Amityville World Exclusive*) printed a story on Ronnie and his Wife, Tracy. The article proclaims that DeFeo says "he ONLY shot to death his father, mother, and sister, Dawn. The latter, he argues, murdered the other siblings, Allison, Marc and John."

    Does Ronnie still have one more story left up his sleeve that will clear up many of the rumors and misconceptions of how the murders took place? Is he even cognizant or capable of telling the truth at this point?

    Weber protests till this day that Ronnie was insane. Even the jury did not buy the insanity plea. Ronnie's mental state was again thoroughly examined on 16 August 1999, by the Office of Mental Health at the Central New York Psychiatric Center at Green Haven Correctional Facility [81]. Their evaluation determined that Ronnie's thinking was logical; his speech: productive and responsive; his behavior: not unusual; his insight: fair; and his judgment: adequate. They also determined that the killings were a result of a conscious decision, not due to a mental dysfunction.

    Ronnie DeFeo truly is the boy who cried wolf. His legitimate gripe with Suffolk County Police and the New York justice system has been overshadowed by his arrogant attitude and his outlandish accounts of the murders. In the years since he's been incarcerated, Ronnie has been busier than many people 'on the outside.' Starting with his 1975 appeal, Ronnie has made several attempts to change his story, along with a plethora of affidavits and letters. Ronnie has blamed Weber; he's blamed his sister Dawn and others; he's blamed his father's abuse; he has even blamed his mother. Surprisingly, at times, DeFeo even blames himself; but that is only brief. Ronald DeFeo, Jr., is still driven by the hope of one day becoming a free man. This drive has led him to invent a multitude of different fabrications as to what happened on that fateful night. But what Ronnie doesn't appear to understand is that the whole world is watching and listening to every word he says. Every contradiction and every fabrication has been thoroughly noted, as well as the fact that he's never really showed any type of emotion or remorse over his six slaughtered family members.

"I think he enjoyed all the attention," Gerard Sullivan, the former assistant district attorney who prosecuted DeFeo, told *Newsday* [58]. "I think it's been several years since he had any of that attention. What the hell else does he have to do in prison?" Ronnie has always claimed that he was not afforded a fair trial back in 1975, and he feels that he got a raw deal from law enforcement officials. There appears to be some truth to this, but this does not take away the fact that Ronnie himself testified in 1975 that he killed his whole family. The sad part is that he blames William Weber, who Ronnie claims told him to testify to this. DeFeo acts as if it's a game he's playing, telling story after story to see which one will set him free. It all seems to be one big "con" to him. However, what he doesn't seem to realize is the only one who's been played all these years is him.

Amityville Realtor on New "Horror"

On 27 May 2010, I wrote an article on *my blog*[4] reporting that the horror house was up for sale. As I was researching the news, I came across a *Newsday* article by Valerie Kellogg entitled, *Broker: 'Amityville Horror' house haunted.* In it was the story of Amityville Realtor, James Smith and his recent claim that the house is, in fact, haunted. In my blog I wrote about the incident; and from that, James Smith contacted me and gave me an exclusive interview.

After exiting the infamous Horror house in Amityville in May 2010, realtor James Smith gave a brief interview to a Channel 4 News reporter who was standing outside the house. In his brief statement, James Smith re-opened a 30-plus year can of worms, claiming that he "got an eerie feeling" while in the home. "It felt like something was there," James said, referring to the evil, unseen resident that has allegedly roamed these grounds for many years. In haste, James told Channel 4, "We took off and got out of there."

For more than a year James Smith has remained silent about the matter. Although he has been contacted by a plethora of news organizations asking him to relay his story; he did not want the publicity. But now he believes that he has a story of importance to tell the world; one that he can no longer keep to himself. Several weeks ago Mr. Smith contacted me and agreed to provide an exclusive taped interview in which he revealed his entire experience in the house that day.

James Smith and his family moved from Manhattan to Amityville in 1978, just down the street from the infamous horror house on Ocean Avenue. James recalls immediately hearing about Ronald DeFeo Jr., killing his entire family in the house and about the family that moved in after the DeFeo's (the Lutz family) having fled from the home after only 28 days, fearing that it was haunted. One night—in a display of anger—young James and his friends decided to go and throw rocks at the house. He also remembers the circus-type atmosphere that followed rumors that the house was haunted.

---

[4] www.willsavive.blogspot.com

James became a real-estate agent in 2003, doing a lot of work in the Amityville area. As a licensed agent, James had the opportunity of not only hearing about listings before the general public got wind of them, but he was also able to view any house that was on the market. On 25 May 2010, James got the news that the Amityville horror house (108 Ocean Ave.) was holding a broker open house.

The broker open house was being facilitated by Laura Zambratto of Daniel Gale Sotheby's International Realty—the firm listing the property. James arrived with his female co-worker (who asked to remain anonymous – we will call her Jane for the purposes of this article). As they entered the home and climbed the stairs to the second floor, Jane said to James, "Something feels weird, doesn't it?" James looked at her and said, "Yeah, it does." However, he was placating Jane at that time; he didn't feel anything. He simply wrote her comments off as angst, on her part, over being in the horror house. They continued previewing the house along with two other agents from another realty company and Laura Zambratto.

Their final previewing destination was the basement area. When they reached the cellar area, where the oil burner is, Jane again got spooked, this time even worse than before. "Did you feel that?" she asked James. "Oh my God!" James replied, "Yeah, I did!" James felt the temperature in the room drop suddenly. He looked up and saw a hole in the wall and felt a very eerie feeling that he still has a hard time describing: he says that this hole was emanating freezing cold air.

James Smith: There was a hole there. It was about 15' by 15' and, hey, Will, I can't even describe it, but it was such an eerie, eerie feeling. Cold air was coming out of this hole…it was very cold, very, very cold. Now we are in the summer, it was the summer; it's probably 90 degrees outside, and the air that was coming out of that hole was like someone opened their freezer door.

In describing the hole a bit further, James said that there was a concrete wall with a square hole in it, as if someone had purposely taken out these bricks. He said that he could see inside the hole only about 12 inches, and he noticed dirt, but it was pitch black otherwise. As he descried the air coming out of the hole, he made it a point to inform me that it wasn't just rushing out of the hole; it was more like someone had just opened up the freezer door of a really big freezer. He said that he immediately got goose bumps and everyone in the basement was experiencing something similar, from his point of view.

James Smith: The room just felt like…I'm trying to describe it exactly. You know that feeling when you are sleeping and you can tell someone is looking over you, someone is standing there before you even see them, and then you open your eyes and you see someone standing there? That's what it felt like. So, we all looked at each other and we took off!

James then says that the entire group decided to leave the house at that time, in a hurry. As they exited the house, a reporter from Channel 4 News scurried over to James—apparently she could see by the way they exited the home that something out of the ordinary was occurring. "What happened, what's going on?" she asked him. Jane was clearly shaken up, and she hurried to the car to gather herself. She didn't move for a few minutes; she just sat in her truck.

According to James, the other two agents, who he had never met before that day, said aloud, as they exited the house, "I am not going back in that house!" And they got in their cars and sped off. He says that they were visibly shaken as well, but did not speak to the media. James then proceeded to give the reporter a brief interview.

James Smith: I am the biggest skeptic that there is, and if I was by myself, I would have just thought that maybe I have too much of the Amityville Horror movies in my head. But because I was with other people and we all were having the same feelings, it legitimized the experience.

James further described the basement experience as feeling as though he was at a high altitude, such as up on a mountain. He said that he didn't get shortness of breath or anything, it just felt like he was high up, as if his ears were going to pop. He also explained that it was not like they just walked into the basement and it was cold. It wasn't until they were down there for a few minutes that they all noticed the drastic temperature change, "as if the ambient temperature just dropped suddenly."

Laura Zambratto also spoke to Channel 4 News, but she gave a different account. "The house is so spectacular—the warmest, most beautifully done, charming house I've been in," Zambratto says. "There's not one thing about the house that makes you feel uncomfortable." She also denied any haunting activity. To this James replied, "Of course she is going to downplay or deny anything that happened; she is trying to sell the house, and there was a lot of money at stake for her in the deal." James swore to me that he is telling the truth about his experience in the house and he sounded very convincing.

Will Savive: So you think that the owner of the house at the time, Brian Wilson; he had to know that there was some occult activity occurring there?

James Smith: [chuckle] Hey, listen, let me tell you something: it's one of those things where, you know how, for example, like a crime will happen in a neighborhood and the police don't know anything about who did it, but everyone in the neighborhood knows who did it? [lol] You know what I mean?

Will Savive: [lol] Right

James Smith: Let me tell you: just living in that area for so many years, everyone was just very hush, hush about that whole incident, because nobody wanted the frenzy. I can tell you back in the 80s, it was just horrendous in that area! The media attention, I mean, there were people coming like trying to pick the shingles off of the house, and camping out. It was to the point where they had the streets blocked off, and if you didn't have ID [identification] you couldn't even go down the block.

Will Savive: Wow!

James Smith: It was so crazy that people didn't want to give a statement. And I know what they mean, Will, because I did that one interview for that woman, and I tell you, I probably...I don't know how people got my cell phone [number], but my cell phone, I had about, at least 16 different news organizations contact me. And my office phone would ring non-stop. I mean people from newspapers in other countries were calling me. Of course, all the local news papers were calling me: Newsday, Daily News, the New York Post, they were all calling me to get this story, and I'm like 'Are you kidding me?' People were showing up at my office looking for an interview.

***

Amityville will never die! It's too deeply ingrained in our culture. As long as people want to know; people will be around to tell. Ironically, the fire will continue to burn in this case, for all time. It will continue to be fueled by 'human interest' and an 'intrinsic' search for truth and justice; for the journey of self-discovery will never be complete: only modified. Amityville encapsulates the entire spectrum of human drama and emotion! Amityville is clearly the "JFK Assassination" of the paranormal world; not to mention JFK-like as far as the DeFeo case! And like JFK; it will be researched, debated, and rehashed for all time.

If curiosity didn't kill the cat then it simply made him wiser. Amityville is a tale of many lessons. Most of all, it teaches us about ourselves and about each other. It teaches us about our world, about our minds, and about our future. Amityville is so many different stories in one; all being important lessons. It's a stark reminder of what can happen when authority is allowed to have absolute power; when demons are let to roam free; when rumors can spin a harmless story into a haunting truth; when family abuse leads to the indifference of life or death; when a beautiful upscale town can be over-run by vandals; and so much more! Where society will ultimately categorize this story in the annals of time has not yet been determined. However, one thing is for sure, Amityville will always be with us! And through all of the debates and speculations, we must remember that *six lives* were taken *violently*; *unnecessarily*.

Although the haunting cannot be proven conclusively, likewise, neither can the hoax. Money has been offered a couple of times for anyone who could offer proof of a hoax or a conspiracy, yet, no one ever has. However, somehow we have collectively deemed this story a hoax, because of the admissions of William Weber and Stephan Kaplan. Don't expect this debate to be resolved anytime soon.

THE END...

END NOTES

A. Testimony of Ronald DeFeo Jr., *People vs. DeFeo*, 1251-74.

B. Testimony of Ronald DeFeo Jr., 1999 Parole Hearing, Inst. # 75-A- 4053

C. Weber, William. 1975 Appeal to the New York Supreme Court.

D. Testimony of Alfred DellaPenna, *People vs. DeFeo*, 1251-74.

E. Crowe, Kenneth E. "Murder: All in the Family." Front Page Detective Mar. 1975: 20+.

F. Complaint and Investigation Report, P.O. Kenneth Greguski. *Time Reported: 1840*. Date Reported: November 13, 1974.

G. National Geographic Channel - Is It Real: *Hauntings*. Monday November 13, 2006, Episode Number: 22; Season Num: 2

H. Moran, Rick. "*OK, I Know You Want to Ask:* Association for the Study of Unexplained Phenomenon."

J. "*Amityville: Horror or Hoax?*" News Close-up, with Senior Correspondent, Marvin Scott. CW Network-WPIX Television. WB11, NY.

K. Flanagan, James. "*Execution of Family Baffles Detectives.*" The Post 15 Nov. 1974: b-5.

L. Affidavit of Barry Springer, October 8, 1975.

M. Tewksbury, Lynn. *Telephone interview*. 30 Dec. 2007.

N. Affidavit of Barry Springer, August 14, 2004.

O. James, Carolyn. *"The Amityville Horror Seekers Begin to Come Around."* Amityville Record. 27 Apr. 2005.

P. Osuna, Ric. *The Night the DeFeos Died*. First ed. Nevada: Noble Kai Media, 2002.

Q. Testimony of Phyllis Procita, *People vs. DeFeo*, 1251-74.

R. Affidavit of: Barry Springer, September 21, 2004. NY, Suffolk.

S. Affidavit of: Geraldine Gates, February 23, 1989. Affidavit of: Richard Romondoe, February 23, 1989

T. Affidavit of: Joseph Poette, July 31, 2003; NY, Dutchess.

U. Affidavit of: Hasson Zarif, August 5, 2003; NY, Dutchess.

V. Affidavit of: Jeffrey Satless, September 3, 2003; NY, Dutchess.

W. Duncan, Blaine, and Eric Walter. *"Interview with Donna Cromarty."* Amityvillefiles.Com. 2008.

X. Affidavit of: Karen Peterson (Assistant District Attorney of Suffolk County, NY), August 28, 1990; NY, Suffolk. (Supreme Court)

Y. Courtesy of: The Amityville Historical Society.

Z. Voluntary statement given by Geraldine Gates. Statement made to Detective Allen Watterson of the Suffolk County Police Department on March 20, 1990.

1. Lorraine Warren, Interview with Paulington. 2005.

2. Craft, E., & Thorne, T. (2005, March 31). Amityville FAQ - Magick Mind Radio. *Amityville FAQ - Magick Mind Radio.* Retrieved 2008, from http://www.amityvillefaq.com/intmmr.html

   Lyons, R. D. (1993, April 30). Ex-Fiance Held in Killing In Hotel Room. *The New York Times.* Retrieved 2008, from http://www.nytimes.com/1993/04/30/nyregion/ex-fiance-held-in-killing-in-hotel room.html

3. *The Real Amityville Horror.* (1 - 6). Dir. Nick Freand Jones.

4. Affidavit of William Davidge, July 24, 1990. Suffolk County, NY.

5. http://www.shattereddreamzz.com/articles.html: includes various Amityville sources: numerous *Newsday* Articles and an interview with William Weber.

6. Testimony of Mindy Weiss, *People vs. DeFeo*, 1251-74.

7. Testimony of Robert Kelske, *People vs. DeFeo*, 1251-74.

8. Osuna, Ric. "*A Grisley Discovery.*" The Amityville Murders.

9. Testimony of Richard Wyssling, *People vs. DeFeo*, 1251-74.

10. Jensen, Bill. "Resident Evil - The Amityville Horror: 25 Years Later." Long Island Voice, 27 Oct. 1999, Volume 3, Number 42 ed.: 1+.

11. Berry-Dee, Christopher. "*Ronald DeFeo Jr. -the Amityville Horror? Maybe a Mass Murderer? But Was He Also a Victim...a Victim of a Corrupt US Judicial System?*"

12. Siegfried, Jacob. Affirmation of J. Siegfried, ESQ. In Support (A 11 to A 13). Court of Suffolk County, NY, January 15, 1975.

13. Osuna, Ric. *"The Injustice That Followed."* The Amityville Murders.

14. Weber, William. Supplemental Omnibus Notice of Motion (pp. A 25 to A 31) Court of Suffolk County, NY, July 22, 1975.

15. Order (Stark, J.) Dated October 6, 1975 Denying suppression after hearings of September 22, et seq: (pp. A 92 to A 94). Court of Suffolk County, NY

16. 1975 DeFeo Trial, Opening statements of the prosecution: "Gerald Sullivan." (pp. 2343 – 2346).

17. Testimony of Dr. Howard C. Adelman [Deputy Chief Medical Examiner of Suffolk County, NY], *People vs. DeFeo*, 1251-74. (p. 2651).

18. Testimony of Herman Race, *People vs. DeFeo*, 1251-74. (p.1124).

19. Godl, John. *"Amityville: the Cultural Impact of Homicide II."* Castle of Spirits

20. Ballistics report.

21. Dawn DeFeo's autopsy report. Office of the Medical Examiner, Suffolk County, New York: Division of Laboratories. (Toxicology Report) ME – 110. The autopsy was performed by Dr. Irving Rappaport at the Suffolk County Morgue on November 14, 1974 in the presence of Dr. Howard Adelman and Det. Schumacher.

22. Alfred DellaPenna giving his analysis of the particles from the gun found on Dawn's nightdress. The link leads to YouTube. The program was originally aired on the A&E Channel. http://www.youtube.com/watch?v=KsKwOl1V8sQ&eurl=http://www.injusticesofamityville.com/ tne/reportsballistic.html.

23. Nixon, John. *Personal interview*. March 2008.

24. http://www.injusticesofamityville.com/tne/reportsballistic.html. Various case-related documents and videos. Dr. Adelman speaks in two of the videos and Det. DellaPenna speaks in one. Also appearing on this page is Ronnie's wife, Tracey DeFeo's, "application for public access records." This submission to the Suffolk County PD (PDCS-5414C), was a request for public records for the tests & results claimed to have been done on Dawn DeFeo's hands. (Site by: Tracey DeFeo).

25. Godl, John. *"Amityville: the Cultural Impact of Homicide."* Castle of Spirits.

26. On May 1, 2000, Ronald DeFeo Jr. wrote a letter to a producer requesting money for an interview. The Producer's name was blackedout. (Site by: Ric Osuna). http://www.amityvillemurders.com/reference/butch_admission.html.

27. Affidavit of Barry Springer, July 23, 1988. Suffolk County, NY.

28. Euro Bank Statement. www.injusticesofamityville.com/eruobnkstment_h_eurobank_ebst_nav.html.

29. Yancey, Tim. *"The Amityville Horror: Interview with George Lutz."* The Amityville Horror: Discover the Truth. 2003.

30. Morris, Steven. "Ronald DeFeo Jr. and the Amityville Murder Case." 22 July 2006. (par. 13). http://www.taph.com/index2.php?option=com_content&do_pdf=1&id=4261.

31. Morris, Steven. *"Ronald DeFeo Jr and the Amityville Murder Case - Autopsy of Dawn DeFeo: Some Details and Questions."*

32. Osuna, Ric. *The Amityville Horror: Discovering the Truth.* Ts.

33. *"The Amityville Horror"* In Search Of. NBC. Hosted by: Leonard Nimoy. 1980.

34. Layne Wilson, Staci. *"Interview with George Lutz" the Man Who Lived 'The Amityville Horror' in the 1970s."* About.Com. 2005.

35. *"Amityville Horror."* The Merv Griffin Show. CBS. YouTube, Las Vegas. 1979.

36. *"Amityville Horror."* Good Morning America. ABC. New York City. 26 July 1979.

37. Unknown. *"Facts Surrounding the: Amityville Horror House"* Amityville Record. 24 Aug. 2000.

38. Vargas, Elizabeth, Diane Sawyer, and Charles Gibson. *"Amityville Horror – Primetime Live."* 1989. ABC News.

39. Case File: The Amityville Horror http://www.warrens.net/amityville.html. The Warrens explain their March 6th investigation of the Amityville house.

40. Brittle, Gerald. *"A Little Extra on Amityville."* The Demonologist.

41. The Lutzes' "Lie Detector Test & Results" in full, along with Chris Gugas's bio, go to: http://www.amityvillehorror.com/docs/docs.htm.

42. Kaplan, S. (1995). L.A. Vampires. *Los Angeles Almanac*. Retrieved 2008, from http://www.laalmanac.com/mysterious/my07.htm

43. Kaplan, Roxanne. Interview with Blaine Duncan. Also, personal phone interviews, including the one with the registrar of Pacific College in San Diego, Troy (taped interview), and other contacts regarding my research of Kaplan's background claims. Kaplan, Roxanne. Interview with Ric Osuna. The Amityville Murders.

44. Nickell, Joe. *"Investigative Files, Amityville: the Horror of It All."*

45. Mayhew, Malcolm. *"The Reel Horror: Amityville house is where it all started"* SignOnSanDiego.Com. 8 May 2005. The Union-Tribune.

46. Smith, Jennifer. *"Ex-Resident of House Debunks Much of Amityville: Horror"* The Seattle Times. 8 May 2005. Newsday; *"Amityville – Hoax or Horror?"* Inside Edition. CBS. New York. 2005.

47. *"Amityville: Horror or Hoax?"* News Closeup, with Senior Correspondent, Marvin Scott. CW Network-WPIX Television. WB11, NY. 2005.

48. Sherbetbizarre. *"Reinvestigating the Flip-Flop."* The Truth About the Amityville Horror.

49. DeFeo. *"Ronnie DeFeo, Jr., Letter."* The Truth About the Amityville Horror.

50. Affidavit of Frank Davidge, October 6, 1988; FL., Volusia.Affidavit of Linnea Nonnewitz, November 6, 1989; PA., Berks. Affidavit of Roger Nonnewitz, October, 1989; PA., Berks.

> In his affidavit, Frank wrote: *"Weber told me during consultation that DeFeo was guilty, but told me he would get DeFeo declared insane by fabricating a defense of insanity... Weber advised me and ordered me to testify at his will, to support his insanity defense, and refused to allow me to testify in any other manner."*

> In her affidavit, Lynn wrote: *"William Weber rehearsed me to testify only about things that were consistent with his insanity defense."* Lynn's husband, Roger, said the exact same thing in his October 1989 affidavit.

51. DeFeo, 1975 Appeal: New York Supreme Court: Appellate Division – Second Department; as argued by, William Weber; Suffolk County Indictment No: 1231- 74.

52. James, Carolyn. *"Why Hollywood'S Version of DeFeo Murders Isn't Amityville'S."* Amityville Record. 26 Oct. 2000. 2008.

    http://www.amityvillerecord.com/news/2000/1026/Front_Page/11.html. "Thus ensued a night of horror that Amityville will never forget during which Ronald DeFeo Jr. was taken into protective cusotody by the Suffolk County Police while the bodies of his slain family were given the last rites of the Catholic Church by Father McNamara."

53. Osuna, Ric. *"Geraldine DeFeo: Amityville's Controversial Figure."* The Amityville Murders. 2008. http://www.amityvillemurders.com/ geraldine.html.

54. Affidavit of: Barry Springer, August 25, 2003; NY, Suffolk.

55. Lotto, Gerald L. Letter to Ronald DeFeo, Jr., 10 Sept. 1992. NY.

56. Nonnewtiz, Linnea. Letter to Hon. Christina A. Sproat (Justice Supreme Court). 5, Sept. 2003. Letter of Complaint. Dutchess County, NY.

57. Boshnack, Mark. "*100 Dogs Taken From Deposit Home.*" The Daily Star: the Newspaper for the Heartland of New York. 13 May 2002. Community Newspaper Holdings Inc.2008. http://old.thedailystar.com/news/stories/2002/05/13/dogs.html.

    Boshnack, Mark. "*Dog Owner Pleads Innocent.*" The Daily Star: the Newspaper for the Heartland of New York. 15 May 2002. Community Newspaper Holdings Inc. 2008. http://old.thedailystar.com/news/stories/2002/05/15/dog.html.

    Boshnack, Mark. "What Was I Going to Do?" The Daily Star: the Newspaper for The Heartland of New York. 2 Oct. 2002. Community Newspaper Holdings Inc. 2008. http://old.thedailystar.com/news/stories/2002/10/02/dog.html.

58. Keeler, Bob. "*A Covict's Tale.*" Newsday 19 Mar. 1986.

59. Testimony of Linnea Nonnewitz, *People vs. DeFeo*, 1251-74.

60. James, Carolyn, and Christina Laquidara. "*Why Hollywood'S Version of DeFeo Murders Isn't Amityville's.*" Amityville Record. 26 Oct. 2000.

61. Stark, Thomas. DNA Denied; Suffolk County Supreme Court. Nov. 24, 1992; 1251-74.

62. DeFeo, Ronald. Leave to Appeal; Suffolk County Supreme Court. July, 19 1993; 1251-74.

63. DeFeo, Tracey. "*Justice for Ronald DeFeo Jr.*" The Injustices of Amityville. http://www.ipetitions.com/petition/dnadefeo.

64. An Investigation of the Suffolk County District Attorney's Office and Police Department. State of New York Commission of Investigation. New York, 1989. 31-42.

65. Mulugeta, S. (1998, January 4). The Fame Demon: In Amityville, Legacy is a Horror in Itself. *Newsday*.

66. Lotto, Gerald. Affirmation; Suffolk County Supreme Court. June 10, 1992; 1251-74.

67. Unknown. "*Indict Son in Slaying of Family.*" Riverhead, N.Y. (UPI) 3 Dec. 1974. Unknown. "*N.Y Man is Indicted.*" Riverhead, N.Y. (AP) 19 Nov. 1974.

68. Unknown. "*House of Evil: Amityville Jinx Hit Actor.*" Amityvillefiles.Com. pgs., 32, 34.

69. Reynolds, Ryan. Interview with Sean Clark. Dread Central.Com. 2005.

70. *"The Amityville Horror."* Box Office Mojo.

71. Unknown. "*Dark Destinations: Amityville Horror Movie House (2005)."* TheCabinet.Com. 21 Mar. 2008.

72. Unknown. "Dark Destinations: Amityville Horror Movie House (1979)." TheCabinet.Com. 11 Aug. 2007.

73. Unknown. "*Haunted House Murder - Attorney: Evil Spirit Pushed Killer.*" Chicago Tribune.

74. Unknown. "Spook Study Adds Scary Side to Life." Hollywood (UPI).

75. Uknown. "*...Simply a Mass Murder Site to Others.*" The San Antonio Light 28 July 1976: 5-B.

76. Unknown. "*'Amityville' Killer Says Sister Did It.*" Riverhead, N.Y. (AP) 1992.

77. Vecsey, George. "*L.I. Slayings Suspect Used Drugs.*" The New York Times 16 Nov. 1974.

78. Gupte, Pranay. "*DeFeos Funeral Attended by 1,000: Son is Indicted on 6 Counts of 2d-Degree Murder.*" The New York Times 19 Nov. 1974: p. 47.

79. Berry-Dee, Christopher, Interview with Ric Osuna. Retrieved from http://www.amityvillemurders.com/interviews/dee.html

80. DeFeo, Jr., Ronald. Letter to Suffolk County Surrogate Court. 16 Sept. 1986. Estate Fraud. New York State.

81. Petrino, Michelle. Ronnie DeFeo'S Mental Health Report. Green Haven Correctional Facility, Mental Health Until. Stormville, New York: May 17, 2000.

82. Vecsey, George. "Neighbors Recall DeFeos as 'Nice, Normal Family'" The New York Times 15 Nov. 1974.

83. Taylor, Troy. Bloody Chicago. London: White Chapel Productions, 2006; Unknown. *"Amityville and Its Resident Al Capone, Capone Lived in Amityville, Then Went to Chicago!"* The True Legends Behind the "Fictional" Movie and Books.

84. Unknown. "Amityville Indians, the Truth of Their Legends & History: the Facts About the Indian Tribes of Suffolk County Including the Shinnecock & Massapequans." The True Legends Behind the "Fictional" Movie and Books. http://truelegends.info/amityville/ indians.htm. *Much of the information used—as provided by the above sources—also appears in a number of other publications. Each source here is listed as a suitable reference.

85. Osuna, Ric. "The Amityville Murders." Internet Archive: Wayback Machine. 18 Feb. 2009 http://web.archive.org/web/20010806163023/www.amityvillemurders.com/2000/pages/author.html (All info under # 85 was provided by Amityville expert and administrator of George Lutzes' old web site, Jason Pyke).

86. "THE LOU GENTILE SHOW--INTERVIEW WITH JOEL MARTIN." Encounters Paranormal Radio Series. 11 Jan. 2009 http://www.timyancey.com/theamityvillefiles.shtml.

87. "Amityville FAQ - The Haunting page 3." Amityville FAQ – Home Page. 2008 http://www.amityvillefaq.com/haunting3.html.

Damiani, Damiano. "Amazon.com: The Amityville Horror Collection (The Amityville Horror/ The Amityville Horror II: The Possession/ The Amityville Horror III: The Demon/ Bonus Disc - Amityville Confidential): James Olson, Burt Young, Tony Roberts, Tess Harper, James Brolin, Margot Kidder, Rutanya Alda, Jack Magner, Andrew Prine, Diane Franklin, Moses Gunn, Ted Ross, Damiano Damiani, Richard Fleischer, Stuart Rosenberg, Dardano Sacchetti, George Lutz, Hans Holzer, Jay Anson, Kathy Lutz: Movies & TV." Amazon.com: Online Shopping for Electronics, Apparel, Computers, Books, DVDs & more. 2008

http://www.amazon.com/dp/B00079Z9WI?tag=thelastwebsit23020&camp=15041&creative=373501&link_code=as3.

Kaplan, Stephen. "Amazon.com: The Amityville Horror Conspiracy: Stephen Kaplan; Roxanne Salch Kaplan: Books." Amazon.com: Online Shopping for Electronics, Apparel, Computers, Books, DVDs & more. 2008
http://www.amazon.com/gp/product/0963749803?ie=UTF8&tag=thelastwebsit20&link_code=as3&camp=211189&creative=373489&creativeASIN=0963749803.

Belanger, Jeff. "Amazon.com: Our Haunted Lives: True Life Ghost Encounters: Jeff Belanger: Books." Amazon.com: Online Shopping for Electronics, Apparel, Computers, Books, DVDs & more. 2008
http://www.amazon.com/gp/product/1564148564?ie=UTF8&tag=thelastwebsit-20&link_code=as3&camp=211189&creative=373489&creativeASIN=1564148564

Lightning Source UK Ltd.
Milton Keynes UK
UKOW04f2310150913

217244UK00001BA/45/P